Fake News on the Internet

This book provides a review of current research on fake news and presents six new empirical research studies examining its impact.

Fake news has garnered immense public attention following the 2016 Brexit referendum, three US elections, the 2019 Indian lynchings, and so on. Fake news undermines public life across the globe, especially in countries where journalistic practices and institutions are weak. Some fake news is created to spread ideological messages or to create mischief, whereas other fake news is created for profit. Research shows that fake news spreads farther, faster, and more broadly than true news and has had major societal impacts. All signs indicate that it will get worse as political activists, scammers, alternative news media, and hostile governments become more sophisticated in their production and targeting of fake news. This book features leading scholars who provide a review of the current research and presents six new empirical research studies examining its impact. Some of this research shows how inventions designed to reduce fake news can actually have the opposite effect, and instead act to increase the spread of fake news. Other research takes a longer-term perspective, by measuring or inserting emotions into headlines, allowing us to examine some of the roots of fake news behaviors for future study. This shows how challenging the fake news phenomenon is to solve.

Fake News on the Internet will be a key resource for academics, researchers, and advanced students of media studies, research methods, information systems, communication studies, management, cultural studies, and sociology. The chapters included in this book were originally published as a special issue of the *Journal of Management Information Systems*.

Alan R. Dennis is Professor of Information Systems and John T. Chambers Chair of Internet Systems at Indiana University. He was named as Fellow of the Association for Information Systems in 2012 and received the LEO Award in 2021. He is a past president of the Association for Information Systems, and also served as Vice President for Conferences.

Dennis F. Galletta is Thomas H. O'Brien Endowed Chair of Information Systems at the Katz Graduate School of Business, University of Pittsburgh. He served as President of the Association for Information Systems (AIS) in 2007, was named an AIS Fellow in 2002, and received a lifetime achievement (LEO) award in 2015. He has served four consecutive terms as Katz Director of Doctoral Programs. His research focuses on human–computer interaction and credibility of online information.

Jane Webster is E. Marie Shantz Chair Emerita in Management Information Systems at Queen's University, Canada, and a fellow of the Association for Information Systems. Jane served as a senior editor for *MIS Quarterly* and VP Publications for the Association for Information Systems. Her current research examines ways to encourage more environmentally sustainable behaviors in organizations.

Fake News on the Internet

Edited by
Alan R. Dennis, Dennis F. Galletta,
and Jane Webster

Routledge
Taylor & Francis Group

LONDON AND NEW YORK

First published 2024
by Routledge
4 Park Square, Milton Park, Abingdon, Oxon OX14 4RN

and by Routledge
605 Third Avenue, New York, NY 10158

Routledge is an imprint of the Taylor & Francis Group, an informa business

British Library Cataloguing in Publication Data
A catalogue record for this book is available from the British Library

ISBN13: 978-1-032-56112-7 (hbk)
ISBN13: 978-1-032-56113-4 (pbk)
ISBN13: 978-1-003-43393-4 (ebk)

DOI: 10.4324/9781003433934

Typeset in Minion Pro
by Newgen Publishing UK

Access the Support Material: www.routledge.com/ 9781032561127

Publisher's Note
The publisher accepts responsibility for any inconsistencies that may have arisen during the conversion of this book from journal articles to book chapters, namely the inclusion of journal terminology.

Disclaimer
Every effort has been made to contact copyright holders for their permission to reprint material in this book. The publishers would be grateful to hear from any copyright holder who is not here acknowledged and will undertake to rectify any errors or omissions in future editions of this book.

Contents

Citation Information

The following chapters were originally published in the *Journal of Management Information Systems*, volume 38, issue 4 (2021). When citing this material, please use the original page numbering for each article, as follows:

For any permission-related enquiries please visit:
www.tandfonline.com/page/help/permissions

Notes on Contributors

Michael Chau is Associate Professor in the Faculty of Business and Economics at the University of Hong Kong, Hong Kong, China. Dr. Chau's research focuses on the cross-disciplinary intersection of information systems, computer science, business analytics, and information science, with an emphasis on the applications of data, text, and web mining in various business, education, and social domains. He has received multiple awards for his research.

Jennifer Crawford is doctoral student in psychology at Bowling Green State University, Bowling Green, Ohio with a specialization in decision-making and narrative construction across adult development. She is skilled in research methods and data analysis using various statistical software such as SPSS, R, and jamovi.

Bingjie Deng is a doctoral student in information systems in the Faculty of Business and Economics at the University of Hong Kong, Hong Kong, China. She is interested in consumer information processing, human–computer interaction, social media, and business analytics.

Alan R. Dennis is Professor of Information Systems and John T. Chambers Chair of Internet Systems at Indiana University, Bloomington, Indiana. He was named as Fellow of the Association for Information Systems in 2012 and received the LEO Award in 2021. He is a past president of the Association for Information Systems and also served as Vice President for Conferences.

Diego Escobari is Associate Professor of Economics in the Robert C. Vackar College of Business and Entrepreneurship at the University of Texas Rio Grande Valley, Edinburg, Texas. His research focuses on pricing, industrial organization, energy, and real estate markets. He has published over 30 articles in such journals as *Journal of Industrial Economics*, *International Journal of Industrial Organization*, *Transportation Research Part A*, *Economics Letters*, *Energy Economics*, *Energy*, and others.

Dennis F. Galletta is Thomas H. O'Brien Endowed Chair of Information Systems at the Katz Graduate School of Business, University of Pittsburgh, Pittsburgh, Pennsylvania. He served as President of the Association for Information Systems (AIS) in 2007, was named an AIS Fellow in 2002, and received a lifetime achievement (LEO) award in 2015. He has served four consecutive terms as Katz Director of Doctoral Programs. His research focuses on human–computer interaction and credibility of online information.

Jordana George is Clinical Assistant Professor of Information Systems in the Mays Business School at Texas A&M University,, College Station, Texas. She earned her Ph.D. in Information Systems at Baylor University. She researches about the societal impact of information systems, including social inclusion, emancipatory technologies, and digital activism.

Natalie Gerhart is Assistant Professor of Business Intelligence and Analytics at Creighton University, Omaha, Nebraska. Her research interests include decision stopping rules, human–computer interaction, business intelligence and analytics, and social networking. She has published in journals such as *MIS Quarterly Executive, Decision Support Systems, International Journal of Human-Computer Interaction*, and *DATA BASE for Advances in Information Systems*.

Christy Galletta Horner is Assistant Professor in the College of Education and Human Development at Bowling Green State University, Bowling Green, Ohio. Her research focuses on the role of emotional culture in the promotion of healthy individual and social functioning. She is Associate Editor of the *Mid-Western Educational Researcher*.

Kelvin K. King is Assistant Professor of Digital Misinformation at Syracuse University, Syracuse, New York. His research leverages econometric models, machine learning algorithms as well as lab and field experiments and consists of two, often overlapping streams. His research work has received several awards. Dr. King has industry experience working with big data.

Dongwon Lee is Assistant Professor in the Information Systems, Business Statistics, and Operations Management Department at the Hong Kong University of Science and Technology (HKUST), Hong Kong, China. His research interests focus on customer analytics, mobile commerce, digital nudging, digital transformation, and economics of information systems. Dr. Lee's work has been appeared in a number of premier journals as well as major conferences and workshops in information systems.

Ka Chung Ng is Assistant Professor in the Department of Management and Marketing, Faculty of Business, Hong Kong Polytechnic University, Hong Kong, China. His research interests lie in fake news, business analytics, and fintech. His work has appeared in the *Journal of Management Information Systems* and *ACM Transactions on Management Information Systems*.

Tamer Oraby is Associate Professor of Statistics and Mathematics in the School of Mathematical and Statistical Sciences at the University of Texas Rio Grande Valley. His research interest is in mathematical and statistical modeling of spread of infectious diseases. He has published several papers in that domain in such journals as *Lancet, Nature's Scientific Reports*, and *Proceedings of the Royal Society B*.

Babajide Osatuyi is Professor of Geography at the University of Geneva, Geneva, Switzerland. She teaches political and cultural geography at the Department of Geography and geography didactics at the Institute of Teacher Education. She specializes in the analysis of landscape policies, mobilization for landscapes, and mediation practices.

Min-Seok Pang is Associate Professor of Management Information Systems and Milton F. Stauffer Research Fellow at Fox School of Business, Temple University, Philadelphia, Pennsylvania. Dr. Pang's research interests include, among others, strategic management of information technology in the public sector, and technology-enabled public policies. He serves as an associate editor for *MIS Quarterly* and *Journal of the Association for Information Systems*.

Paul A. Pavlou is the Dean of the C.T. Bauer College of Business at the University of Houston, Houston, Texas. He is also the Cullen Distinguished Chair Professor of Information Sciences. Dr. Pavlou's research has been cited about 68,000 times according to Google Scholar, and he was recognized among the "World's Most Influential Scientific Minds" by Thomson Reuters based on an analysis of "Highly Cited" authors in *Economics & Business* for 2002–2012.

Abhijeet Shirsat is Assistant Professor in the Department of Recreation, Parks and Tourism Administration at California State University, Sacramento. Dr. Shirsat intends to build upon the human behavioral body of literature that identifies the problems and challenges of the hospitality industry, and his research interests focus on human behavioral topics including fake news on social media.

Jie Tang is a Ph.D. student in information systems in HKU Business School at the University of Hong Kong, Hong Kong, China. Her research interests include social media, information privacy, and human–computer interaction. Her research has appeared in the proceedings of several international conferences including International Conference on Information Systems and Pacific Asia Conference on Information Systems.

Russell Torres is Assistant Professor of Business Analytics in the Department of Information Technology and Decision Sciences at the University of North Texas, Denton, Texas and a Society for Information Management (SIM) research fellow. His research interests include data-driven decision-making, organizational impacts of business intelligence and analytics, the use and governance of artificial intelligence, and a wide variety of information technology management topics.

Ofir Turel is Professor of Geography at the University of Geneva. She teaches political and cultural geography at the Department of Geography and geography didactics at the Institute of Teacher Education. She specializes in the analysis of landscape policies, mobilization for landscapes, and mediation practices.

Bin Wang is the endowed Robert C. Vackar College of Business and Entrepreneurship Professor of Business and Professor of Information Systems at the University of Texas Rio Grande Valley. Her research focuses on social media and social commerce, crowdfunding, electronic commerce, mobile commerce, IT adoption, and performance of IT-focused firms.

Shuting (Ada) Wang is Assistant Professor of Information Systems at Zicklin School of Business of Baruch College, City University of New York, New York. She received her Ph.D. in Management Information Systems from Temple University, . Dr. Wang's research examines the impact of social media on the businesses and society and her work has been mentioned by multiple media such as NPR and BizPhilly.

Jane Webster is E. Marie Shantz Chair Emerita in Management Information Systems at Queen's University, Canada, and a fellow of the Association for Information Systems. Jane served as a senior editor for *MIS Quarterly* and VP Publications for the Association for Information Systems. Her current research examines ways to encourage more environmentally sustainable behaviors in organizations.

Vladimir Zwass is Gregory Olsen Endowed Chair and University Distinguished Professor of Computer Science and Management Information Systems at Fairleigh Dickinson University, USA. He is the founding and present editor-in-chief of the *Journal of Management Information Systems*.

Preface

Approaching the fifth decade of its publication, *JMIS* has always stood for a broad understanding of the remit of our discipline and for the multiplicity of research methodologies that undergird its sociotechnical approach to the study of information systems (IS). Indeed, we have been privileged to contribute significantly to the definition of our boundaries. The recent years, combining a broad societal change with the vastly enhanced role of IS in society whose transformations it is driving in many ways, validate this approach to our field.

The present issue of the *Journal* contributes to our understanding and, one hopes, action in a crucial realm. The Special Issue focusing on fake news (FN) we present to you offers a comprehensive (insofar as special issues can do that) analysis of a global societal ill enabled by the Internet. As we study the deleterious effects of FN, we should always keep in mind the good that the Internet-Web compound has brought the world in the societal growth and in the economic development.

The Special Issue on Fake News on the Internet, guest edited by Alan R. Dennis, Dennis F. Galletta, and Jane Webster, offers a multidisciplinary analysis of the destructive global phenomenon. The Guest Editors provide a valuable introduction to the issue they have edited to which 80 submissions were received. It is my place here to add some context and perspective.

"Fake News" is a shorthand for the production, dissemination, and amplification of misinformation originated with an intent to deceive. On the Internet, it may be a fake product review, placed by a competitor, and conceivably integrated into a hostile campaign by a firm specializing in such services. It may also be fake information about a political candidate deployed as a component in a political campaign devised to pervert the democratic process of an election. The first FN may damage a brand, the second may distort the outcome of the election and, beyond that, shake people's faith in democracy. The actors may be individuals or it may be the Russian Internet Research Agency specializing in disinformation as a state organization formed for influence and propaganda purposes. In fact, state actors may be joined by unaffiliated individuals to diffuse and obscure responsibility, and to provide deniability.

FN is not a novel phenomenon. The arrival of new media technologies always has dual, Janus-like, effects, with the dark side being the reverse of the bright coin. The invention of the printing press in the 15th century did not only bring access to the Bible and literacy to the now more enlightened populace. For centuries, it has also brought threats and transformation to the established orders. Jean-Jacques Rousseau, a philosopher who was no particular friend of his contemporary order, had this to say in 1750 for the ages: "If we consider the horrible disorders that printing press has already produced in Europe . . . " (cited in Rauch [6], p.120). Scurrilous printed pamphlets bearing salacious FN about the respective royal consorts kindled the flames of two revolutions, French and Russian, by delegitimizing and "de-majestifying" the reigning houses. Some FN books have lasted centuries, in the ever new editions.

However, there is a huge difference. Powerful technologies have powerful consequences. The power of the Internet and associated information technologies lends the online FN a particular weight. Social media are the principal means of the unholy spiral in spreading FN. Yet the phenomenon of rapid social amplification on the Internet was identified well before the arrival of social media [10]. Here are the principal reasons the FN on today's Internet present a threat to social order and its democratic transformation. The public sphere created by the Internet-Web is massive and global. The global and dense network of networks and software-stack connectivity can import impacts across distant borders. The smartphone as an edge device is accessible to billions of people around the globe. Social media, with the prevailing anonymity of the actors, are based on platforms owned by colossal tech companies that absorb huge profits and massive data. Big data aggregates allow microtargeting of algorithmically personalized real or fake news at the algorithmically defined best responders. Thus, frictionless access to powerful social media platforms facilitates the origination and spreading of FN. Monetization of FN through advertising is a potent driver of their ubiquity. Softbots delivering news to the users according to their profile, magnify the phenomenon. Business models of smaller rogue firms, actually based on exploiting FN, are particularly effective in disseminating online falsehoods at a profit when the costs of communications approach zero.

The onymous author of an article in established print media bears the mantle of expertise, experience, and authority, and her reputation and career prospects are at stake when she publishes. The bearer of FN on the Internet can be just about anyone. And many in the reading public are not equipped to tell the difference and are prone to share and endorse. With that, we have what has been called "a hype machine" [1]. The problem we are dealing with here is that much of what is being hyped is false and there are many falsities that are being hyped.

It is important to recognize and study all these factors in the blooming of FN in order to seek the points and means of intervention and countermeasures. Like the interdisciplinary study that is required, the measures will entail laws and regulations, a variety of technological means, international cooperation, and education. A fundamental issue is that the spread of FN is based on IT and driven algorithmically. To match this, Facebook employs 15,000 moderators to battle misinformation [3] – and that is woefully insufficient if only in matching the speed of the spread (also, who said that the online big tech does not generate jobs?). Any movement towards solutions has to encompass a variety of means, certainly technological and algorithmic, but going well beyond that.

On the demand side, we should recognize the susceptibility to the false belief lent to FN. This is particularly so during the years of the pandemic that bear social isolation, cliquishness, and sense of vulnerability. Of a lie there is an infinite variety; there is only one truth. A lie can be made infinitely colorful; truth attracts the adjective "stark." Lie then entices attention; attention can be sold. The very nature and the often skillful design of FN bear more novelty or sensationalism than the real information, which makes them attractive algorithmically and otherwise to the platforms supported by advertisement. Conspiracy theories are more exciting to many than straight news. Confirmation bias makes people susceptible to the FN reaffirming their prior beliefs. To reproduce the apt title of one of the empirically grounded publications of our field: "People believe what they want to believe when it makes no sense at all" [4]. The empirics confirm that FN spread faster and more broadly than real news [8]. The virality of lies has been well expressed by Jonathan Swift: "Falsehood flies, and truth comes limping after it" [7].

The FN phenomenon has marked societal effects. The post-factuality we experience damages the epistemic order and open societies. The erosion of trust in a society has been linked by extensive research to the damages to social order and to economic prosperity.

Owing to its sociotechnical nature, our discipline has much to offer in seeking out the roots and solutions to the scourge of FN. For example, social norms have been found effective in combating FN on social media [2]. Formal modeling has been deployed to recommend platform policies to counteract FN [5]. Rating the reliability of news sources, labeling individual messages, blocking messages deemed unreliable by various criteria, limiting the number of repostings or "likes" certainly address the issue, but certainly do not scale up to the multifaceted problem. Our research must inform the promulgation of laws and regulations that will necessarily accompany the technological fixes. Over the recent years, *JMIS* has published a series of papers proposing and testing solutions to some of the deception problems in various contexts, some as early as 2004 [9]. We shall continue to do so.

The papers in the present Special Issue analyze numerous problems associated with the supply of FN and the demand for them, mutually reinforcing actions. One of the papers offers a valuable systematization of the multidisciplinary (as necessary) research on FN and induces an integrated research model. Some of the papers also propose solutions and study empirically their effectiveness. The efforts are valiant and present valuable remedies. We need to stress the obvious: at present there is no comprehensive solution. This is another of the massive problems we are faced with since the Internet has been overlaid by the Web, such as security and privacy. The combination of multiple methodologies, positivist, interpretive, and design-scientific included, is at our disposal. We must persevere, since our discipline has much light to shed in all of these dark areas, and so we hope.

Disclosure statement

No potential conflict of interest was reported by the author(s).

References

1. Aral, S. *The Hype Machine*. New York: Currency, 2020.
2. Gimpel H.; Heger, S.; Olenberger, C.: and Utz, L. The effectiveness of social norms in fighting fake news on social media. *Journal of Management Information Systems*, 38, 1 (2021), 196–221.
3. "It's all connected, man," *The Economist*, September 4, 2021, pp. 47–48.
4. Moravec, P.L., Minas, R.K, and Dennis, A. Fake news on social media: People believe what they want to believe when it makes no sense at all. *MIS Quarterly*, 43: 4 (2019), pp.1343–1360.
5. Papanastasiou Y. Fake news propagation and detection: A sequential model, *Management Science*, 66, 5 (2020), pp. 1826–1846.
6. Rauch, J. *The Constitution of Knowledge: A Defense of Truth*. Washington, D.C., Brookings Institution Press, 2021.
7. Swift, J. Political lying, in Craik, H., ed., *English Prose*, 1916. https://www.bartleby.com/209/633.html (accessed on 9/23/2021).
8. Vasoughi, S., Roy, D., and Aral, S. The spread of true and false news online, *Science 359*, 6380 (2018), 1146–1151.
9. Zhou, L., Burgoon, J.K., Twitchell, D.P., Qin, T., Nunamaker Jr., J.F. A comparison of classification methods for predicting deception in computer-mediated communication, *Journal of Management Information Systems*, 20, 4 (2004), 139–165.
10. Zwass, V. Electronic commerce: structures and issues, *International Journal of Electronic Commerce*, 1, 1 (1996), 3–23.

Vladimir Zwass

Introduction to Fake News on the Internet

Alan R. Dennis, Dennis F. Galletta, and Jane Webster

The online generation and dissemination of false information (e.g., through Facebook, Twitter, Snapchat and other Internet media), commonly referred to as "fake news", has garnered immense public attention following the 2016 Brexit referendum, three US elections, the 2019 Indian lynchings, and the 2019 rise in polio cases in Pakistan. Fake news undermines public life across the globe, especially in countries where journalistic practices and institutions are weak [3]. Some fake news is created to spread ideological messages or to create mischief, whereas other fake news is created for profit, such as the Macedonian teenagers who created fake news sites during the 2016 US election to drive advertising [22].

Research shows that fake news spreads "significantly farther, faster, deeper, and more broadly" than true news [24:1146] and has had major societal impacts [15]. All signs indicate that it will get worse as political activists, scammers, alternative news media, and hostile governments become more sophisticated in their production and targeting of fake news.

Fake news and other types of false information are also a matter of concern for business and management research and practice [2,9,10,11,12,19]. Businesses have engaged in deceptive communications such as greenwashing, astroturfing, false advertising and other types of false messages [4,5,14], but false content presented as news presents a novel range of issues for individuals, organizations, and societies [1,18].

The widespread adoption and use of information and communication technologies, particularly social and digital media, play a key role in the current wave of fake news and false information sweeping the globe [1,7,13]. We believe that the IS discipline can contribute significantly to the discourse, as it already has in related areas such as cyberdeviance [23,24] and deception [e.g., 5]. Our field can draw on its intellectual core of theories and empirical findings on the design, use, and impacts of IT artifacts at different levels of analysis. A nascent body of IS research on this topic is emerging [6,8,16–18,20,21]. Related areas such as review manipulation [e.g., 11] and social behaviors in online social networks [e.g., 10,12,21] can provide valuable lessons to apply to online fake news and false information more generally. Yet there is a dearth of evidence about many aspects, and many issues remain open to debate.

We received 80 submissions, which went through three rounds of review and revision. The papers spanned a diverse set of experimental, qualitative, econometric, and analytical methods, and focused on fake news around the globe. The set of accepted papers are also diverse in methods and focus. We would like to say that collectively the articles offer several viable solutions to the problem of fake news. However, this is not the case in all instances.

Access the Support Material: www.routledge.com/ 9781032561127

Some of the articles show how inventions designed to reduce fake news actually have the opposite effect, and instead act to increase the spreading of fake news. Other articles take a longer-term perspective, by measuring or inserting emotions into headlines, allowing us to examine some of the roots of fake news behaviors for future study. Another approach was to prime readers to think more objectively and fairly (which only helped liberal participants), as well as to measure perceptions of what their peers want. Some examined various antecedents of sharing or suppression behaviors. Taken together, this set of articles allows our field to take a significant step forward, but simultaneously shows how challenging the fake news phenomenon is to solve. Clearly, more research is needed before we will be able to reduce the effects of fake news.

Ka Chung Ng, Jie Tang and Dongwon Lee applied two platform interventions to try and combat fake news, in a large-scale archival study of Sina Weibo, the largest social network in China. One intervention targets the *content*, as a flag applying to a single fake news post. Another targets the *person* posting the fake news, imposing a restriction on forwarding further items. After reducing their large sample obtained over a 12-day period, their study of 1,014 matched pairs of truthful fake news posts found that a flag on the content enabled fake news to disseminate in a central manner, encouraging influential users to forward the item. On the other hand, a forwarding restriction kept fake news more dispersed in nature, with a shorter survival time.

Ofir Turel and Babajide Osatuyi took the point of view that users post not only because of their own interests, but also because of their perceptions of the interests of others. In an experiment involving 408 Facebook-using students, they imposed a personal objectivity priming questionnaire that asked them to reflect on their own objectivity, fairness, and rationality in making judgments. This was done to increase the availability and salience of such assessments. Their model also took into account their own credibility bias and political orientation as well as their perceptions of their peers' political orientation, to ultimately predict their sharing bias. Interestingly, the objectivity prime only had an impact on liberal-leaning participants. Also, the consistency of fake news with people's political orientation increased credibility bias and sharing bias, and credibility bias increased sharing bias. Finally, the perceived alignment between a user and their peers' political orientation reduced the effect of credibility bias on sharing bias.

Bingjie Deng and Michael Chau focused on the previously-neglected area of emotions that are expressed in fake news headlines, by testing headlines expressing anger or sadness. Their experiment involved two pretests for instrument development and two main studies of US participants (N=335 and 633, respectively) from Amazon's Mechanical Turk. The authors hypothesized that embedding angry or sad phrases into the headlines would impact the perceived effort of the author and the believability of the headlines, and in turn impact four ultimate behaviors: reading, commenting, sharing, and liking. They found that anger expressed in a headline lowered the perceived effort of the author and lowered the believability of the headline. Sadness, however, did not have the same effect. Finally, believability did impact the ultimate behaviors, as hypothesized.

Kelvin King, Bin Wang, Diego Esobari, and Tamer Oraby use a combination of analytical modeling and data from Twitter to examine the effects of actively combatting fake news by providing correct information to dispel specific fake news stories. They first develop a theoretical model of the diffusion of both falsehoods and correction messages on Twitter and their mutual relationship. They then use Twitter data from Hurricane Harvey in 2017 and Hurricane Florence in 2018 to examine the bidirectional relationships between the diffusion of falsehoods and their correction messages. The results show that correction messages do not reduce the spread of fake news, but instead have the opposite effect of *increasing* the spread of fake news; intervening to correct fake news backfires and instead increases its reach. These results suggest that leaving falsehoods to run their course may be the most effective course of action.

Ada Wang, Min-Seok Pang, and Paul Pavlou use data from Weibo in China (combined with surveys of Chinese and American social media users) to examine the effects of identity verification on the spread of fake news. Many social media platforms are attempting to reduce the relative anonymity of those posting news stories by verifying users' identity, with the idea that after disclosing their identity, users would be less likely to deliberately create and share fake news. The results suggest that identity verification (without a publically viewable verification badge) reduces users' propensity to post fake news. However, if users receive a verification badge, identity verification has no effect. Moreover, if identity verification is voluntary (rather than mandatory), users who seek an identity verification badge, post *more* fake news after they receive it. Thus, identity verification backfires, and increases the spread of fake news.

Rather than focusing on interventions to reduce fake news, Christy Galletta Horner, Dennis Galletta, Jennifer Crawford, and Abhijeet Shirsat theorize relations between emotions and the sharing of fake news. In the context of U.S. elections, they conduct a mixed methods study to investigate the process by which individuals experience discrete emotional reactions to political fake news headlines and how these emotions contribute to the perpetuation of fake news. They find through the use of an emotion inventory that strong, activating emotions lead to either the further spread of fake news through actions such as sharing, or suppression by publicly or privately refuting the post. In contrast, deactivating emotions lead to inaction, where readers are more likely to ignore or disengage from the spread of false news. Other findings point out that different headlines appear to stimulate different emotions, depending on the nature of the story, but conservatives did react with strikingly different patterns than liberals. They synthesize their findings into a process model to help drive future research to mitigate fake news.

Jordana George, Natalie Gerhart, and Russell Torres also help set directions for the future by inducing a research model for the investigation of fake news from their analysis of the multidisciplinary fake news literature. They synthesize the literature and then develop a research framework and related propositions to help spark future research. They highlight key research themes for IS researchers, in which potential theoretical perspectives and research questions are proposed. We expect that this paper will become required reading for all future IS research on fake news.

We would like to thank the hundreds of reviewers, the five individuals who served as Associate Editors (Hailiang Chen, Atanu Lahri, Kai Larson, Mingfeng Lin, and Antino Kim), and Indrani Karmakar, who served as Review Coordinator. Without them, this Special Issue would not have been possible.

Disclosure statement

No potential conflict of interest was reported by the author(s).

References

1. Allcott, H. and Gentzkow, M. Social media and fake news in the 2016 election. *Journal of Economic Perspectives, 31,* 2 (May 2017), 211–236.
2. Aral, S. Truth, Disrupted. *Harvard Business Review,* July 2018, 3–11.
3. Bradshaw, S. and Howard, P.N. Challenging truth and trust: A global inventory of organized social media manipulation. *The Computational Propaganda Project,* (2018).
4. Dunlap, R.R. and McCright, A.M. Organized climate change denial. In J.S. Dryzek, R.B. Norgaard and D. Schlosberg, eds., *The Oxford handbook of climate change and society.* Oxford University Press, 2011.
5. George, J.F., Gupta, M., Giordano, G., Mills, A.M., Tennant, V.M., and Lewis, C.C. The effects of communication media and culture on deception detection accuracy. *MIS Quarterly, 42,* 2 (February 2018), 551–575.
6. Gimpel, H., Heger, S., Olenberger, C., & Utz, L. The effectiveness of social norms in fighting fake news on social media. *Journal of Management Information Systems, 38,* 1 (2021), 196–221.

7. Humprecht, E. Where "fake news" flourishes: a comparison across four Western democracies. *Information, Communication & Society*, (May 2018), 1–16.

8. Kim, A. and Dennis, A.R. Says who? The effects of presentation format and source rating on fake news in social media. *MIS Quarterly*, 43, 3 (September 2019).

9. Knight, E. and Tsoukas, H. When fiction trumps truth: What "post-truth" and "alternative facts" mean for management studies. *Organization Studies*, 40, 2 (February 2019), 183–197.

10. Kuem, J., Ray, S., Siponen, M., and Kim, S.S. What leads to prosocial behaviors on social networking services: A tripartite model. *Journal of Management Information Systems*, 34, 1 (January 2017), 40–70.

11. Kumar, N., Venugopal, D., Qiu, L., and Kumar, S. Detecting review manipulation on online platforms with hierarchical supervised learning. *Journal of Management Information Systems*, 35, 1 (January 2018), 350–380.

12. Kwon, H.E., Oh, W., and Kim, T. Platform structures, homing preferences, and homophilous propensities in online social networks. *Journal of Management Information Systems*, 34, 3 (July 2017), 768–802.

13. Lazer, D.M.J., Baum, M.A., Benkler, Y., et al. The science of fake news. *Science*, 359, 6380 (March 2018), 1094–1096.

14. Lyon, T.P. and Montgomery, A.W. The means and end of greenwash. *Organization & Environment*, 28, 2 (June 2015), 223–249.

15. Mathew, I. Most Americans say they have lost trust in the media. *Columbia Journalism Review*, 2018. https://www.cjr.org/the_media_today/trust-in-media-down.php.

16. Moravec, P., Kim, A., and Dennis, A.R. Behind the stars: The effects of news source ratings on fake news in social media. *Journal of Management Information Systems*, (in press).

17. Moravec, P., Kim, A., and Dennis, A.R. Flagging fake news: System 1 vs. System 2. In *ICIS 2018 Proceedings*. Association for Information Systems, San Francisco, CA, US, 2018.

18. Moravec, P., Minas, R.A., and Dennis, A.R. Fake news on social media: People believe what they want to believe when it makes no sense at all. *MIS Quarterly*, (in press).

19. Murphy, M. Study: Fake news hits the workplace. *Leadership IQ*, 2017. https://www.leadershipiq.com/blogs/leadershipiq/study-fake-news-hits-the-workplace.

20. Murungi, D., Puaro, S., and Yates, D.J. Beyond facts: A new spin on fake news in the age of social media. In *AMCIS 2018 Proceedings*. Association for Information Systems, New Orleans, LA, US, 2018.

21. Pan, Z., Lu, Y., Wang, B., and Chau, P.Y.K. Who do you think you are? Common and differential effects of social self-identity on social media usage. *Journal of Management Information Systems*, 34, 1 (January 2017), 71–101.

22. Subramanian, S. Inside the Macedonian fake-news complex. *Wired*, 2017. https://www.wired.com/2017/02/veles-macedonia-fake-news/.

23. Venkatraman, S., M. K. Cheung, C., Lee, Z.W.Y., D. Davis, F., and Venkatesh, V. The "Darth" side of technology use: An inductively derived typology of cyberdeviance. *Journal of Management Information Systems*, 35, 4 (October 2018), 1060–1091.

24. Vosoughi, S., Roy, D., and Aral, S. The spread of true and false news online. *Science*, 359, 6380 (March 2018), 1146–1151.

The Effect of Platform Intervention Policies on Fake News Dissemination and Survival: An Empirical Examination

Ka Chung Ng ⓘ, Jie Tang ⓘ, and Dongwon Lee ⓘ

ABSTRACT

Fake news on social media has become a serious problem, and social media platforms have started to actively implement various interventions to mitigate its impact. This paper focuses on the effectiveness of two platform interventions, namely a content-level intervention (i.e., a fake news flag that applies to a single post) and an account-level intervention (i.e., a forwarding restriction policy that applies to the entire account). Collecting data from China's largest social media platform, we study the impact of a fake news flag on three fake news dissemination patterns using a propensity score matching method with a difference-in-differences approach. We find that implementing a policy of using fake news flag influences the dissemination of fake news in a more centralized manner via direct forwards and in a less dispersed manner via indirect forwards, and that fake news posts are forwarded more often by influential users. In addition, compared with truthful news, fake news is disseminated in a less centralized and more dispersed manner and survives for a shorter period after a forwarding restriction policy is implemented. This study provides causal empirical evidence of the effect of a fake news flag on fake news dissemination. We also expand the literature on platform interventions to combat fake news by investigating a less studied account-level intervention. We discuss the practical implications of our results for social media platform owners and policymakers.

Introduction

Online channels such as social media play an important role in information acquisition and dissemination [62]. However, these channels are increasingly affected by the spread of fake news, which should be addressed through substantial efforts, especially during serious social, political, and epidemiological crises like the COVID-19 pandemic of 2020. Unlike content disseminated through traditional channels such as newspapers and broadcasts, social media content can be created, modified, and spread in a much less rigorous way. It can be published by a layperson without sufficient knowledge of a topic, modified, and even distorted during dissemination, ultimately leading to serious and undesirable consequences.

Access the Support Material: www.routledge.com/ 9781032561127

For instance, as reported by CNN,[1] a man in Phoenix, U.S., died of chloroquine phosphate poisoning after taking a product intended for cleaning fish tanks in the hope of recovering from COVID-19, after reading a post on social media advocating this as a treatment. Antonio Guterres, Secretary-General of the United Nations, alerted people to the "dangerous epidemic of fake news" on COVID-19 in the current situation and stressed that social media companies should take responsibility for tackling the spread of fake news.[2]

In line with this alert, social media platforms have implemented various interventions in recent years, including WhatsApp's forwarding restriction to slow the spread of fake news,[3] Sina Weibo's launch of its Community Management Center to detect fake news by social reporting,[4] and Facebook's fact-checking teams that verify the factuality of news stories.[5] Although these efforts to protect the credibility of information are recognized, the effectiveness of platform interventions remains unclear [2,41,57]. We believe that it is urgent and important to examine the effectiveness of platform interventions with empirical evidence. This study thus performs a series of analyses to evaluate the effectiveness of platform interventions to limit the spread of fake news. Specifically, we study the effectiveness of platform interventions in terms of fake news dissemination and survival. We further divide fake news dissemination into three patterns to better understand the more nuanced impacts of platform interventions.

Previous studies focused primarily on the content-level platform intervention, which applies to a single piece of information. A fake news flag is a good example of the content-level intervention; it attaches a label to a post to indicate that the post is fake news [44,45,49]. The results of previous studies on its effectiveness mainly focus on the cognitive level. Several studies have shown that flagging fake news can reduce its believability and sharing intentions [17,44]. However, other studies have found that a fake news flag can be ineffective due to confirmation bias [45] and people's habit of disregarding warnings [55]. These seemingly inconsistent findings based on psychological outcomes motivate us to investigate the influence of a fake news flag on people's actual behavior in a more generalizable setting. Many social media platforms, such as Twitter, do not prevent the spread of flagged fake news to ensure the practice of free speech, unless the harm caused by such fake news is extremely serious (i.e., a threat to national security).[6] Besides, fake news may be continuously forwarded even after being flagged as it is most often more novel than real news [69]. Therefore, it is of great interest to understand how a fake news flag works in the real world. Instead of focusing on the psychological outcomes induced by a fake news flag, we take a different approach by using large-scale archival data collected from the field and exploiting a quasi-experiment to establish a causal relationship between a fake news flag and people's sharing behaviors.

In addition to studying a fake news flag, we identify an important research gap in the relevant literature. As the impact of fake news has become increasingly serious,[7] platforms have started to implement stricter regulations by imposing activity restrictions on accounts that publish fake news. We refer to this type of restriction as an account-level platform intervention. Unlike a fake news flag, which mitigates fake news by focusing on people's cognitive processes [25], the restriction intervention directly controls the spread of fake news by limiting people's engagement with fake news and inducing deterrence among accounts that intend to create and distribute fake news. However, there are concerns about the negative impacts of this intervention, as it may unintentionally restrict freedom of speech and block legitimate contents.[8] It also takes time for the platform to discern the legitimacy of a post [12]. Therefore, our work fills this research gap by empirically examining the effectiveness of the account-level intervention on fake news dissemination. As little is known about the impact of the account-level intervention, we also examine its effectiveness in shortening the survival time of fake news. Contrary to popular belief, fake news may not be overwhelmed by a huge amount of information online and disappear quickly (within days) [58,66]. If fake news can survive for an extended period, it is more likely to be spread through likes, sharing, comments, and, more importantly, reading. Exposure to fake news is dangerous, as people may take action without seeking the truth. Therefore, stopping the early spread of fake news is important to minimize its damage and negative social impact. In this regard, in addition to scholarly implications, we believe that understanding the impact of the account-level platform intervention on the survival time of fake news is of great importance for practice.

This study leverages two interventions implemented by Sina Weibo, the largest social media platform in China: a fake news flag as a content-level intervention and a forwarding restriction policy as an account-level intervention. To this end, we empirically examine how these two platform interventions affect fake news and answer the following two research questions:

1. *How does a content-level platform policy, i.e., fake news flags, affect fake news dissemination?*

2. *How does an account-level platform policy, i.e., forwarding restrictions, affect fake news dissemination and fake news survival?*

Using natural language processing and propensity score matching (PSM), we obtain a matched sample of fake news and truthful news to alleviate potential endogeneity issues for empirical analysis. We first study the impact of a fake news flag by using a difference-in-differences (DiD) approach. This specification helps us to identify a causal relationship between a fake news flag and fake news dissemination. We find that a post is distributed through more direct forwards than indirect forwards after being marked as "fake news." Furthermore, a fake news flag encourages influential users to spread fake news posts to confirm its falsehood. Next, we estimate the impact of implementing a forwarding restriction policy by using the matched sample and controlling for the observable characteristics of the post and the user. Our results show that a forwarding restriction policy affects fake news and truthful news differently. Compared with truthful news, fake news is disseminated in a less centralized but more dispersed manner and has a significantly shorter survival time after the implementation of a forwarding restriction policy.

Overall, we find that a fake news flag and a forwarding restriction policy have different effects on fake news, with the former leading to more centralized and less dispersed dissemination of fake news and the latter yielding the opposite pattern. These results are not contradictory, as fake news flag and forwarding restriction policy are theorized as two different types of platform intervention. Therefore, their different influences on fake news dissemination are expected and can be explained by two mechanisms. The impact of a fake news flag on fake news is explained by the reduction of content ambiguity [35], which affects the weak ties of the fake news publishing account, whereas the impact of a forwarding restriction policy on fake news is explained by relational concerns arising from the strong ties [71]. In practice, these findings can inform social media platforms about designing interventions to combat the spread of fake news. Although the account-level intervention seems to represent a "one-size-fits-all" policy, our results suggest that it does not affect the normal and desirable dissemination of truthful news.

This study contributes to the literature on platform interventions to combat fake news on social media. We provide empirical evidence based on field data of the causal impact of the content-level intervention (i.e., fake news flag) on fake news dissemination, which extends previous findings based on cognitive outcomes to actual behaviors by examining the practical importance of and capacity for flagging fake news to reduce its harm and social impact. We further investigate a less studied account-level intervention (i.e., forwarding restriction policy) and shed light on its effectiveness in mitigating the spread of fake news.

The rest of this paper is organized as follows. In the next section, we summarize the related literature and identify research gaps. In Section 3, we theorize the impacts of the two platform intervention policies on fake news. In Section 4, we introduce the research context and describe the data collected for the study. In Section 5, we propose our identification strategies. In Section 6, we present and discuss the research results. We discuss the contributions and limitations of this study in Section 7 and conclude our study in Section 8.

Related Literature

Fake News on Social Media

Fake news refers to news posts with deceptive intentions and false content [1,34]. Fake news also strongly overlaps with other deceptive information such as misinformation (false or misleading information) and disinformation (false information that is purposely spread to deceive people) [41]. As social media has changed the way news is created and consumed, such that people typically only read headlines or watch short videos,[9] we define fake news in a broader sense as any information that is intentionally and verifiably false and could mislead readers.

The issue of fake news on social media has received much attention in previous studies [1,33,45,69], given its huge impact on politics, social crises, and other aspects of social life. One strand of the literature focuses on the empirical analysis of fake news dissemination, using descriptive analyses to examine dissemination patterns in terms of post and user characteristics [42,46,65,69]. For instance, Vosoughi et al. [69] found that fake news spreads farther, faster, deeper, and more broadly than truthful news across various topics, including politics, terrorism, and natural disasters. In addition to these static characteristics, previous studies have adopted a dynamic perspective to study fake news dissemination with informative results [32,65]. For example, Sutton et al. [64] explored how users' follower-followee networks can influence the transmission of crisis information from a social network perspective. Tang and Ng [66] examined the forwarding behavior of users and found that more forwards are associated with a longer survival time of fake news on social media. The characteristics of fake news recipients have also been examined. For example, in the context of the 2016 U.S. presidential election, studies have shown that people who were older [21,23], politically conservative [21,23], and heavily involved in political news [21] were more likely to engage with fake news.

Another strand of the literature focuses on the psychological mechanisms or consequences of users exposed to fake news on social media. Several studies have posited the existence of confirmation bias, arguing that users tend to believe news that confirms their prior beliefs, regardless of the authenticity of its content [33,34]. When encountering information that does not align with their prior beliefs, individuals experience cognitive dissonance [24] and tend to resolve such dissonance by rejecting new information, as this often requires less effort than changing one's beliefs. Other mechanisms, such as fluency via prior exposure [50], laziness or lack of reasoning [51], and cognitive and affective engagement [42], have also been proposed to explain why people are susceptible to fake news. In terms of outcomes, previous studies have focused on perceived believability [33,34,45], engagement with the news (e.g., read, like, comment, and share) [33,34,43,45,47,49], and fact-checking behavior [68].

In summary, studies have investigated several aspects of fake news, including the characteristics of fake news content, publishers, and receivers; the mechanisms behind people's susceptibility to fake news; and individuals' attitudes and behavioral outcomes when exposed to fake news on social media. However, to the best of our knowledge, relatively few studies have used field data to investigate platform interventions aimed at changing people's behavior toward fake news.

Platform Interventions to Combat Fake News

Aside from understanding the phenomenon of fake news per se, previous studies have focused on platform interventions as mitigation strategies to detect [23,34] and stop [1,2,14,18,33] the spread of fake news. Most empirical studies of platform interventions, as summarized in Table 1, have focused on the content-level intervention, which only regulates one piece of information on social media. A fake news flag is a commonly studied content-level intervention, but the results of previous studies on its effectiveness are mixed.

For instance, Moravec et al. [44] showed that flagging fake news along with training on the meaning of the flag could significantly reduce the believability of fake news. They also showed that conducting flagging interventions to trigger subconscious processing (i.e., by displaying a visual "stop" sign when flagging fake news), deliberative reasoning (i.e., by displaying a text argument when flagging fake news), or a combination of these two approaches can effectively reduce the believability of fake news on social media. Garrett and Poulsen [17] reported that publishers' self-identified flags could reduce people's beliefs and sharing intentions regarding inaccurate messages. However, Moravec et al. [45] found that although a fake news flag can trigger increased cognitive activity in people, it cannot affect their judgments about the truth due to confirmation bias. In the same vein, Ross et al. [55] studied a fake news flag with additional manipulation (either a normal warning message indicating that the focal information was disputed by the third party or a negatively framed risk-handling advice) and found no significant effect of the flag on fake news. Considering the interaction between a fake news flag and the reputation of the information source, Figl et al. [14] found that although the flag may reduce the believability of fake news, this effect is weakened if the source of that fake news has a good reputation. Recently, Pennycook et al. [49] suggested that a fake news flag induces an implied truth effect so that unflagged fake news headlines are considered valid and more accurate by default.

Table 1. Existing Empirical Studies on Platform Intervention against Fake News

Reference	Platform Intervention	Dependent Variable	Data	Fake vs. Truthful News Comparison
This study	**Content-level: fake news flag** **Account-level: forwarding restriction policy**	**Dissemination pattern and survival time**	**Field**	**Yes**
Pennycook et al. [49]	Content-level: fake news flag	Accuracy judgment and social media sharing	Behavioral experiment	Yes
Figl et al. [14]	Content-level: fake news flag	News believability	Behavioral experiment	No
Kim and Dennis [33]	Content-level: highlighting source	Engagement with news (read, like, comment, and share)	Behavioral experiment	No
Kim et al. [34]	Content-level: source rating	Engagement with news (read, like, comment, and share)	Behavioral experiment	No
Moravec et al. [45]	Content-level: fake news flag	News believability	Behavioral experiment	Yes
Tang and Ng [66]	Community-level: launch of the social reporting system	Survival time	Field	No
Moravec et al. [44]	Content-level: fake news flag	News believability	Behavioral experiment	No
Ross et al. [55]	Content-level: fake news flag (warning message with/without risk-framed advice)	Number of hits and false alarms identified by a user	Behavioral experiment	No

The literature mainly addresses the effectiveness of a fake news flag based on cognitive and psychological outcomes, such as content believability and sharing intentions. To the best of our knowledge, little research has focused on changes in people's actual behavior in response to a fake news flag. Understanding this effect is crucial for fake news research, as the ultimate goal of any platform intervention is to stop the spread of fake news. In this regard, this study considers a more generalizable setting that exploits field data to investigate the effectiveness of flagging deceptive content by examining changes in people's sharing behavior. In particular, we aim to understand how a post is disseminated after being flagged as fake news.

In light of the huge impact of fake news on society, social media platforms have started to take a proactive approach by restricting the activities of accounts that publish deceptive information. This imposition of restrictions is considered an account-level intervention. Algorithms have been developed to detect and remove malicious and bot accounts created solely to spread fake news [59]. In addition, network-based methods have been proposed to stop the spread of fake news by identifying a set of accounts to monitor [59] or by controlling the flow of information through suspicious accounts [3]. Nevertheless, the effectiveness of this type of platform intervention has been less studied, as shown in Table 1. The account-level intervention is expected to be a better fake news mitigation strategy, as it not only regulates isolated fake news but also prevents the account publishing this fake news from performing activities such as forwarding posts or being followed by other accounts. This intervention should trigger inhibitory emotions such as fear and dread among accounts with the intent to deceive, effectively deterring them from creating and spreading fake news [52]. However, this account-level intervention may be detrimental to the freedom of speech and might inevitably hinder the normal circulation of credible information, i.e., truthful news. Therefore, it is theoretically and practically important to study the account-level intervention and its impact on the dissemination of fake and truthful news.

Hypothesis Development

Conceptualization of Dissemination Characteristics

The main objective of this study is to examine how content-level and account-level platform interventions affect fake news dissemination. We define "the dissemination of a post" as a directed network, with each node representing an account and each link representing a forwarding of the post by the account. We then divide the dissemination of posts into three patterns, namely *centrality*, *dispersibility*, and *influenceability*.

Centrality captures the centralized distribution of a post by counting its direct forwards. This pattern is commonly considered when studying information diffusion [18,21,25]. In our context, high centrality indicates that a post receives more direct forwards than indirect forwards. Dispersibility captures how far and deep a post is distributed in its dissemination network. Vosoughi et al. [69] captured this dissemination characteristic through structural virality [19] and documented that fake news spreads significantly farther, deeper, and more broadly than truthful news. In this study, we propose a similar but more accurate measure than structural virality to represent the dispersibility of fake news, in which a post with high dispersibility indicates that it spreads farther and deeper than a post with low dispersibility.

Finally, influenceability captures whether a post is widely disseminated to other accounts through a few direct forwards. The literature suggests that influential users help to facilitate the cascade and spread of information [11,72]. Therefore, a few direct forwards of a fake news post can also reach many other accounts if it is forwarded by influential users. We represent influenceability as the reach of a post that is distributed through influential users.

Our three proposed dissemination patterns correspond to basic and commonly used measures in social networks, namely degree centrality, closeness centrality, and eigenvector centrality [19,56,73]. These three measures use various concepts of social networks, such as degree [56], shortest path, interconnectedness [40], social influence [73], and power [15], to capture the main aspects of a post dissemination network.

Effect of the Content-Level Intervention: Fake News Flag

To identify the effect of a fake news flag on post dissemination patterns in terms of centrality and dispersibility, we first draw on social tie theory and define two types of social ties for an account: strong ties and weak ties [20]. Strong ties refer to proximate followers who can forward posts directly from the focal account, and weak ties refer to other users with more than one degree of separation from the focal account [71]. Due to the homophily of strong ties, followers are more likely to have the same views and beliefs as the focal account [22,38,48]. Therefore, the forwarding behavior of strong ties is not affected by a fake news flag due to confirmation bias [33,34,45].

In contrast, weak ties are distant followers who are less likely to have the same views and beliefs as the focal account. The forwarding behavior of weak ties is thus affected by a fake news flag that reduces the ambiguity of the post and eliminates the followers' need for information verification. Rumor theory suggests that ambiguity is an important factor that leads to fake news dissemination [35]. For example, Rosnow [54] proposed that uncertainty is a major predictor of rumor generation and transmission. Oh et al. [46] found that the ambiguity of the information source is a significant predictor of rumor dissemination in the context of a social crisis. Therefore, before a post is identified as fake news, its authenticity is ambiguous to its audience. As individuals experience a lack of reliable information in an ambiguous situation, they tend to engage in information seeking, sharing, and elaboration to resolve information uncertainty, incompleteness, or incongruence [32,46]. With a fake news flag, the ambiguity is lifted because the post is verified as fake news. In line with this reasoning, we predict that flagging fake news will reduce its ambiguity, preventing it from spreading farther and more broadly through weak ties. Therefore, we expect that a fake news flag leads to more centralized and less dispersed dissemination of fake news and propose the following hypotheses:

H1a: A fake news flag increases the centrality of the fake news dissemination network.

H1b: A fake news flag decreases the dispersibility of the fake news dissemination network.

Regarding the influenceability of the fake news dissemination network, influential users with many followers are expected to behave more cautiously to protect their authenticity, good reputation, and good public relations [4,13]. They tend to avoid disseminating an ambiguous post until it has been verified but will forward verified fake news to help dispel it so that their followers are not fooled or confused by fake news posts. As a result, we expect influential users to be more likely to spread a post after it is flagged as fake news, as the ambiguity regarding its authenticity is removed. Accordingly, we propose the following hypothesis:

H1c: A fake news flag increases the influenceability of the fake news dissemination network.

Effect of the Account-Level Intervention: Forwarding Restriction Policy

Unlike the content-level intervention that targets post of questionable reliability, the account-level intervention targets malicious accounts and imposes severe punishment to combat the spread of fake news. It can be a very efficient strategy to fight the wave of fake news, as accounts are completely blocked from posting deceptive information. However, as mentioned above, this intervention can also cause fear and concern among legitimate accounts about publishing trustworthy content and may restrict freedom of speech and the spread of truthful news. Research has also suggested that blocking malicious accounts is problematic if the decision is not transparent and publicly assessable [41]. We thus aim to empirically investigate this less studied platform intervention for better policy design.

To explain the relationship between a forwarding restriction policy and fake news dissemination, we argue that the strong ties and weak ties of an account differ with respect to their relational aspect [71]. Specifically, compared with weak ties, strong ties have a high level of emotional closeness and a strong proximate interpersonal relationship with the focal account [63,71]. When an account publishes a post whose authenticity is uncertain, strong ties tend to avoid forwarding that post by considering that the account may be punished with an activity restriction. For weak ties with less relational consideration, their forwarding behavior is less likely to be affected by a forwarding restriction policy. Taken together, there will be fewer direct forwards made by the strong ties but relatively more indirect forwards made by the weak ties, leading to less centralized and more dispersed dissemination of fake news. Therefore, we propose the following hypotheses:

H2a: Fake news is disseminated in a less centralized manner after the implementation of a forwarding restriction policy.

H2b: Fake news is disseminated in a more dispersed manner after the implementation of a forwarding restriction policy.

In terms of influenceability, as discussed earlier, influential users' forwarding behavior tends to be largely affected by reputational concerns because they feel more accountable for their behavior in the presence of a large audience. In other words, influential users decide to forward a post by considering whether this forwarding will harm their reputation or not. Unlike a fake news flag, which clearly alleviates the problem of sharing fake news by reducing its ambiguity, a forwarding restriction policy does not affect the forwarding behavior of influential users in a predictable direction. On the one hand, influential users may become more active in forwarding posts to protect the practice of free speech [5]. On the other hand, they may choose to share fewer posts to avoid forwarding fake news that would damage their reputation [4,13]. In line with this reasoning, we consider the effect of a forwarding restriction policy on the influenceability of fake news dissemination as an empirical question, and we do not formally propose a hypothesis here.

Using a forwarding restriction policy is an effective way to stop the spread of fake news, as it restricts the activities of the fake news publishing account instead of just warning others about fake news. Although our above hypotheses posit that fake news will be disseminated in a more dispersed manner with a forwarding restriction policy, the impact of fake news should be limited because the strong ties of the fake news publishing account are unlikely to forward fake news due to relational concerns. As a result, the number of fake news forwards will be significantly reduced, ultimately leading to the faster and earlier disappearance of the post. Therefore, we propose the following hypothesis:

H2c: Fake news has a shorter survival time after the implementation of a forwarding restriction policy.

The next section describes the empirical context and data to test the proposed hypotheses.

Empirical Context and Data

Sina Weibo and Sina Community Management Center

Sina Weibo is one of China's largest and most popular microblogging websites. Launched by Sina Corporation on August 14, 2009, Sina Weibo has grown dramatically and had over 497 million monthly active users in the third quarter of 2019.[10] Faced with the growing threat of fake news, Sina Weibo launched a Community Management Center[11] in May 2012 to take advantage of the collective intelligence of community users to control the spread of fake news. The center relies on a social reporting system, through which users can report a post if they believe it to be harmful information (e.g., a threat to national security, misleading advertising, or obscene information), a message related to personal attacks, or fake news ("misinformation").[12] This report is posted publicly, with details including the reporting user's ID, reasons for reporting, reported post, and processing stage (e.g., stage of proof, judgment, and publicity).

According to Sina Weibo Community Management Regulations,[13] a reported post will be accepted for validation only if 1) the post has been forwarded more than 100 times or 2) the post has been reported by more than 10 users. We believe that this rule validates our study, as we can avoid issues such as malicious and indiscriminate reporting. We focus on posts that are reported and verified as fake news and exclude those being reported as harmful information, as the latter will be directly assessed and removed by the platform and will not be allowed to be freely distributed. We also exclude all posts related to personal attacks, as they do not necessarily contain fake content.

Content-level and Account-level Platform Interventions on Sina Weibo

Using the launch of this Community Management Center, we focus on two interventions implemented by Sina Weibo: a content-level intervention, i.e., fake news flag, and an account-level intervention, i.e., forwarding restriction policy.

Sina Weibo introduced the fake news flag on May 28, 2012, alongside the launch of its Community Management Center. Fake news is flagged with a message stating that "this post is identified as fake" after being reported and verified. Along with this warning message, users can follow the hyperlink, which directs them to the web page of the Community Management Center. This page provides users with various information about the fake news post, including the reporting time, the reporter, the reported proof, and the assessment process. Figure 1 shows a screenshot of this assessment page.

On August 30, 2013, Sina Weibo implemented a forwarding restriction policy based on a credit scoring system. The credit scoring system punishes users with score deductions for misbehavior, such as publishing fake news, and the number of deductions increases with the number of fake news forwards. As the number of forwards increases, an account's credit score will be continuously reduced until it reaches a certain low value and the account's activities are restricted, e.g., posts can no longer be forwarded by others. Before August 30, 2013, no form of punishment prevented users from engaging with accounts with low credit scores. However, after the implementation of the forwarding restriction policy (August 30, 2013), accounts with a credit score of fewer than 60 points are restricted automatically by preventing their posts from being forwarded by others, regardless of the content. Accounts with a credit score of fewer than 40 points are further restricted by hiding all their posts from their followers. To emphasize again, the forwarding restriction policy intervention takes effect at the account level and naturally influences all posts from restricted accounts, even if the content is truthful. As this platform intervention is unexpected or unpredictable, we consider it an exogenous shock to platform users and examine its impact on the dissemination of both fake and truthful news. Figure 2 shows how the intervention works to prevent platform users from forwarding fake news.

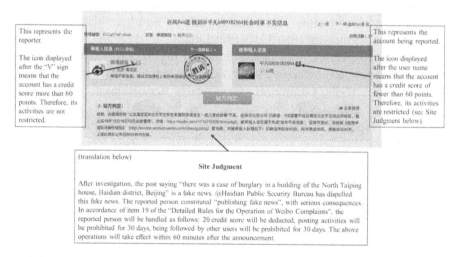

Figure 1. Fake News Assessment Page from Sina Weibo

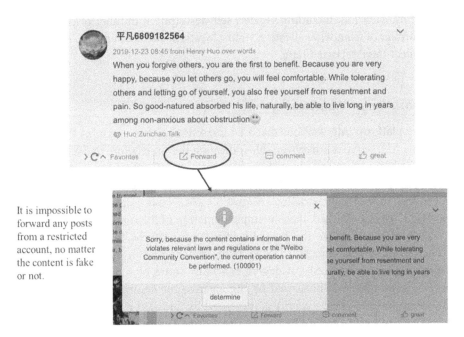

It is impossible to forward any posts from a restricted account, no matter the content is fake or not.

Figure 2. Forwarding Restriction Policy Intervention from Sina Weibo

Sina Weibo Datasets

To analyze the effects of the two platform interventions on fake news, we obtain our datasets from Sina Weibo through its open API.[14] The Sina Weibo API provides a comprehensive interface to capture all relevant information of a post and its forwards. We restrict our sample to all posts published after June 2012, as the Community Management Center was officially launched on May 28, 2012. We then focus on a 2-year period, from June 2012 to May 2014. We identify a set of known fake news posts from the Community Management Center and only focus on posts reported as fake news by users. Notably, in addition to user reporting, Sina Weibo proactively identifies fake news either manually or by using machine learning algorithms. These fake news posts are likely to be identified quickly after publication due to sensitive keywords and images and then be deleted immediately. Therefore, they are unlikely to be disseminated and are not appropriate for our analysis of fake news dissemination pattern and survival. This proactive detection of fake news can also be seen as a form of censorship and is out of our scope. Therefore, we limit our scope to only fake news identified by the social reporting system rather than the platform. Based on our screening process, our dataset contains 1,514 fake news posts and all their forward/comment messages from 409,020 Weibo users. This sample of fake news posts covers various topics such as local news, international politics, and life-related news. In addition, we collect over 50,000 truthful news posts published during the same sample period.

For each post, we have information on the number of forwards, comments, likes received, and pictures included. We also know from which source the post is published (e.g., iPhone, website, or desktop app). In addition to post-specific information, we obtain user-specific information, including gender, self-description, number of posts, number of followers, number of friends, verification status, location, and account age. For all fake news posts, we collect their reported date.

Operationalization of Variables

We study two platform interventions that are represented by two variables. For the fake news flag, we define *Marked* as a binary variable indicating the time before and after the flag, with a value of 1 when a post was flagged as fake news and 0 otherwise. For the forwarding restriction policy, we define *Restriction* as equal to 1 if a post was published after the implementation date of the restriction (August 30, 2013) and 0 otherwise. Of the 1,514 fake news posts, 137 were published after the implementation of the forwarding restriction policy.

For variables that capture the post dissemination patterns, two are directly adopted from the literature and one is adapted with minor modifications [40]. *Centrality* is measured by the standardized out-degree centrality score of a post in its dissemination network. *Influenceability* is measured by the eigenvector centrality score of a post in its dissemination network. *Dispersibility* is measured by taking the reciprocal of the standardized closeness centrality score of a post. As mentioned earlier, previous studies have used structural virality to capture the dispersibility of the spread of fake news [69]. This measure considers the average distance between all pairs of nodes in the dissemination network and is less accurate and reliable than our proposed measure that only considers the average distance between the focal node and all other nodes. When measuring the dispersibility of a post, we treat its dissemination network as an undirected network because forwarding is unidirectional, which causes a problem when calculating the shortest paths between nodes. Note that *Centrality* and *Dispersibility* are defined in a relative sense, as the two variables are based on standardized scores, although their rates of change are different. For example, centrality can decrease dramatically without a significant increase in dispersibility if indirect forwards occur within a few degrees of the focal account.

Following Tang and Ng [66], we operationalize fake news survival by two variables: *Discovery time* and *Stopping time*. *Discovery time* is measured (in minutes) by the time between the published time and the reported time. It captures how fast a post is identified and reported to the platform as fake news. *Stopping time* is measured (in minutes) by the time between the reported time and the time of the last reply (either a forward or comment), which serves as a proxy for fake news survival rather than an exact measure. As fake news has an effect when people read, comment, and forward it, an exact survival time should be measured by the time between the reported time and the time when no more users interact with that fake news post. However, it is impossible to identify whether any individual has read that fake news post or not. Thus, we consider the last observable user engagement as the length of time that fake news can survive after being verified and labeled.

Fake is a binary variable indicating whether a post is a fake news or not. Finally, to account for the heterogeneity of the post and user characteristics, we use a comprehensive set of control variables. The definitions of all variables used in this study are summarized in Appendix A. The summary statistics of the fake news variables are reported in Table 2.

Table 2. Summary Statistics of Variables for Fake News

Variable Name	Overall (n = 1,514)				Before Restriction (n = 1,377)				After Restriction (n = 137)			
	Mean	Std. Dev.	Max.	Min.	Mean	Std. Dev.	Max.	Min.	Mean	Std. Dev.	Max.	Min.
Stopping Time (in min.)	115,731	216,957	1,714,810	0	124,395	223,064	1,714,810	0	28,653	108,750	1,006,050	0
Discovery Time (in min.)	38,152	253,520	2,513,535	1	39,461	259,680	2,513,535	1	24,992	180,461	1,501,583	4
Centrality	0.540	0.196	0.981	0.075	0.543	0.189	0.981	0.100	0.517	0.254	0.965	0.075
Dispersibility	2.000	0.866	9.576	1.019	1.972	0.791	9.126	1.019	2.279	1.388	9.576	1.038
Influenceability	0.004	0.002	0.014	0.001	0.004	0.002	0.014	0.001	0.004	0.003	0.012	0.001
Forward	336	230	999	0	335	229	999	0	347	238	974	78
Comment	92	127	2629	0	90	128	2629	0	115	116	577	0
Like	11	41	605	0	5	16	605	0	68	111	605	0
Picture	0.935	0.726	9	0	0.907	0.676	9	0	1.212	1.074	7	0
Description	0.933	0.251	1	0	0.934	0.249	1	0	0.920	0.273	1	0
Gender	0.631	0.483	1	0	0.630	0.483	1	0	0.635	0.483	1	0
Message	17,664	30,933	358,663	0	17,837	31,792	358,663	0	15,925	20,389	107,017	0
Follower	345,527	1,184,097	26,630,301	17	335,779	1,190,912	26,630,301	17	443,505	1,112,658	7,591,558	19
Friend	1,044	893	4,981	0	1,043	886	4,981	0	1,055	965	4,745	17
Account Age (in hr.)	15,945	7,808	40,329	1	15,344	7,383	34,854	1	21,984	9,291	40,329	912
Length	110	44	193	3	111	44	193	3	94	48	172	9
Number	0.606	0.489	1	0	0.614	0.487	1	0	0.518	0.502	1	0

Empirical Methodology

We first use two matching strategies to alleviate potential selection bias and heterogeneity concerns to examine how the two platform interventions affect fake news dissemination.

Matching Strategies

Content-Based Matching: Latent Semantic Analysis

The first matching strategy is based on the idea of textual similarity, in which we match fake news and truthful news so that they are semantically similar. The basic logic is to quantify the news content in a numerical representation using natural language processing techniques and then apply similarity measures (e.g., cosine similarity and Euclidean distance) to infer semantic similarity between news posts. This approach has been implemented in various applications, such as collaborative filtering [29], incident risk factor identification [60], business proximity analysis [61], copycat detection [70], and customer agility measurement [74].

We start with truthful news posts. Due to the highly noisy dataset, a preliminary step is implemented to manually remove all posts that are (1) meaningless (with only emojis, numbers, or fewer than five words), (2) advertisements, and (3) forwarded posts. We remove all meaningless posts because they are not suitable for our content-based matching strategy. We ignore advertisements to avoid comparison with fake news posts, which are expected to be different from truthful news posts. Finally, we exclude forwarded posts because they are used to construct the post dissemination network. As a result, we obtain 23,535 truthful news posts, which are matched to our 1,514 fake news posts for further processing. We then tokenize all posts into a bag-of-words dictionary and remove all stop words and punctuation. Thus, each post is represented by a word vector, and each vector value indicates the frequency of a word occurring in the corresponding post. The term frequency-inverse document frequency (TF-IDF) technique is applied to all posts to normalize their corresponding word vectors. The result is a word-by-post matrix, with each row representing a post, each column representing a unique word, and each cell representing the TF-IDF value of the word in the post.

Next, we apply latent semantic analysis (LSA)[15] to the word-by-post matrix to reduce the dimensionality and independency between words [39]. A dimensionality of 300 is chosen for LSA so that each word vector of a post is decomposed into a 300-dimensional feature vector. Finally, we match each fake news post to one or two truthful news posts based on the smallest angle calculated from the cosine similarity between their feature vectors. As a result, we obtain a matched sample of 1,586 truthful news posts and 1,514 fake news posts. The performance of the content-based matching method is reported in Appendix B1. Table 3 reports the summary statistics for truthful news posts after content-based matching.

Post-Based Matching: Propensity Score Matching

Based on the content-based matched sample, we implement a second matching strategy to control for post and user characteristics using the propensity score matching (PSM) approach [53]. This strategy helps us remove non-comparable fake and truthful news posts to minimize estimation bias arising from the post and user characteristics. One-to-

Table 3. Summary Statistics of Variables for Truthful News After Content-Based Matching

Variable Name	Overall (n = 1,586)				Before Restriction (n = 1,246)				After Restriction (n = 340)			
	Mean	Std. Dev.	Max.	Min.	Mean	Std. Dev.	Max.	Min.	Mean	Std. Dev.	Max.	Min.
Centrality	0.667	0.233	1.000	0.028	0.674	0.229	1.000	0.028	0.644	0.246	1.000	0.030
Dispersibility	1.583	0.818	16.746	1.000	1.561	0.651	8.727	1.000	1.665	1.250	16.746	1.000
Influenceability	0.006	0.050	1.000	0.001	0.006	0.041	1.000	0.001	0.009	0.076	1.000	0.001
Forward	463	250	999	13	449	251	999	13	514	242	982	13
Comment	198	329	5,285	0	183	307	5,285	0	253	393	4,816	0
Like	74	240	4,348	0	24	91	1,551	0	257	443	4,348	0
Picture	1.067	1.187	9	0	0.885	0.551	9	0	1.732	2.216	9	0
Description	0.970	0.170	1	0	0.967	0.178	1	0	0.982	0.132	1	0
Gender	0.602	0.490	1	0	0.601	0.490	1	0	0.603	0.490	1	0
Message	40,429	42,461	295,309	40	40,797	43,447	295,309	40	39,081	38,664	228,462	95
Follower	5,814,669	10,140,082	50,910,636	0	5,544,103	10,021,889	50,910,636	0	6,806,215	10,517,658	48,251,168	0
Friend	805	849	5,000	0	805	838	5,000	0	807	891	5,000	0
Account Age (in hr.)	20,138	8,886	39,985	1	18,364	7,841	34,933	1	26,641	9,457	39,985	1,386
Length	113	41	226	10	112	41	226	10	116	41	194	14
Number	0.512	0.500	1	0	0.509	0.500	1	0	0.524	0.500	1	0

one matching is implemented with a caliper size of 0.01. The matching procedures and performance assessment are reported in Appendix B2. With both matching strategies, we obtained a matched sample of 703 fake news posts and 703 truthful news posts for regression analysis.

Regression Analysis

We first use the fake news flag intervention implemented by Sina Weibo to establish the causal impact of the platform intervention on fake news dissemination. As the fake news flag is only applied to fake news but not truthful news, we can consider a quasi-experimental design based on a matched DiD sample to tease out unobservable characteristics of posts that may bias our estimation [10,37]. The matched sample of truthful news posts is then used as the quasi-control group to reveal the impact of flagging on fake news dissemination. The following model specification is estimated:

$$Dissemination_{it} = \beta_0 + \beta_1 Fake_i + \beta_2 Marked_t + \beta_3 Fake_i \times Marked_t + \varepsilon_{it}, \qquad (1)$$

where $Dissemination_{it}$ is one of the three dissemination variables of post i measured up to time t, $Fake_i$ indicates whether post i is fake news, $Marked_t$ is coded as 0 if t is before the flagged time and 1 otherwise, and t represents the daily time range from three days before to three days after the flagged time. A major challenge is that fake news posts have different discovery and end times. For instance, one fake news post may be identified three days after its publication and stop spreading five days after, and another fake news post may be identified two months after its publication and stop spreading one month later. To overcome this challenge, we focus on the dissemination patterns three days before and three days after the flagged date of a fake news post, which corresponds to one week. To do so, we perform time matching between the matched fake news and truthful news pairs to align the unflagged period before the fake news post is identified. Figure 3 illustrates our identification strategy. Consider a pair of matched posts. The fake news post was published on April 12, 2013, and

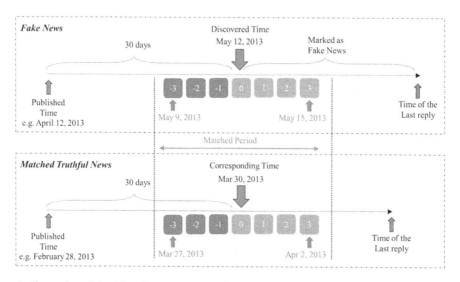

Figure 3. Illustration of the Identification Strategy for the Fake News Flag

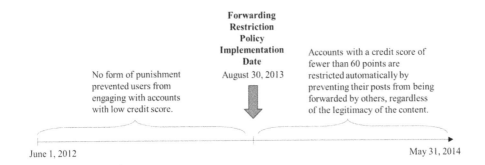

We compare **matched** fake and truthful news before and after the implementation of the forwarding restriction policy.

Figure 4. Illustration of the Identification Strategy for the Forwarding Restriction Policy

discovered on May 12, 2013, and the truthful news post was published on February 28, 2013. We compare the dissemination patterns of the fake news post three days before and after May 12, 2013. As it took 30 days for the fake news post to be discovered, we also use 30 days to identify a matched period of the matched truthful news post for comparison. From Figure 3, we subsample fake news posts between May 9, 2013, and May 15, 2013, and truthful news posts between March 27, 2013, and April 2, 2013, and specify a DiD strategy during this matched period. As some fake news posts only last for a very short time (e.g., less than a day), we exclude these and their matched truthful news posts, which leads to a matched sample of 1,014 pairs for our DiD analysis.

Our next model uses the forwarding restriction policy intervention implemented on August 30, 2013. As this intervention affects both fake and truthful news, we are interested in examining its different impacts on the dissemination of fake and truthful news. Our regression framework is specified below:

$$Dissemination_{it} = \beta_0 + \beta_1 Fake_i + \beta_2 Restriction_t + \beta_3 Fake_i \times Restriction_t + ControlVars_i + \gamma_t + \varepsilon_{it}, \tag{2}$$

where $Dissemination_{it}$ is one of the three dissemination variables of post i published at time t, measured up to the post's end time; $Restriction_t$ is coded as 0 if t is before the implementation date of the forwarding restriction policy and 1 otherwise; $ControlVars_i$ represents time-invariant post control variables; γ_t represents week fixed effects; and t represents the daily time range throughout our analysis period. The coefficient of the interaction term revealed by β_3 helps us to determine how fake news is disseminated after the forwarding restriction policy is implemented. We use our matched sample of 1,406 pairs obtained from the content-based and post-based matching approaches for this model specification. An illustration of this analysis framework is presented in Figure 4.

Finally, to examine the impact of the forwarding restriction policy on fake news survival, we specify two regression frameworks for a more comprehensive analysis. The first regression is an ordinary least squares (OLS) regression specified below:

$$Time_{it} = \beta_0 + \beta_1 Restriction_t + ControlVars_i + \gamma_t + \varepsilon_{it}, \tag{3}$$

where $Time_{it}$ represents either the logarithm of *Discovery time* or *Stopping time* of fake news i measured at time t, and t represents the daily time range throughout our analysis period. The advantage of this framework is that we can incorporate time fixed effects γ_t to account for potential time-induced and trend effects. The second regression is a Cox proportional-hazards framework commonly used to investigate how multiple covariates are simulta-neously related to survival time:

$$h(Time_{it}) = h_0(Time_{it}) \times exp\big(\beta_1 Restriction_t + ControlVars_i\big), \qquad (4)$$

where $h(\cdot)$ is the hazard function and $h_0(.)$ the baseline hazard function with all variables set to 0. This framework is a natural choice because our variable of interest is the survival time of fake news. However, the two limitations of this framework are the lack of data censoring,

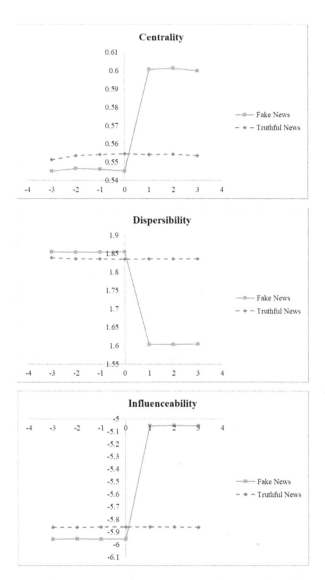

Figure 5. Model-Free Evidence of the Effect of the Fake News Flag on Fake News Dissemination

Table 4. Effect of the Fake News Flag on Fake News Dissemination

	Centrality	Dispersibility	Influenceability
Fake	-0.007	0.017	-0.093***
	(0.005)	(0.030)	(0.030)
Marked	0.000	0.000	0.000
	(0.007)	(0.032)	(0.033)
Fake × Marked	0.055***	-0.250***	0.903***
	(0.012)	(0.045)	(0.012)
Log Likelihood	68	-9,639	-9,788
Observations	1,014	1,014	1,014

Notes. *, ** and *** indicate statistical significance at the 10%, 5% and 1% levels, respectively. Standard errors are displayed in parentheses under the coefficient estimates.

as all fake news posts are eventually identified, and the proportional hazards assumption, which precludes the incorporation of time fixed effects. Therefore, we implement both frameworks to complement each other's limitations for a robust analysis of the impact of this platform intervention.

Results

Effect of the Fake News Flag on Fake News Dissemination

We present the results of our main analyses in this section. We first assess the parallel trend assumption in Figure 5. Figure 5 shows a sharp change in centrality, dispersibility, and influenceability after the intervention, which provides us with model-free evidence of the effect of the fake news flag. We also analyze pre-treatment trends to verify the parallel trend assumption and report the results in Appendix C. Table 4 reports the DiD regression results. We find that the intervention has a positive and significant impact on the centrality ($\beta = 0.055$, $p<0.01$) of fake news, which means that after a fake news post is flagged as such, it is more likely to be disseminated through direct forwards (H1a is supported). We also find that the flag has a significant and negative effect on the dispersibility ($\beta = -0.250, p<0.01$) of fake news, which means that fake news is less likely to be forwarded to distant others after the intervention (H1b is supported). Moreover, the intervention has a significant and positive impact on the influenceability ($\beta = 0.903, p< 0.01$) of fake news. In other words, the flag encourages influential users to forward fake news posts (H1c is supported).

To identify the underlying mechanism, we test whether the ambiguity of fake news decreases after being flagged as such. We perform a content analysis on all fake news forwarding comments. We use a popular psycholinguistic dictionary, the Linguistic Inquiry and Word Count (LIWC) constructed by Tausczik and Pennebaker [67], to infer the extent of ambiguity for each fake news forwarding comment [27, 28]. We consider the two most

Table 5. Ambiguity Analysis

Condition	Tentative Word Usage	Affective Word Usage
Before fake news flag	0.137 (0.401)	7.282 (5.595)
After fake news flag	0.100 (0.339)	5.036 (5.456)
Within-subject *t*-test	2.671***	13.048***
Observations	1,250	1,250

Notes. *** indicates statistical significance at the 1% level. Mean values are displayed with standard errors in parentheses.

Table 6. Examples of Fake News Forwarded by an Influencer

Original Fake News	Forwarding Comment from the Influencer
In summer, watermelon is the top choice of refreshing food, but malicious merchants seek to make a profit from unripe watermelons. They inject the banned food additives, cyclamate and carmine! The injected watermelon is red and juicy but tasteless. The additives used contain toxic substances that destroy the function of the liver and kidneys and affect the intellectual development of children!	To the blogger and the latest forwarder, couldn't you use your brain? It is so annoying that you post fake news every year. Please be conscientious when posting on Weibo to make money.
China's Bone Marrow Bank, sponsored by the Red Cross Society of China, calls for bone marrow donations in the name of charity and creates a bank of samples. If there are matching patients, they will contact volunteers to donate bone marrow. How wonderful! However, the patient will be charged 500 yuan for each inquiry and at least 50,000 yuan for obtaining bone marrow! Therefore, Peking University students were outraged and set up a private bone marrow bank. From inquiry to transplantation, the process is free, and the bank is called "Sunshine Marrow Bank."	China's Bone Marrow Bank search is free: 500 yuan is the HLA typing test fee for each blood sample in the bank, which is currently funded by the financial department, and the Bone Marrow Bank has never charged it. The number "50,000 yuan" is also wrong. Due to the international principle that donors should not meet patients, we collect 20,000 yuan from patients to be used for transportation, collection, and other donor expenses, and any overpayment will be refunded and any deficit will be repaid. The Bone Marrow Bank has never kept any money. China's Bone Marrow Bank will hold an opening day in the morning of May 8. Welcome on-site consultation.
Although I am not a celebrity, I notice that there are more and more bad people in this society, and I hope to do my best to get your attention. This child has just been abducted from RT-Mart Supermarket in Xiaolan. I hope more people can follow and forward this post.	After due diligence, the information source is identified: user @storm0109 reported at around 8 a.m. that the daughter of his/her friend's coworker was abducted near RT-Mart Supermarket, Plaza South Road, Nanchang City, Jiangxi Province. Some certified users in Jiangxi Province forwarded this post. At around 12 p.m., the child was found. All information was provided by this single user, and its factuality could not be verified. However, Shinnosuke Nohara is to be blamed for posting this fake news.

relevant word categories: *Tentative* and *Affect*. We expect the reduced ambiguity of fake news after being flagged to be reflected by the reduced use of tentative words, such as "maybe," "perhaps," and "guess," in forwarding comments. We also expect a reduced use of affective words in forwarding comments, as ambiguity is strongly associated with various emotions such as anxiety and worry [9,16]. We only focus on fake news with forwarding comments containing at least one tentative or affective word, resulting in a sample of 1,250 fake news posts for analysis. We then perform a within-subjects t-test to statistically compare the proportions of tentative or affective words used in fake news forwarding comments before and after the implementation of the fake news flag. Table 5 shows a significant decrease in the use of tentative and affective words in forwarding comments after a post is flagged as fake news, which supports our conjecture that the fake news flag can reduce the ambiguity of fake news.

Table 7. Effect of the Forwarding Restriction Policy on Fake News Dissemination

	Centrality		Dispersibility		Influenceability	
Fake	0.042	0.108	-0.182	-0.450	-0.230***	0.051
	(0.029)	(0.103)	(0.119)	(0.424)	(0.068)	(0.240)
Restriction	-0.058	-0.069	0.356	0.248	-0.298	-0.259
	(0.090)	(0.101)	(0.366)	(0.413)	(0.211)	(0.233)
Fake × Restriction		-0.338*		1.471**		-0.102
		(0.179)		(0.736)		(0.416)
ln(Forward)	-0.102***	-0.098***	0.274***	0.259***	-0.879***	-0.894***
	(0.008)	(0.008)	(0.034)	(0.035)	(0.020)	(0.020)
ln(Comment)	0.068***	0.067***	-0.104***	-0.108***	-0.095***	-0.095***
	(0.006)	(0.006)	(0.026)	(0.026)	(0.015)	(0.015)
ln(Like)	0.005	0.009	-0.084***	-0.075***	-0.041***	-0.021
	(0.006)	(0.006)	(0.022)	(0.023)	(0.013)	(0.013)
ln(Picture)	-0.010	-0.012	-0.201**	-0.143	0.220***	0.252***
	(0.023)	(0.023)	(0.094)	(0.093)	(0.054)	(0.053)
Description	0.018	0.002	-0.206**	-0.160	-0.055	-0.050
	(0.025)	(0.025)	(0.102)	(0.101)	(0.059)	(0.057)
Gender	0.034***	0.033***	-0.079*	-0.089**	0.009	0.015
	(0.011)	(0.010)	(0.043)	(0.042)	(0.025)	(0.024)
ln(Message)	-0.018***	-0.012***	0.115***	0.122***	-0.043***	-0.037***
	(0.004)	(0.004)	(0.017)	(0.018)	(0.010)	(0.010)
ln(Follower)	0.039***	0.041***	-0.152***	-0.155***	0.042***	0.034***
	(0.003)	(0.003)	(0.012)	(0.012)	(0.007)	(0.007)
ln(Friend)	-0.020***	-0.017***	0.036**	0.030*	-0.009	0.000
	(0.004)	(0.004)	(0.018)	(0.018)	(0.010)	(0.010)
ln(Account Age)	0.001	-0.006	-0.041	-0.027	-0.011	-0.024
	(0.007)	(0.007)	(0.029)	(0.030)	(0.017)	(0.017)
ln(Length)	0.002	0.009	-0.004	-0.026	0.015	0.008
	(0.009)	(0.008)	(0.035)	(0.035)	(0.020)	(0.020)
Number	0.003	0.005	-0.068	-0.061	0.035	0.055**
	(0.011)	(0.011)	(0.044)	(0.044)	(0.026)	(0.025)
Verified Type	Yes	Yes	Yes	Yes	Yes	Yes
Location	Yes	Yes	Yes	Yes	Yes	Yes
Source	Yes	Yes	Yes	Yes	Yes	Yes
Week Fixed Effect	Yes	Yes	Yes	Yes	Yes	Yes
Log Likelihood	662	761	-1,305	-1,223	-529	-420
Observations	1,406	1,406	1,406	1,406	1,406	1,406

Notes. 1. *, ** and *** indicate statistical significance at the 10%, 5% and 1% levels, respectively. Standard errors are displayed in parentheses under the coefficient estimates.

2. For fake news, the sample sizes before and after restriction are 623 and 80, respectively. For truthful news, the sample sizes before and after restriction are 586 and 117, respectively.

In summary, we find that the fake news flag leads the fake news dissemination network to be more centralized through direct forwards than dispersed through indirect forwards. These results confirm our theorization based on the basic law of rumor [35] that flagging fake news can reduce its ambiguity and prevent it from being disseminated farther and deeper. In terms of the effect of the fake news flag on fake news influenceability, influential users with a large number of followers are expected to behave more cautiously. Therefore, they tend to avoid disseminating an ambiguous post until it has been verified. The increased influenceability of fake news after the implementation of the fake news flag highlights the effort of influential users to help dispel fake news. Table 6 qualitatively supports this claim, as we find that influential users forward fake news posts with an intention to confirm their falsehood. In short, the fake news flag significantly alters the spread of fake news by generating more direct than indirect forwards, causing fake news posts to be disseminated more by influential users.

Effect of the Forwarding Restriction Policy on Fake News Dissemination

We now examine the impact of the forwarding restriction policy on post dissemination patterns. We first provide a descriptive analysis to understand how the forwarding restriction policy shapes the post dissemination network. We randomly select 24 fake news and 24 truthful news dissemination networks before and after the intervention for visual comparison, as shown in Appendix D. Before the intervention, the fake news dissemination networks were more centralized, and only a relatively small portion spread to distant accounts. A similar pattern can be observed for truthful news, with their dissemination network showing high centrality but low dispersibility. In general, both fake news and truthful news dissemination networks involved some degree of influenceability. However, after the implementation of the forwarding restriction policy, a clear distinction can be observed: the fake news dissemination networks become more dispersed with longer tails (i.e., more indirect forwards) and less centralized (i.e., fewer direct forwards). We observe no significant change in the truthful news dissemination networks from before to after the intervention. In short, the visualization of these networks is consistent with our expectation that the forwarding restriction policy influences fake news and truthful news differently.

We present the regression results in Table 7. The significant and negative coefficient of *Fake × Restriction* on the centrality ($\beta = -0.338$, $p < 0.1$) of fake news indicates that compared with truthful news, fake news is disseminated via less direct forwards after the implementation of the forwarding restriction policy (H2a is supported). However, the significant and positive coefficient of *Fake × Restriction* on the dispersibility ($\beta = 1.471$, $p < 0.05$) of fake news suggests that compared with truthful news, fake news is disseminated in a more dispersed manner after the intervention (H2b is supported). We find no significant effect ($\beta = -0.102$, $p > 0.1$) of the forwarding restriction policy on the influenceability of fake news. Taken together, the forwarding restriction policy leads to significantly less centralized and more dispersed dissemination of fake news as compared with truthful news.

The above results are consistent with our theorization based on the social tie theory. After the implementation of the forwarding restriction policy, the strong ties of fake news publishing accounts are prevented from forwarding fake news posts by relational concerns, whereas their weak ties are not affected by relational concerns and continue to forward fake news posts. Thus, the dissemination of fake news becomes less centralized and more dispersed than truthful news.

Robustness Checks

We run two additional tests to check whether the impact of the forwarding restriction policy on fake news dissemination changes based on the topic and sentiment. The results are reported in Appendix E. We find that the forwarding restriction policy only affects life-related fake news posts but does not affect international and local fake news posts (Table E2). Relational concerns are not likely to occur among the strong ties of fake news publishing accounts that publish international and local fake news, as these types of posts have more effect on society than life-related fake news posts. This finding indirectly supports our proposed mechanism of relational concerns arising from strong ties. In addition, we find that fake news sentiment does not affect the dissemination patterns of fake news, which confirms that the identified effect is not driven by the emotions expressed in the content of fake news (Table E4).

Another major concern regarding the dissemination of fake news is whether social bot accounts spread fake news on social media on a large scale [59]. Previous research has shown that social bots play a significant role in promoting fake news that distorts various social events [6], such as the 2016 U.S. election. However, this is not a concern in our study due to the real-name policy implemented by Sina Weibo since 2011.[16] The policy states that Weibo users must verify their accounts by using their real names for account registration. This policy was formally launched on March 3, 2012, before our analysis period. According to this real-name policy, accounts registered without real-name verification can only read posts on Weibo but cannot publish, comment, or forward posts. We believe that the real-name policy alleviates the concern that our findings might be contaminated by social bots.

In summary, this study reveals that the fake news flag and the forwarding restriction policy have different effects on fake news dissemination. In a broader sense, the fake news flag (content-level intervention) affects the spread of fake news by reducing its ambiguity, leading to more centralized and less dispersed dissemination of fake news and more forwards by influential users. The forwarding restriction policy (account-level intervention) creates relational concerns among the strong ties of fake news publishing accounts, leading to less centralized and more dispersed dissemination of fake news. These findings provide insights into the effectiveness of different types of platform interventions in fake news mitigation.

Effect of the Forwarding Restriction Policy on Fake News Survival

As little research focuses on the impact of account-level interventions (e.g., forwarding restriction policy), we conducted an additional analysis to examine how the forwarding restriction policy influences fake news survival, which is a more direct way to examine the effectiveness of this type of intervention. We report the results in Table 8. As the lifespans of some fake news posts may overlap with the intervention implementation date, we remove these posts for a more robust analysis, which reduces our sample to 1,368 fake news posts. We obtain consistent results across the two regression models. For the linear regression model, the significant and negative coefficient of *Restriction* on *Stopping time* ($\beta = -8.779$,

Table 8. Effect of the Forwarding Restriction Policy on Fake News Survival

	OLS		Cox Proportional-Hazards Model	
	log(Stopping Time)	log(Discovery Time)	Stopping Hazard	Discovery Hazard
Restriction	-8.779***	-0.673	0.899***	0.013
	(2.848)	(2.341)	(0.154)	(0.122)
log(Forward)	0.817***	-0.010	-0.427***	-0.098*
	(0.142)	(0.116)	(0.052)	(0.052)
log(Comment)	-0.175*	-0.106	0.037	0.051
	(0.099)	(0.081)	(0.039)	(0.039)
log(Like)	0.148	0.013	0.082**	0.081**
	(0.094)	(0.077)	(0.037)	(0.032)
log(Picture)	0.042	0.267	0.651***	-0.216
	(0.436)	(0.359)	(0.170)	(0.146)
Description	-0.359	0.355	-0.108	-0.085
	(0.339)	(0.278)	(0.142)	(0.120)
Gender	-0.311*	-0.011	0.130*	-0.002
	(0.167)	(0.138)	(0.072)	(0.063)
log(Message)	-0.147***	-0.001	0.100***	-0.009
	(0.056)	(0.046)	(0.024)	(0.020)
log(Follower)	-0.058	0.033	-0.061***	0.001
	(0.050)	(0.041)	(0.021)	(0.017)
log(Friend)	0.068	-0.083	-0.019	0.023
	(0.070)	(0.057)	(0.031)	(0.025)
log(Account Age)	0.157	-0.166*	0.089*	0.050
	(0.112)	(0.092)	(0.048)	(0.039)
log(Length)	-0.073	0.279***	-0.077	-0.106**
	(0.128)	(0.106)	(0.052)	(0.045)
Number	0.005	-0.275*	0.137*	0.053
	(0.179)	(0.147)	(0.077)	(0.066)
Verified Type	Yes	Yes	Yes	Yes
Location	Yes	Yes	Yes	Yes
Source	Yes	Yes	Yes	Yes
Week Fixed Effect	Yes	Yes	No	No
Log Likelihood	-3,111	-2,843	-8,244	-8,535
Observations	1,368	1,368	1,368	1,368

Notes. *, ** and *** indicate statistical significance at the 10%, 5% and 1% levels, respectively. Standard errors are displayed in parentheses under the coefficient estimates.

$p < 0.01$) indicates that fake news has a shorter average survival time after the intervention. In the Cox proportional-hazards model analysis, the positive and significant coefficient of *Restriction* on *Stopping time* ($\beta = 0.899, p < 0.01$) suggests a higher hazard rate of fake news after the intervention. Specifically, the expected hazard of fake news increases by 146% after the intervention, compared with that before the intervention. We find no evidence of the impact of the forwarding restriction policy on the discovery time of fake news. In all cases, we examine the Kaplan-Meier curves of the Cox proportional-hazards models and find no violation of the proportional hazard assumption [26].

We find that the forwarding restriction policy effectively combats the spread of fake news by shortening its lifespan because relational concerns of strong ties prevent the further spread of fake news. However, the forwarding restriction policy has no effect on the discovery time of fake news, likely because there are no relational concerns before the verification of fake news. We also conduct a placebo test by repeating the same regression analyses on truthful news as a robustness check and find that the forwarding restriction policy has no effect on the lifespan of truthful news. The placebo test is presented in Appendix F.

Overall, after the implementation of the forwarding restriction policy, 1) fake news is disseminated in a less centralized and more dispersed manner, compared with truthful news, and 2) fake news survives for a much shorter time but is not discovered sooner. These findings have several implications for social media platforms, as they show how the account-level intervention affects user engagement with fake news and suggest that this type of platform intervention can effectively mitigate fake news by shortening its survival time.

Discussion

Contributions

The study makes two main contributions to the literature. First, we extend the fake news literature by establishing a causal relationship between the fake news flag and fake news dissemination using empirical field data. To the best of our knowledge, previous studies have mainly focused on the cognitive and psychological impacts of the fake news flag by using experimental laboratory data, and few have addressed the actual behavior change caused by this flag. Thus, we complement the literature by using field data and providing causal empirical evidence to better understand the effectiveness of the fake news flag.

Second, we extend the literature on platform interventions that target fake news by examining the impact of the forwarding restriction policy on fake news dissemination and survival time. Previous studies have mainly focused on the content-level intervention (i.e., fake news flag) from a cognitive perspective to reduce people's willingness to engage with fake news [25]. We find that the forwarding restriction policy, a type of stricter platform intervention applied at the account level, can shorten the survival time of fake news, with no detrimental effect on the dissemination of truthful news. Furthermore, we highlight the different impacts of the two interventions on fake news dissemination, thereby solving a conundrum that has never been adequately addressed. This missing piece of the puzzle advances our understanding of the effectiveness of platform interventions by providing a holistic view of how content-level and account-level interventions work differently to combat the spread of fake news.

From a practical perspective, our findings provide important insights for online platform owners and policymakers. Today, the Internet and social media have become the primary sources of information consumption for most people. Online platforms are important mediators that ensure the quality of information to prevent consumers from exposure to misleading and manipulative news. However, the effectiveness and efficacy of platform interventions are questionable [41], and more effort should be devoted to better understanding how different policies work. Our study responds to this call by empirically examining the effects of two platform interventions in a rigorous framework. Our analysis of the fake news flag provides a result consistent with that of Moravec et al. [45], indicating that people continue to forward fake news posts even after they are identified as fake news. Our proposed mechanism is supported, showing that the fake news flag reduces the ambiguity of fake news posts and, therefore, helps control the spread of fake news within a smaller network, i.e., direct forwards within one degree of separation. However, our findings also suggest a possible consequence of the increased echo chamber, as the flagged fake news posts are likely to be forwarded more by like-minded people [38], adversely reinforcing polarization and fueling extreme emotions within the online user community. In brief, the fake news flag may have both positive and potential negative effects on controlling the spread of fake news. Contrary to the concern that the account-level intervention may interfere with the spread of truthful news due to its strict "one-size-fits-all" approach, our results reveal different effects for fake and truthful news. Although we find that fake news spreads much farther and more broadly after the implementation of the forwarding restriction policy, it stops the spread of fake news much more quickly. Altogether, these findings have important implications for online platforms in designing interventions to mitigate the spread of fake news.

For policymakers, this study suggests that platform interventions on social media are an effective way to combat the spread of fake news. Specifically, the two platform interventions have different objectives. The fake news flag is effective because it can prevent fake news from spreading farther and deeper within the dissemination network. In addition, as the fake news flag encourages influential users to spread fake news posts, we recommend that the platform develop an effective policy to motivate influential users to dispel fake news. This study reveals that the account-level intervention can effectively mitigate fake news by shortening its survival time. As this intervention only affects the dissemination of fake news but not truthful news, platform owners may consider implementing this account-level intervention to stop the spread of fake news quickly.

Limitations and Future Research

We acknowledge that this paper has several limitations. Measuring the fake news survival time may be of concern, as users may remember a post after several years and forward or comment on it, which may potentially compromise our survival time measure. We address this concern with two points. First, we ensure that all forwards and comments collected from the posts cover the period up to 2018, so any forward or comment after a sufficiently long period is unlikely to happen. Second, the mean and standard deviation of the number of forwards are very similar before and after the implementation of the forwarding restriction policy (Before: $M = 335$, $SD = 229$; After: $M = 347$, $SD = 238$).[17] Thus, we believe that the effect of the forwarding restriction policy on the survival time of fake news is unlikely to be affected by forwards or comments omitted during data collection.

Another limitation is that this study only investigates one social media platform in China. Although Sina Weibo offers the opportunity to investigate the effectiveness of both platform interventions, the findings of this study may not be widely generalizable to other cultures, e.g., the United States. Referring to the influential theory of cultural dimensions [30, 31], we suggest that two dimensions should be taken into consideration when applying our findings to other cultures. One dimension is power distance, which is defined as "the extent to which the members of a society accept that power in institutions and organizations is distributed unequally" [30]. Brockner et al. [8] showed that people tend to react unfavorably when they have little voice in a decision-making process, but this tendency is weaker for people in high power distance cultures (e.g., China) than in low power distance cultures (e.g., the United States). Therefore, Chinese people might be more willing to accept a fake news flag verified by a reliable or mainstream information source. In contrast, people in low power distance cultures may not react favorably to the fake news flag, as they have little say in investigating and claiming the authenticity of a post.

The second cultural dimension is individualism/collectivism, which is defined as the extent to which members of a society emphasize their own needs over those of the group and tend to act as individuals rather than as members of a group [30]. It has been argued that members of a collectivist culture like China value harmony and group consensus more than freedom of expression, compared with members of an individualistic culture like the United States [36]. Hence, social media users in individualistic cultures may be more tolerant of extreme, irrational, and harmful posts and may be less likely to spontaneously report such posts.

Our results show that the fake news flag leads to more centralized and less dispersed dissemination of fake news. We argue that this observation can be explained by the reduced ambiguity of fake news content and provide empirical evidence to support this proposed mechanism. However, we note that the more centralized fake news dissemination network can also be explained by alternative theories such as the echo chamber [38] or social bot sharing [7]. Social bot sharing is less likely to be a concern due to the above-mentioned real-name policy implemented by Sina Weibo. Regarding the echo chamber, like-minded individuals may be more likely to forward fake news posts after flagging. Multiple mechanisms may occur simultaneously to explain why individuals continue to engage with fake news after it is flagged as such, and our study proposes and empirically tests one mechanism, reduced ambiguity. Therefore, future research could conduct a more in-depth investigation to determine how different mechanisms interact to strengthen our study results.

Our study offers several research opportunities for future studies. First, our sample of fake news posts relies on a social reporting system operated through the collective intelligence of the crowd, but social media platforms are increasingly using machine learning-based fake news detection systems. Future research could compare the effectiveness of these two types of systems in terms of fake news mitigation. Second, our study only focuses on a simple type of fake news flag. More empirical studies should be conducted to examine a fake news flag with various manipulations, such as a strong warning or a high level of severity, which is expected to have a more salient deterrent effect on fake news dissemination. Third, as the forwarding restriction policy depends on a credit scoring system, future research could explore the impact of the credit score on users' fake news posting and forwarding behavior and study its interaction with the platform intervention. Fourth, future research could investigate the dynamic change in the survival time of fake news. An interesting research question would be to study how two fake news posts with the same survival time differ if one is disseminated with an initial surge followed by a decline and the other is disseminated with a slow start followed by a huge surge.

Conclusions

This study exploits fake news data and two types of platform interventions in Sina Weibo to study the impact of platform interventions on fake news dissemination and survival. First, we exploit a natural experiment using a DiD approach to identify the causal relationship between the fake news flag (content-level intervention) and three fake news dissemination patterns. We show that after a post is flagged as fake news, its dissemination network instantly becomes more centralized and less dispersed. Furthermore, fake news is more likely to be spread by influential users. We attribute these findings to the reduced ambiguity of fake news [35]. Second, we investigate how the forwarding restriction policy (account-level intervention) influences the spread of fake and truthful news. We show that the implementation of the forwarding restriction policy leads to less direct and more indirect forwards of fake news, compared with truthful news. This phenomenon can be explained by social tie theory [20], as relational concerns prevent the strong ties of fake news publishing accounts from spreading fake news but have no effect on the weak ties. We also show that the forwarding restriction policy shortens the survival time of fake news. This study is among the first to provide empirical evidence of the effectiveness of platform interventions in combating the spread of fake news. Thus, our study constitutes an early effort, and we hope that our work will shed light on subsequent understandings of platform interventions and fake news dissemination.

Notes

1. https://edition.cnn.com/2020/03/23/health/arizona-coronavirus-chloroquine-death/index. html
2. https://news.un.org/en/story/2020/04/1061682
3. https://www.theguardian.com/technology/2020/apr/07/whatsapp-to-impose-new-limit-on-forwarding-to-fight-fake-news
4. https://chinacopyrightandmedia.wordpress.com/2012/05/08/sina-weibo-community-management-regulations-trial/
5. https://www.facebook.com/journalismproject/programs/third-party-fact-checking
6. https://blog.twitter.com/en_us/topics/product/2020/updating-our-approach-to-misleading-information.html; https://economictimes.indiatimes.com/magazines/panache/twitter-tightens-rules-will-label-tweets-that-spread-fake-news-to-ensure-a-fair-us-election/articleshow/78617901.cms
7. https://www.bbc.com/news/blogs-trending-37846860
8. https://theconversation.com/governments-are-making-fake-news-a-crime-but-it-could-stifle-free-speech-117654
9. https://www.forbes.com/sites/nicolemartin1/2018/11/30/how-social-media-has-changed-how-we-consume-news/?sh=18400d243c3c
10. https://www.chinainternetwatch.com/statistics/weibo-mau/
11. http://service.account.weibo.com/?type=0&status=4
12. Full details of the difference between harmful information and fake news can be found in this policy document: https://chinacopyrightandmedia.wordpress.com/2012/05/08/sina-weibo-community-management-regulations-trial/
13. https://chinacopyrightandmedia.wordpress.com/2012/05/08/sina-weibo-community-management-regulations-trial/
14. http://www.open.weibo.com/
15. https://radimrehurek.com/gensim/models/lsimodel.html
16. https://baike.baidu.com/item/%E5%BE%AE%E5%8D%9A%E5%AE%9E%E5%90%8D%E5%88%B6; https://www.globaltimes.cn/content/700489.shtml
17. The mean difference is not statistically significant based on independent two-samples t-tests (t-statistic = -0.564).

Disclosure statement

No potential conflict of interest was reported by the author(s).

ORCID

Ka Chung Ng (iD) http://orcid.org/0000-0001-7875-8194
Jie Tang (iD) http://orcid.org/0000-0002-9588-8756
Dongwon Lee (iD) http://orcid.org/0000-0001-7450-4437

References

1. Allcott, H. and Gentzkow, M. Social media and fake news in the 2016 election. *Journal of Economic Perspectives, 31,* 2 (2017), 211–236.
2. Allcott, H., Gentzkow, M., and Yu, C. Trends in the diffusion of misinformation on social media. *Research and Politics, 6,* 2 (2019), 1–8.
3. Amoruso, M., Anello, D., Auletta, V., Cerulli, R., Ferraioli, D., and Raiconi, A. Contrasting the spread of misinformation in online social networks. In K. Larson, M. Winikoff, S. Das and E. Durfee (eds.), *Journal of Artificial Intelligence Research.* International Foundation for Autonomous Agents and Multiagent Systems, São Paulo, Brazil, 2020, pp. 847–879.
4. Audrezet, A., de Kerviler, G., and Guidry Moulard, J. Authenticity under threat: When social media influencers need to go beyond self-presentation. *Journal of Business Research, 117,* (2020), 557–569.
5. Balkin, J.M. Free speech in the algorithmic society: Big data, private governance, and new school speech regulation. *SSRN Electronic Journal, 51,* (2017), 1149–1210.
6. Bessi, A. and Ferrara, E. Social bots distort the 2016 U.S. Presidential election online discussion. *First Monday, 21,* 11 (2016).
7. Boichak, O., Jackson, S., Hemsley, J., and Tanupabrungsun, S. Automated diffusion? Bots and their influence during the 2016 U.S. Presidential election. In G. Chowdhury, J. McLeod, V. Gillet and P. Willett (eds.), *Lecture Notes in Computer* Science *(including subseries Lecture Notes in Artificial* Intelligence *and* Lecture Notes in Bioinformatics). Springer, Cham, 2018, pp. 17–26.
8. Brockner, J., Ackerman, G., Greenberg, J., et al. Culture and procedural justice: The influence of power distance on reactions to voice. *Journal of Experimental Social Psychology, 37,* 4 (2001), 300–315.
9. Buhr, K. and Dugas, M.J. The intolerance of uncertainty scale: Psychometric properties of the English version. *Behaviour Research and Therapy, 40,* 8 (2002), 931–945.

10. Chan, J. and Wang, J. Hiring preferences in online labor markets: Evidence of a female hiring bias. *Management Science, 64,* 7 (2018), 2973–2994.

11. Chen, D., Lü, L., Shang, M.S., Zhang, Y.C., and Zhou, T. Identifying influential nodes in complex networks. *Physica A: Statistical Mechanics and its Applications, 391,* 4 (2012), 1777–1787.

12. Craig, S. This analysis shows how viral fake election news stories outperformed real news on Facebook. *BuzzFeed News,* 2016, 1–7. https://www.buzzfeednews.com/article/craigsilverman/viral-fake-election-news-outperformed-real-news-on-facebook.

13. Enke, N. and Borchers, N.S. Social media influencers in strategic communication: A conceptual framework for strategic social media influencer communication. *International Journal of Strategic Communication, 13,* 4 (2019), 261–277.

14. Figl, K., Rank, C., Kießling, S., and Vakulenko, S. Fake news flags, cognitive dissonance, and the believability of social media posts. In H. Krcmar, J. Fedorowicz, W.F. Boh, J.M. Leimeister, and S. Wattal (eds.), *International Conference on Information Systems, Munich, Germany,* 2019.

15. Friedkin, N.E. Theoretical Foundations for Centrality Measures. *American Journal of Sociology, 96,* 6 (1991), 1478–1504.

16. Gao, G. and Gudykunst, W.B. Uncertainty, anxiety, and adaptation. *International Journal of Intercultural Relations, 14,* (1990), 301–317.

17. Garrett, R.K. and Poulsen, S. Flagging Facebook falsehoods: Self-identified humor warnings outperform fact checker and peer warnings. *Journal of Computer-Mediated Communication, 24,* 5 (2019), 240–258.

18. Gimpel, H., Heger, S., Olenberger, C., and Utz, L. The effectiveness of social norms in fighting fake news on social media. *Journal of Management Information Systems, 38,* 1 (2021), 196–221.

19. Goel, S., Anderson, A., Hofman, J., and Watts, D.J. The structural virality of online diffusion. *Management Science, 62,* 1 (2016), 180–196.

20. Granovetter, M. The strength of weak ties: A network theory revisited. *Sociological Theory, 1,* (1983), 201.

21. Grinberg, N., Joseph, K., Friedland, L., Swire-Thompson, B., and Lazer, D. Political science: Fake news on Twitter during the 2016 U.S. presidential election. *Science, 363,* 6425, (2019) 374–378.

22. Gu, B., Konana, P., Raghunathan, R., and Chen, H.M. The allure of homophily in social media: Evidence from investor responses on virtual communities. *Information Systems Research, 25,* 3 (2014), 604–617.

23. Guess, A., Nyhan, B., and Reifler, J. *Selective exposure to misinformation: Evidence from the consumption of fake news during the 2016 US presidential campaign.* European Research Council 9.3 (2018): 4.

24. Harmon-Jones, E. and Mills, J. *An introduction to cognitive dissonance theory and an overview of current perspectives on the theory.* Stanford University Press, 2004.

25. Hartley, K. and Vu, M.K. Fighting fake news in the COVID-19 era: policy insights from an equilibrium model. *Policy Sciences, 53,* 4 (2020), 735–758.

26. Hess, K.R. Graphical methods for assessing violations of the proportional hazards assumption in cox regression. *Statistics in Medicine, 14,* 15, (1995), 1707–1723.

27. Hinz, O. and Spann, M. The impact of information diffusion on bidding behavior in secret reserve price auctions. *Information Systems Research, 19,* 3 (2008), 351–368.

28. Ho, S.M., Hancock, J.T., Booth, C., and Liu, X. Computer-mediated deception: Strategies revealed by language-action cues in spontaneous communication. *Journal of Management Information Systems, 33,* 2 (2016), 393–420.

29. Hofmann, T. Latent semantic models for collaborative filtering. *ACM Transactions on Information Systems, 22,* 1 (2004), 89–115.

30. Hofstede, G. The interaction between national and organizational value systems[1]. *Journal of Management Studies, 22,* 4 (1985), 347–357.

31. Jalili, M. and Perc, M. Information cascades in complex networks. *Journal of Complex Networks, 5,* 5 (2017), 665–693.

32. Katz, E. and Shibutani, T. *Improvised News: A Sociological Study of Rumor*. The Bobbs-Merrill Company Inc., 1969.

33. Kim, A. and Dennis, A.R. Says who? The effects of presentation format and source rating on fake news in social media. *MIS Quarterly*, 43, 3 (2019), 1025–1039.

34. Kim, A., Moravec, P.L., and Dennis, A.R. Combating fake news on social media with source ratings: The effects of user and expert reputation ratings. *Journal of Management Information Systems*, 36, 3 (2019), 931–968.

35. Knapp, R.H. A psychology of rumor. *Public Opinion Quarterly*, 8, 1 (1944), 22–37.

36. Koh, N.S., Hu, N., and Clemons, E.K. Do online reviews reflect a product's true perceived quality? An investigation of online movie reviews across cultures. *Electronic Commerce Research and Applications*, 9, 5 (2010), 374–385.

37. Kuang, L., Huang, N., Hong, Y., and Yan, Z. Spillover effects of financial incentives on non-incentivized user engagement: Evidence from an online knowledge exchange platform. *Journal of Management Information Systems*, 36, 1 (2019), 289–320.

38. Kwon, H.E., Oh, W., and Kim, T. Platform structures, homing preferences, and homophilous propensities in online social networks. *Journal of Management Information Systems*, 34, 3 (2017), 768–802.

39. Landauer, T.K., Foltz, P.W., and Laham, D. An introduction to latent semantic analysis. *Discourse Processes*, 25, 2–3 (1998), 259–284.

40. Landherr, A., Friedl, B., and Heidemann, J. A critical review of centrality measures in social networks. *Business & Information Systems Engineering*, 2, 6 (2010), 371–385.

41. Lazer, D.M.J., Baum, M.A., Benkler, Y., et al. The science of fake news. *Science*, 359, 6380 (2018), 1094–1096.

42. Maasberg, M., Ayaburi, E., Liu, C., and Au, Y. Exploring the propagation of fake cyber news: An experimental approach. In *Proceedings of the 51st Hawaii International Conference on System Sciences*. Curran Associates Inc., Hawaii, USA, 2018.

43. Marett, K. and Joshi, K.D. The decision to share information and rumors: Examining the role of motivation in an online discussion forum. *Communications of the Association for Information Systems*, 24, 1 (2009), 47–68.

44. Moravec, P.L., Kim, A., and Dennis, A.R. Flagging fake news: System 1 vs. System 2. In J.P. Heje, S. Ram, and M. Rosemann (eds.), *International Conference on Information Systems*, San Francisco, USA, 2018.

45. Moravec, P.L., Minas, R.K., and Dennis, A.R. Fake news on social media: People believe what they want to believe when it makes no sense at All. *MIS Quarterly*, 43, 4 (2019), 1343–1360.

46. Oh, O., Agrawal, M., and Rao, H.R. Community intelligence and social media services: A rumor theoretic analysis of tweets during social crises. *MIS Quarterly*, 37, 2 (2013), 407–426.

47. Papanastasiou, Y. Fake news propagation and detection: A sequential model. *Management Science*, 66, 5, (2020), 1826–1846.

48. Park, J.H., Konana, P., Gu, B., Kumar, A., and Raghunathan, R. Information valuation and confirmation bias in virtual communities: Evidence from stock message boards. *Information Systems Research*, 24, 4 (2013), 1050–1067.

49. Pennycook, G., Bear, A., Collins, E.T., and Rand, D.G. The implied truth effect: Attaching warnings to a subset of fake news headlines increases perceived accuracy of headlines without warnings. *Management Science*, 66, 11 (2020), 4944–4957.

50. Pennycook, G., Cannon, T.D., and Rand, D.G. Prior exposure increases perceived accuracy of fake news. *Journal of Experimental Psychology: General*, 147, 12, (2018), 1865–1880.

51. Pennycook, G. and Rand, D.G. Lazy, not biased: Susceptibility to partisan fake news is better explained by lack of reasoning than by motivated reasoning. *Cognition*, 188, (2019), 39–50.

52. Pickett, J.T., Roche, S.P., and Pogarsky, G. Toward a Bifurcated Theory of Emotional Deterrence. *Criminology*, 56, 1 (2018), 27–58.

53. Rosenbaum, P.R. and Rubin, D.B. The central role of the propensity score in observational studies for causal effects. *Biometrika*, 70, 1 (1983), 41–55.

54. Rosnow, R.L. Inside rumor: A personal journey. *American Psychologist*, 46, 5 (1991), 484–496.

55. Ross, B., Heisel, J., Jung, A.K., and Stieglitz, S. Fake news on social media: The (in)effectiveness of warning messages. In J.P. Heje, S. Ram, and M. Rosemann (eds.), *International Conference on Information Systems*, San Francisco, USA, 2018.

56. Sarker, S., Ahuja, M., Sarker, S., and Kirkeby, S. The role of communication and trust in global virtual teams: A social network perspective. *Journal of Management Information Systems, 28*, 1 (2011), 273–310.

57. Schulze, E. EU tells Facebook, Google and Twitter to take more action on fake news. In *CNBC*. 2019.

58. Shao, C., Hui, P.M., Cui, P., Jiang, X., and Peng, Y. Tracking and characterizing the competition of fact checking and misinformation: Case Studies. *IEEE Access, 6*, (2018), 75327–75341.

59. Sharma, K., Qian, F., Jiang, H., Ruchansky, N., Zhang, M., and Liu, Y. Combating fake news: A survey on identification and mitigation techniques. *ACM Transactions on Intelligent Systems and Technology, 10*, 3 (2019), 1–41.

60. Shi, D., Guan, J., Zurada, J., and Manikas, A. A data-mining approach to identification of risk factors in safety management systems. *Journal of Management Information Systems, 34*, 4 (2017), 1054–1081.

61. Shi, Z.M., Lee, G.M., and Whinston, A.B. Toward a better measure of business proximity: Topic modeling for industry intelligence. *MIS Quarterly, 40*, 4 (2020), 1035–1056.

62. Stieglitz, S. and Dang-Xuan, L. Emotions and information diffusion in social media - Sentiment of microblogs and sharing behavior. *Journal of Management Information Systems, 29*, 4 (2013), 217–248.

63. Suh, A., Shin, K.S., Ahuja, M., and Kim, M. The influence of virtuality on social networks within and across work groups: A multilevel approach. *Journal of Management Information Systems, 28*, 1 (2011), 351–386.

64. Sutton, J., Spiro, E.S., Fitzhugh, S., Johnson, B., Gibson, B., and Butts, C.T. Terse message amplification in the Boston bombing response. In S.R. Hiltz, M.S. Pfaff, L. Plotnick and P.C. Shih (eds.), *ISCRAM 2014 Conference Proceedings - 11th International Conference on Information Systems for Crisis Response and Management*. University Park, USA, 2014, pp. 612–621.

65. Sutton, J., Spiro, E.S., Johnson, B., Fitzhugh, S., Gibson, B., and Butts, C.T. Warning tweets: serial transmission of messages during the warning phase of a disaster event. *Information Communication and Society, 17*, 6 (2014), 765–787.

66. Tang, J., and Ng, K.C. Reposts influencing the effectiveness of social reporting system: An empirical study from sina weibo. In H. Krcmar, J. Fedorowicz, W.F. Boh, J.M. Leimeister, and S. Wattal (eds.), *International Conference on Information Systems*, Munich, Germany, 2019.

67. Tausczik, Y.R. and Pennebaker, J.W. The psychological meaning of words: LIWC and computerized text analysis methods. *Journal of Language and Social Psychology, 29*, 1 (2010), 24–54.

68. Torres, R., Gerhart, N., and Negahban, A. Combating fake news: An investigation of information verification behaviors on social networking sites. In *Proceedings of the 51st Hawaii International Conference on System Sciences*. Curran Associates Inc., Hawaii, USA, 2018.

69. Vosoughi, S., Roy, D., and Aral, S. The spread of true and false news online. *Science, 359*, 6380 (2018), 1146–1151.

70. Wang, Q., Li, B., and Singh, P.V. Copycats vs. original mobile apps: A machine learning copycat-detection method and empirical analysis. *Information Systems Research, 29*, 2 (2018), 273–291.

71. Zhang, X. and Venkatesh, V. Explaining employee job performance: The role of online and offline workplace communication networks. *MIS Quarterly, 37*, 3 (2013), 695–722.

72. Zhang, X., Zhu, J., Wang, Q., and Zhao, H. Identifying influential nodes in complex networks with community structure. *Knowledge-Based Systems, 42*, (2013), 74–84.

73. Zhang, X.M. and Wang, C. Network positions and contributions to online public goods: The case of Chinese wikipedia. *Journal of Management Information Systems, 29*, 2 (2012), 11–40.

74. Zhou, S., Qiao, Z., Du, Q., Wang, G.A., Fan, W., and Yan, X. Measuring customer agility from online reviews using big data text analytics. *Journal of Management Information Systems, 35*, 2 (2018), 510–539.

Biased Credibility and Sharing of Fake News on Social Media: Considering Peer Context and Self-Objectivity State

Ofir Turel ⓘ and Babajide Osatuyi ⓘ

ABSTRACT
Several studies have examined the consumption and spread of fake news on social media. Two notable gaps, though, exist in the extant literature. First, prior research has focused on the political orientation of users while ignoring the broader context of sharing, namely the perceived political orientation of their social media peers. Second, there is limited insight about how user states, especially those related to their judgment abilities, influence the critical evaluation of fake news on social media. This paper addresses these gaps by theorizing the roles of perceived peer political orientation and self-objectivity states of users in translating biased credibility assessments of fake news into biased sharing intentions. It reports on an 7experiment (n=408) that primed self-perceived objectivity (a state) in half of the participants to examine its efficacy in moderating the influence of credibility bias (the extent to which users believe the news that high-light ideas that are consistent with their political orientation more than fake news articles that highlight ideas that are inconsistent with their political orientation) on sharing bias (the extent to which they are likely to share fake news that highlight ideas that are consistent with their political orientation more than fake news that highlight ideas that are inconsistent with their political orientation) while accounting for the moderating effect of perceived peer political orientation (a contextual factor). We found that consistency of fake news with peo-ple's political orientation increased credibility bias and sharing bias and that credibility bias increased sharing bias. We also found that perceived alignment between a user and their peers' political orienta-tion, as a social context, reduced the effect of credibility bias on sharing bias. Finally, we found mixed support for the moderating effects of primed self-objectivity on the influence of credibility bias on sharing bias; it affected only liberal-leaning participants.

Introduction

The presidential election in 2016 popularized the generation and dissemination of fake news on a global scale. Fake news refers to "news stories that have no factual basis but are presented as news" [3–4]. Although researchers identified the topic of fake news before the 2016 election, its prevalence, especially in the social media context, grew after the election and rose to the global stage [24–25]. While only a tiny percentage of people share fake news, the ease of spreading such news on social media can harm individuals and societies; false news spread faster and to more people than true news [35,108]. Consequently, many studies

Access the Support Material: www.routledge.com/ 9781032561127

have been conducted to shed light on the different aspects of fake news generation [65, 66], sharing motivation and intentions [96], detection [86–87], and tracking [45], to develop an understanding of its influence among users [13].

Especially in the political context, fake news is an inexpensive and effective means to sway election results [24] because 68% of adults consume news on social media, with projections of increases ahead [91]. The challenge here is that while the number of users that consume news online continues to grow, their ability to detect fake news is barely slimmer than chance [73]. This is partly because social media and other online platforms that afford news dissemination can be heavily polarized [117], and people tend to believe and share news in accordance to the political party with which they self-identify (i.e., own political orientation) [106]. As such, about 60% of U.S. adults who prefer to get their news through social media have participated directly or indirectly in spreading fake news [111], which leads us to believe that the spread of politically charged information on social media is a digital pandemic (what some may call "infodemic") that needs to be curbed [44].

While a majority of prior studies on fake news in the social media context have focused on the consumers of fake news and their characteristics, the ability of technologies to spread, detect and limit fake news, and the consequences of fake news [13], limited attention has been given to the *social context* in which the information exchanges occur. The social context, which manifests in peer implicit or explicit opinions and behaviors, is presumed to be important in social media for two reasons. First, social media is very efficient at conveying social ideas, pressures, and acceptable behaviors [77]. Second, the social context influences people's beliefs, attitudes, and behaviors [9–11], as people try to adopt beliefs, perceptions, and behaviors that are internally consistent, to manage unpleasant cognitive dissonance [30, 63], and externally conforming to their peers, to fit-in and strengthen their in-group identity [94–95]. After all, social approval by peers is a highly potent reward that, together with social punishment avoidance, motivates action aimed at being aligned with peers [61].

Thus, building on social identity theory [94], we expect that perceived peer political orientation, which is effectively signaled and/or implied via social media actions of peers, is a potential source of influence (driver or inhibitor) on user motivations and behaviors on social media. Simply put, a fake news item is more likely to be shared when it is aligned with one's political orientation *AND* with perceived peer political orientation than in other situations (e.g., when it is not aligned with the perceived political orientation of peers). Here, we focus on two such outcomes in the context of political news: (1) the extent to which a user believes news that highlight ideas consistent with one's political ideology more than fake news that highlight ideas that are inconsistent with one's political ideology (credibility bias), and (2) the extent to which they are likely to share fake news that highlight ideas consistent with their political ideology more than fake news that highlight ideas that are inconsistent with their political ideology (sharing bias).

Having acknowledged the possible role of perceived peer political orientation in disseminating fake news online, we further venture to examine another research gap, namely the need to understand underlying preconditions of biased believability and sharing of fake news. This is important because such an understanding can help IS scholars create a better society [13] or create awareness of possible consequences of the technologies people use. Prior research indicates that biased decisions that are not based on facts, like discrimination at the workplace, may be influenced by people's state of self-objectivity [102]. We extend this view and theorize that priming a self-objectivity state in people can alter how they process fake news and the weights they put on their own vs. external beliefs. Self-objectivity refers to an individual's confidence in his or her beliefs. Importantly, priming can change the accessibility people have to relevant information, which ultimately changes how they process biased decisions [68,102]. As such, we expect that priming a self-objectivity state in social media users will alter the way they scrutinize fake news articles.

To address the gaps identified above, we integrate the perspectives on the roles of peers and self-objectivity in changing how people scrutinize information and develop a theoretical model. We test it in a between-subjects experiment (n=408) that examines how one's political orientation increases credibility and sharing biases. The experiment also primes self-perceived objectivity and captures perceived peer political orientation to examine their efficacy in moderating the influence of a user's credibility bias on sharing bias in the context of fake political news on social media.

Theoretical Background

This section reviews social identity theory as a progressive perspective on social learning theories and discusses how the processes it posits help us understand how people interact with fake political news on social media within the perceived context of peer political orientation. To do so, we present a social-contextual factor, perceived peer political orientation, and a cognitive state, perceived self-objectivity, as two moderators that regulate how individuals interact with fake news on social media.

Social Identity Theory

Identity theories describe how people self-identify relative to other groups or classifications [15–16,94]. A critical theory in this area of research is social identity theory [103]; it describes the socio-cognitive processes individuals use to form their social identity and the actions they take to reinforce it. The theory posits *self-categorization* and *self-enhancement* as two processes that produce different outcomes and enable people to assume different roles to interact with other groups in which they belong [42]. Aiming at self-enhancement, an individual can self-identify with a political party or stance (i.e., own political orientation) such that he or she creates a desired social affiliation (e.g., I belong to a group of like-minded people who endorse a specific set of policies). People that ideologically belong to the same political party (i.e., having similar peer political orientation) share a similarity with the self, and this creates what is labeled as a sense of "in-group." This sense of feeling socially acceptable within a group is highly gratifying and activates the reward centers in the brain [28]. It drives, in part, the formation of "echo chambers" on social media [31], as people prefer to surround themselves with like-minded people.

In contrast, other people that belong to different political parties are labeled as the "out-group." The premise of self-enhancement is to inform social categorization such that the beliefs, norms, and practices favor the in-group compared to the out-group. Self-enhancement, therefore, enacts evaluative (self-esteem) and psychological (commitment) components in its categorization approach. While self-enhancement can be viewed as taking a micro-level perspective of categorization, self-categorization focuses on meso- or macro-level categorization, such that people place themselves in established categories that are parts of a structured society [94]. Self-categorization is typically described as a dehumanization of the self in that a person cognitively assumes the identity of the group he or she identifies with rather than an integral part of the large group. For instance, a supporter of party A will self-identify with the party (self-categorization) by voting for a party candidate running for office rather than voting for a member of another party running to improve the chances of his party filling that position as well as to legitimize their voting right as a responsible citizen (self-enhancement). Such individuals will often not even care who is running for their party because the affiliation with the party rather than nuanced beliefs will dictate their choice [33]. This process is in line with social dissonance theory in that it dictates that people will act in a way that ensures consistency with beliefs about group affiliation as a means to avoid unpleasant feelings of dissonance [70].

Social media presents the opportunity for people from diverse backgrounds and classifications to interact based on a shared interest or identity, making it suitable for studying the influences of self-categorization and social comparison processes [81–83]. Osyerman [80] shows that people make decisions based on their identity, and that context can influence this process as it can cue identities. Thus, we focus on examining how these socio-cognitive processes influence the credibility evaluation and sharing of fake news on social media, both of which can be viewed as motivated by one's desire to maintain and strengthen the political facets of their social media identity.

Although there is consensus on the efficacy of examining individual behaviors on social media using a social identity lens, researchers have focused mainly on one of the socio-cognitive processes, namely self-categorization. For instance, prior research examined how self-categorization processes explain social media use [19,29,57,81], community contribution [20,98], branding [5,67], and knowledge exchange [112] behaviors on social media. Consequently, social comparison processes have been largely overlooked, and there are limited insights regarding the simultaneous influence of both processes on behavioral outcomes. Identity theorists posit that these processes may lead to different outcomes and therefore warrant a simultaneous investigation to fully understand how social identity explains the behavior of interest [94].

Simply put, while social self-categorization is an essential and informative process, the influence of peers or the context in which these categorization processes take place has been largely overlooked [115]. Nonetheless, the social context is an essential determinant of human cognition, perception, and behavior [113–114]. Many theoretical lenses suggest that humans [60,80] and animals [31] adapt thoughts and actions while considering social rewards and punishments; that is, the peer context. This study addresses this gap and examines how the abovementioned socio-cognitive processes influence credibility evaluations and sharing behaviors of fake political news on social media within the given social context of peers' political orientation.

Moderators

Social identity theory implies that many social and individual factors can serve to regulate (inhibit or enhance) how people think and act [37] through controlling people's approach and avoidance tendencies [1]. Focusing on such moderators, including social-contextual and individual states, is essential because it allows identifying boundary conditions that enrich our understanding of individual information technology use behaviors [101]. As an umbrella framework, social identity theory does not point to specific social-contextual and individual states [95]. Thus, we relied on the context of this study, prior research on political news on social media [21,92,99], and previous works on individual states that can sway decision-making processes [39,92,104] to select a critical social-context factor that is presumably highly relevant for the context of this study, and a critical state that can affect decision making. These choices were also guided by the theoretical gap discussed in the introduction section, which implies a need to consider the stance of one's peers for better understanding why a person does not always act upon his or her internal beliefs [14,64].

Specifically, considering the social media context of this study, we examine perceived peer political orientation (a social-contextual factor) and self-perceived objectivity (a cognitive state factor) as moderators of how an individual evaluates the credibility of fake news articles and decisions to share such news articles on social media. It is important to note that credibility assessment and sharing behaviors are distinctly different in that the former informs a personal cognitive evaluation of news articles, which is not visible to others (i.e., internal to the person, implicit), while the latter is an external exhibition that is visible to other users (i.e., an explicit declaration). These differences in visibility are important because research shows that people process information differently when their contributions are visible compared to when they are not visible to others [78]. Therefore, it is essential to understand the interplay between internal evaluative mechanisms and external sources of influence since it can provide a nuanced view on how social media users interact with fake news on social media.

Social Context Factor: Perceived Peer Political Orientation

Perceived peer political orientation captures one's summative assessment of the general political leaning of his or her peers on the social networking site. Through self-enhancement processes, individuals evaluate their commitment and self-esteem with their referent in-group members to maintain and sustain their reputation. Thus, we expect that individuals will be encouraged to favor their in-group beliefs and norms when evaluating the credibility of fake news and sharing fake news on social media. Although social-environment factors such as social norm [17,79], social matching [6–7], prosocial behaviors [62], sense of belonging [46–52], and community behaviors [19] have been examined in the IS literature, no known research explores how such factors (e.g., context as set by peers) influence how people interact with fake news on social media. This is an important gap because people's information processing and decision-making processes are influenced by the social context [101–103].

Indeed, IS research has demonstrated the importance of including social-influence factors in behavioral models [26,104,105,109,110]. Especially in the social media context where users are exposed to the influence of their social network, it is important to account for such factors to inform how people process and respond to fake news articles. Existing literature on fake news on social media has focused mainly on individual-focused factors and processes, including confirmation bias [55–56], source reputation validation [56], and the ability for users to detect fake vs. true news articles [73]. Therefore, exploring how perceived peer political orientation influences the evaluation and sharing processes extends prior research on fake news in the social media context in an important direction. It does so by accounting for a critical social factor, as dictated by social identity theory, and providing a rich explanation, based on individual *and* social factors, of the dissemination of fake news. A recent study [34] reported that social norms (injunctive and descriptive) influence reporting of fake news. Injunctive social norms refer to behaviors most people approve or disapprove while descriptive social norms describe what other people do in specific situations. Although we focus on sharing of fake news and not reporting, findings from the study emphasize the role of social context in influencing people's behavior in the context of fake news and warrant further investigation.

Individual State: Self-Perceived Objectivity

Self-perceived objectivity describes how individuals perceive themselves given their unbiased interpretation and evaluation of surrounding factors. We focus on the focal person's perceptions of peer orientation because it drives the person's decisions more directly than actual peer orientation, which might be hidden, nuanced, or change under certain circumstances that are unforeseen by the focal person. The importance of this perception stems from its biasing (decision swaying) power; when people perceive themselves as objective, they become confident in their immunity to biases that may unjustly influence their ability to make fair judgment calls. We suggest that self-objectivity is a state because its accessibility and consequent expression fluctuate and depend on external stimuli. While the perception is relatively high in most individuals, its expression varies within individuals and can be primed. That is, a person may change the expression of self-objectivity beliefs within the same day, for instance, after being primed, and through this, alter the impact of beliefs on decisions [104].

The effect of self-perceived objectivity is rooted in the notion that it results in an "I think it, therefore it's true" mentality in people since it validates their bias-immune beliefs and imaginations [104]. It *does not* change people's beliefs, but instead, it makes information that is aligned with one's own beliefs more accessible, and through this, affords narrow and focused ("tunnel vision") deliberation [104]. That is, it does not shift the impulsiveness of decisions or reduce deliberation (i.e., shifting from an emphasis on system 2 processes to system 1 processes, see Dennis and Minas [23]). Instead, it biases inputs to the deliberation process by putting a stronger emphasis on internally consistent beliefs. Internal inconsistent beliefs do not disappear or change; they are simply suppressed and reduced in salience and less often make it an essential input for decision-making. Consequently, self-perceived objectivity is a moderator of the effect of peoples' stereotypic beliefs on behaviors. It attenuates the inputs for decision making, and through this, can increase reliance on stereotypic, non-fact-based beliefs [102].

Importantly, research indicates that the unobtrusive priming of concepts such as self-perceived objectivity in individuals can have significant implications for their cognitive evaluation capabilities and actions [10,11]. In our case, we expect that priming an individual's sense of objectivity will cause the individual to put different weights on credibility judgments when deciding to share (or not) fake news articles. As such, we theorize on and examine the moderating role of self-perceived objectivity. We took this focus because self-objectivity is a good vehicle for altering accessibility to important non-factual cognitions and beliefs [102].

Hypotheses Development

Social Identity and Credibility Calculus

Credibility bias captures the extent to which a person believes fake news headlines aligned with his or her political orientation more than equally fake news headlines aligned with a competing political orientation. *Sharing bias* captures the extent to which a person is willing to share fake news headlines aligned with his or her political orientation more than equally fake news headlines aligned with a competing political orientation. Self-reported willingness to share political news articles is essential, as it is a reasonable proxy for actual sharing behavior [73]. Thus, even though based on willingness levels, sharing bias is a good proxy for one's actual behavioral bias.

Social identity theory explains how individuals view themselves as members of a community or a group through self-categorization. We argue that the extent to which an individual self-identifies with a group will determine biases in his or her beliefs and intended actions. Self-categorization posits that people cognitively represent the social groups they belong to in terms of assuming the social group's beliefs, norms, and behaviors [43]. This suggests that an individual that self-identifies with a political party will find news articles that promote the party's causes to be credible because they want to believe in them, regardless of their true credibility [72]; this prevents cognitive dissonance and drives selective exposure to content that is consistent with one's orientations and attitudes, and to self-affirmation [36, 37,59,74,93]. Therefore, individuals that self-identify with a political party will present credibility bias in the direction of their political orientation and engage in sharing on social media news articles leaning in the direction of their political affiliation. This way, their credibility assessment and sharing behaviors are more consistent with their beliefs and prevent unpleasant cognitive dissonance. This tendency indicates a blind loyalty to the group with which one self-identifies. It suggests that such assessments and decisions are influenced by peripheral considerations, such as wanting to fit in (through sharing), wanting to reduce cognitive dissonance (through adjusting beliefs and behaviors), and self-affirmation (through both changing beliefs and sharing behaviors), and not by the actual credibility of the message or the source. Thus, we hypothesize:

$H1_{a,b}$: People's political orientation would increase their (a) credibility and (b) sharing biases in the direction of their political orientation.

Liberal-leaning individuals will assign higher credibility to and share more liberal-leaning fake news than conservative-leaning fake news. Conservative-leaning individuals will assign higher credibility to and share more conservative-leaning fake news than liberal-leaning fake news.

Credibility Bias and Sharing Bias

Credibility bias should influence one's sharing bias because people are more likely to share information that they consider to be more credible [48] and have avoidance attitudes toward non-credible information [71]. Sharing information on social media is a behavior that is, based on various behavioral theories, informed by beliefs [2,113]. As such, individuals are likely to find liberal or conservative news articles to be more credible than conservative or liberal ones, respectively, and consequently are more likely to share those articles on social media than share the news articles that are less compatible with their political orientation [88–89]. We, therefore, expect that the more credible liberal (or conservative) news are perceived compared to equally fake conservative (or liberal) news, the more people will be likely to share them, over and above their willingness to share news headlines that are aligned with the competing political orientations. Thus:

H2: Credibility bias would increase sharing bias.

Liberal credibility bias would increase liberal sharing bias among liberal-leaning individuals. Conservative credibility bias would increase conservative sharing bias among conservative-leaning individuals.

The Role of Perceived Peer Political Orientation

Perceived peer political orientation captures the perceived general political leaning of one's peers as one group. Political news is transmitted through social interactions and is therefore susceptible to social influence where an individual's decisions could be shaped by the groups of peers he or she identifies with [32,58]. Thus, perceived peer political orientation represents a proximal and influential social context in which credibility and sharing decisions are made. As such, we reason that peer political orientation can have both direct and moderating roles.

First, we suggest that perceived peer political orientation can influence sharing bias directly. According to social identity theory, people engage in self-categorization processes, emphasizing the perceived similarities between the self and other in-group members. This affords them to strengthen in-group support and cohesion, and at the same time, highlight the differences between the self and out-group members, which triggers distinction actions such as selective avoidance [114]. As such, people are more likely to behave in ways consistent with the norms, attitudes, and beliefs of their in-group [107]. In contrast, when the political orientation of a user and his or her peers are different, the user is less likely to engage in sharing behaviors because it undermines his or her social media group affiliation [32]. Consequently, if a person's peers are largely leaning in one political direction, he or she will be more likely to share news, even fake ones that are consistent with this political direction. Thus, we hypothesize:

H3a: Perceived peer political orientation will increase one's sharing bias in the direction of the peers' political orientation.

Perceived peer's liberal political orientation would increase liberal sharing bias among liberal-leaning individuals. Perceived peer's conservative political orientation would increase conservative sharing bias among conservative-leaning individuals.

Second, we reason that perceived peer orientation can serve as a regulator that controls how much attention people would pay to their credibility beliefs in light of the social pressures implied by peers' opinions. The environment-behavior interface of social cognitive theory [9] suggests that if peers are strongly oriented toward one political party, then sharing decisions should be more influenced by peers and less by one's judgment. In contrast, if peers are not strongly oriented toward one political party (i.e., they are more centrist), their judgments and biases should more strongly guide sharing behaviors. This is because sharing news is an act that is visible to peers on social media [53]. According to social identity theory, when sharing is aligned with the in-group's political orientation, it signals in-group fit and support and strengthens self-affirmation [97]. When it is not, it signals lower in-group loyalty and fit [22] and deviates from normative in-group scripts [40, 41]. Such in-group scripts, norms, and expectations are likely more salient when peers are strongly oriented toward one political party instead of when they are not. Consequently, perceived peer political orientation and credibility bias serve as substitute sources of influence on one's sharing bias; when one factor's influence is strong, the other factor's effect becomes weak. In other words, the tendency to conform to peers [6] rather than logically evaluating news articles before sharing them [84–85] can strengthen the reliance on peer political orientation rather than on one's own credibility biases when formulating intentions to share news articles. We hence hypothesize:

H3$_b$: Perceived peer political orientation will moderate (decrease) the effect of credibility bias on sharing bias, such that the effect is less pronounced when peers are more strongly politically oriented in the direction of one's political affiliation.

Perceived peer's liberal political orientation would decrease the effect of liberal credibility bias on liberal sharing bias in liberal-leaning individuals. Perceived peer's conservative political orientation would reduce the effect of conservative credibility bias on conservative sharing bias in conservative-leaning individuals.

The Role of Self-Objectivity

Individuals who perceive themselves to be self-objective are confident in constructing the reality about their thoughts and beliefs, which informs their information processing and decisions [102]. Specifically, increasing one's self-objectivity state (as primed in our case) should increase reliance on one's credibility bias when formulating sharing intentions. We expect an invoked sense of self-objectivity to change people's accessibility to relevant information that will attenuate the weight they give to it in decision making and reduce their motivation to elaborate on other factors [102]. Indeed, primed-to-feel objective individuals are encouraged to act more on their implicit and explicit biases and ignore others' beliefs [102].

This happens because self-objectivity effects are enacted via three related mechanisms. Firstly, people consider their beliefs valid and perceive those who hold a different belief to be poorly informed or biased [54]. Secondly, individuals that believe themselves to be objective accept evidence that confirms their beliefs with little or no scrutiny but dismiss external influences [69–77]. They are, therefore, less motivated to elaborate on external information when self-perceived objectivity is high [39,75, 77]. Finally, people with high perceived self-objectivity view themselves as invulnerable to common biases because they are overly confident in their objectivity and unbiased evaluation of facts to inform their decisions [27,90]. Taken together, the effect of self-objectivity priming is in the form of increasing one's reliance in decision making on his or her own beliefs, even when biased, misinformed,

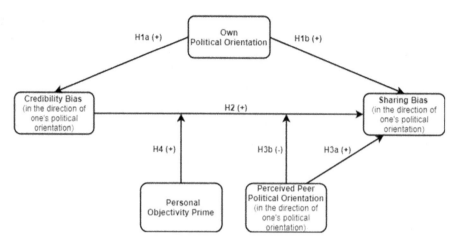

Figure 1. Research Model

or unsupported. In our case, it means that priming self-objectivity should increase the emphasis people put on their own biased beliefs when they develop sharing intentions. Thus, we hypothesize that:

H4: Priming a sense of personal objectivity will moderate (*increase*) the effect of credibility bias on sharing bias, such that the effect is more pronounced when self-objectivity is high.

A primed sense of personal objectivity in liberal-leaning individuals would increase the effect of liberal credibility bias on liberal sharing bias. A primed sense of personal objectivity in conservative-leaning individuals would increase the effect of conservative credibility bias on conservative sharing bias.

The implied research model for this study is depicted in Figure 1.

Methods

Participants

Participants were recruited from a population of U.S. university students who were Facebook users. The study was announced on a course portal, and participation was encouraged with course bonus points. Inclusion criteria were being at least 18 years old and using Facebook. We decided to focus on Facebook users given the high prevalence of use of this platform, including for disseminating, reading, and sharing fake news [65]. Of the 487 invitees, 408 met the inclusion criteria and completed the study (83.7% response rate). Because the meaning of constructs, hypothesis testing, and interpretation of associations depend on the participant's political orientation, the sample was divided based on self-reported political orientation on a 5-point Likert-type scale into liberal-leaning (n=223) and conservative-leaning (n=158) subgroups. We dropped 27 records of people with exact centric scores. The pure centrist group was of no theoretical interest based on our

Table 1. Descriptive Statistics

	Analytical Sample (n=381)	Liberal-leaning (n=223)	Conservative-leaning (n=158)	P-values for Difference
Age	25.95 (6.55)	25.17 (6.47)	27.06 (6.53)	**0.005**
Sex	176 Women [46.2%]	120 Women [53.8%]	56 Women [35.4%]	**0.000**
# of Social Media Sites Used	4.21 (1.26)	4.18 (1.21)	4.27 (1.33)	0.532
Hours/Day on Facebook	1.51 (1.14)	1.75 (1.23)	1.17 (0.84)	**0.001**
Own Political Orientation	3.32 (1.01)	4.07 (0.52)	2.25 (0.39)	**0.001**
Peer Political Orientation	3.73 (0.75)	3.88 (0.70)	3.50 (0.75)	**0.001**
Interest in U.S. Politics	4.03 (1.44)	4.18 (1.45)	3.82 (1.41)	**0.014**

*Own and perceived peer political orientations were measured on a 5-point Likert type scale, with one being more conservative and 5 being more liberal. Interest in U.S. politics was measured on a 1 (very low) to 7 (very high) Likert scale.
**p-values <0.05 are bolded

hypotheses and was too small to be analyzed. Consequently, the analytical sample included 381 records. Descriptive statistics for the analytical sample as a whole and by political affiliation group are provided in Table 1.

The descriptive statistics point to notable differences between the liberal-leaning and conservative-leaning people in our sample. The liberal group was female dominant, younger, more interested in U.S. politics, and spent more time on Facebook than the conservative group. This is consistent with notable differences between the groups [8,18]. The liberal group also reported higher peer liberal political orientation than the conservative group, which is consistent with the idea that people, especially liberal-leaning, surround themselves with like-minded people, also known as "filter bubbles" [37].

Procedures

The study employed an online survey. The survey included three parts: (1) demographic and descriptive statistics, (2) a fake news task, and (3) a self-perceived objectivity prime. After reporting demographic information and descriptive statistics, all participants completed the same fake news task that required them to rate the credibility of 12 fake news headlines, presented in a random order, and state the likelihood of them sharing these headlines. Following [102], we employed a between-subjects design, with self-perceived objectivity manipulation (prime) delivered to a random half of the sample. The rest served as a control group and completed the self-perceived objectivity scale at the end of the survey. That is, we asked a randomly selected set of 50% of the participants to report their self-perceived objectivity *before* completing the fake news task, and the others completed the self-perceived objectivity scale at the end of the survey, *after* the fake news task. The self-perceived objectivity scores were higher ($p=0.003$) in the conservative group (M=6.02, SD=0.57) compared to the liberal group (M=5.79, SD=0.82). Importantly, they did not differ ($p=0.430$) between the prime (M=5.86, SD=0.66) and control/no-prime (M=5.92, SD=0.80) groups. The prime and no-prime groups did not differ in age, sex, political orientation, and perceived peer political orientation (all with $p>0.15$). Thus, the key differentiator between the prime and no-prime groups was that one received a prime before the fake news task, and the other did not.

Survey

Participants first reported descriptive statistics (age, sex, social media sites they use, and daily hours on Facebook). They then reported their interest in U.S. politics by answering the question "Overall, how would you rate your interest in U.S. politics?" with answers ranging from 1= very low to 7=very high. They next disclosed their own and perceived peer political orientations on 5-point Likert-type scales that used synonyms to create three-item measures. Specifically, people were asked what they consider their political orientation to be: (1) [a] right, [b] conservative, and [c] Republican party, to (5) [a] left, [b] liberal, and [c] Democratic party. Similarly, they were asked to report whether they believed that most of their Facebook contacts are: (1) [a] leaning to the right, politically, [b] conservative, and [c] prefer the Republican party, too (5) [a] leaning to the left, politically, [b] liberal, and [c] prefer the Democratic party[1]. Given the sensitivity of self-reporting such orientations, we ensured response anonymity and asked for honest reports. Note that we avoided using scales that infer complex multi-dimensional political stance [e.g., 4] because multi-dimensional political ideology structures are beyond the scope of this study. Both scales were reliable, with corresponding Cronbach's alphas of 0.90 and 0.82. The scale scores were positively correlated ($r=0.25$, $p=0.001$), which indicated that people tend to affiliate online with somewhat, but not exactly, like-minded people in terms of political orientation.

Fake News Task

The fake news part of the study asked individuals to report the perceived credibility of 12 fictitious news item headlines related to U.S. politics (i.e., fake news; six left/liberal-leaning and the other six right/conservative-leaning and state their likelihood of sharing them. No headline source was provided, such that assessments focused only on the content of the headline. Each statement was presented on a separate screen in random order and was followed by perceived credibility and sharing likelihood scales. Perceived credibility was measured with three 7-point Likert scale items [55,72] as adapted from [12]. Respondents were asked to state how (1) believable, (2) truthful, and (3) credible they found the headline to be. The likelihood of sharing was measured with two items extended from Kim and Dennis [55]. People were asked how (1) likely are they to share and (2) how probable it is that they share the news item headline. Cronbach's alphas for credibility and sharing likelihood were adequate (0.88 and 0.90, respectively). When calculated separately for liberal and conservative news items, all αs were still above 0.88. As such, index scores were created independently for liberal-leaning and conservative-leaning news headlines, with higher scores reflecting higher perceived credibility and the likelihood of sharing.

The 12 news headlines were selected by an expert panel (10 American social media users interested in U.S. politics) from a pool of topics in [63] that reflects divergent (typical liberal-leaning and conservative-leaning) political opinions. Choice of the specific six

Table 2. Fake News Headlines Used in This Study*

Following are 12 news headlines. Each will appear on a separate page. For each news headline, you are asked to state whether you find it to be credible and the likelihood of you sharing it.

- the U.S. congress is going to discuss next month the need for income redistribution (L)
- the U.S. congress is going to discuss next month the idea that the average income tax rate for high incomes should be increased (L)
- the U.S. congress will discuss next month the idea that to protect workers, labor unions in the U.S. should have more power (L)
- The U.S. congress will discuss next month the idea that it should be made more difficult for employers to lay-off employees (L)
- The U.S. congress will discuss next month the idea that poor people should receive free healthcare (L)
- The U.S. congress will discuss next month the idea that landlords should not be free to raise rent by as much as they want (L)
- The U.S. congress will discuss next month the idea that soft drugs should NOT be legalized (C)
- The U.S. congress will discuss next month the need for increased investment in the military, despite budget constraints (C)
- The U.S. congress will discuss next month the idea that a person that refuses to work should not receive welfare money (C)
- The U.S. congress will discuss next month the idea that to decrease the debt burden of future generations, and the retirement age should be increased to 75 (C)
- The U.S. congress will discuss next month the view that minimum wages should be abolished (C)
- The U.S. congress will discuss next month the idea that the death penalty should be reinforced in all states (C)

*L=Liberal leaning, C= Conservative-leaning; order of presentation was random

liberal-leaning and six conservative-leaning items was guided by fit to the U.S. context. The statements were developed initially to capture political beliefs. They were adapted to represent news headlines about the U.S. congress going to discuss these topics next month (all fictitious, i.e., equally fake). The statements are provided in Table 2.

To operationalize one's credibility and sharing biases, we subtracted the credibility and sharing intentions attributed to one group of news from those attributed to the other. For participants in the liberal-leaning group, it was Credibility$_{Liberal news}$ – Credibility$_{Conservative news}$, and Sharing$_{Liberal news}$ – Sharing$_{Conservative news}$. For participants in the conservative-leaning group, biases were calculated as Credibility$_{Conservative news}$ – Credibility$_{Liberal news}$, and Sharing$_{Conservative news}$ – Sharing$_{Liberal news}$. Credibility bias scores reflected how much people find news leaning in the direction of their political preference to be more credible than news headlines in the opposite direction. Sharing bias scores reflected how much people are willing to share news aligned with their political orientation more than they are eager to share the news that does not align with their political orientation. Credibility and sharing biases were positively correlated ($r=0.49$, $p=0.001$), which provides preliminary support for H2.

Prime

We used four items to prime individuals with a sense of personal objectivity [102]. These items were: (1) In most situations, I try to do what seems reasonable and logical, (2) When forming an opinion, I try to objectively consider all of the facts I have access to, (3) My judgments are based on a logical analysis of the facts, and (4) My decision making is rational and objective (1 = strongly disagree, 7 = strongly agree; $\alpha=0.83$). A random half of the participants completed these items before the fake news task, and the other half after the fake news task. Consistent with [102], the prime was not to change the participants' beliefs in their objectivity because it is expected that people already have a naturally inflated sense of objectivity [89]. Instead, the prime aimed at improving temporary availability, accessibility to, and salience of personal objectivity assessments and relevant information [41].

Pilot Study and Analytical Approach

A pilot study was performed with 50 Facebook users in the U.S. Results supported the validity and reliability of the scales, as well as our assumption that biases in credibility and sharing are primarily (but not fully) in the direction of a person's political orientation. See details in Appendix A. Appendix B outlines our analytical approach.

Results

Test of Assumption about Direction of Biases

Repeating the pilot study procedure, we noted that the proportions of positive bias scores (i.e., in the direction of one's political orientation) were significantly (all $p<0.0001$) larger than this of negative bias scores in the whole dataset, as well as independently for liberal and conservative-leaning individuals. See Table 3. These results further support the assumption that credibility and sharing biases are mostly, but imperfectly, in the direction of users' political orientation.

Sex did not correlate with credibility and sharing biases or political orientation (all $p>0.13$). Age correlated negatively with political orientation ($r=-0.19$, $p=0.001$), indicating that younger people reported more centrist and less extreme political preferences. Interest in U.S. politics was not associated with credibility and sharing biases or with political orientation (all $p>0.08$). Partial correlations (after controlling for age, sex, and interest in U.S. politics) between political orientation and credibility bias was 0.151 ($p=0.003$). Hence, H1a was supported. Partial correlations between political orientation and sharing bias were 0.256 ($p=0.001$). Hence, H1b was supported. Together, the findings support the idea that people are cognitively and behaviorally biased in the direction of their political orientation.

Direct Effects Model (H1 and H3a)

Unstandardized estimates for the hypothesized direct effects (H2 and H3a) are given in Figure 2, separately for the liberal-leaning and the conservative-leaning datasets. Control variables effects had $p>0.05$ and are hence not included in the figure. The results support H2 (credibility bias → sharing bias) for conservative-leaning participants, but not for liberal-leaning participants. It is therefore conceivable that the credibility effect on sharing can be contingent on factors such as perceived peer orientation and primed self-objectivity, especially among liberal-leaning participants. Note that we expected a positive effect of peer political orientation on sharing (H3a), and we observed a negative one in the case of

Table 3. Tests of Assumptions about Direction of Biases

		Liberal-Leaning	Conservative-Leaning	All
Credibility Bias	Positive	66.80%	65.20%	66.10%
	Negative	33.20%	34.80%	33.90%
	p-value (diff)	<0.0001	<0.0001	<0.0001
Sharing Bias	Positive	81.60%	81.00%	81.40%
	Negative	18.40%	19.00%	18.60%
	p-value (diff)	<0.0001	<0.0001	<0.0001

Source of Biases (H1)

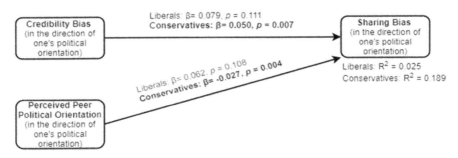

Figure 2. Direct Effects Model

conservative-leaning participants and a null effect in the case of liberal-leaning participants. It is still possible that peer political orientation does not directly increase one's sharing bias but instead moderates the effect of credibility bias on sharing bias.

* Values with $p<0.05$ are bolded.

Moderation Effects Model (H3b and H4)

Unstandardized estimates are provided in Figure 3, separately for the liberal-leaning and the conservative-leaning datasets. The results support H3b for both conservatives and liberals by showing that perceived peer political orientation reduces the effect of credibility bias on sharing bias. The results also support H4 for liberal-leaning participants, but not conservative-leaning participants, by showing that personal objectivity prime applied to liberals increased the effect of credibility bias on sharing bias. In both samples, women (coded as 1) presented a lower sharing bias, regardless of credibility bias. Younger conservative-leaning participants showed a higher sharing bias and interest in politics, but not among liberal-leaning participants, sheltered against sharing bias.

* Values with $p<0.05$ are bolded. Dashed lines represent control variables.

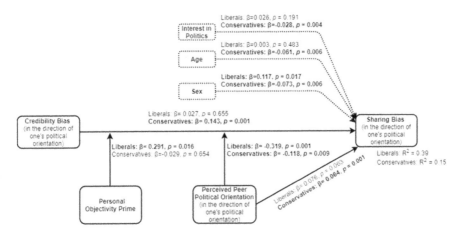

Figure 3. Moderation Model*

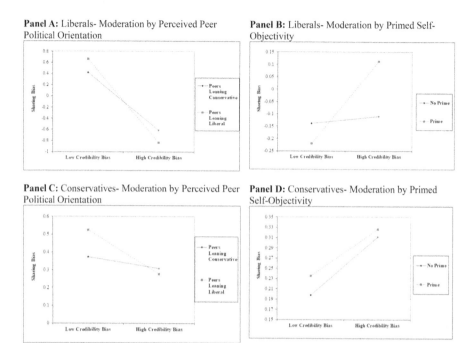

Panel A: Liberals- Moderation by Perceived Peer Political Orientation

Panel B: Liberals- Moderation by Primed Self-Objectivity

Panel C: Conservatives- Moderation by Perceived Peer Political Orientation

Panel D: Conservatives- Moderation by Primed Self-Objectivity

Figure 4. Two-way Interaction Plots

Next, we generated interaction plots that depict the association between credibility bias (on the x-axis) and sharing bias (on the y-axis), at different levels (low=-1SD and high=+1SD) of perceived peer political orientation (Figure 4, panels A [liberals] and C [conservatives]) and the prime (no prime vs. prime) (Figure 4, Panels B [liberals] and D [conservatives]). The results and figures imply that for liberal-leaning participants, the effect of credibility bias on sharing bias is contingent on perceived peer political orientation (panel A) and primed personal objectivity (panel B). The results and figure also imply that for conservative-leaning participants, the effect of credibility bias on sharing bias is contingent only on perceived peer political orientation (panel C); and not on primed self-objectivity (panel D).

Post-hoc Analysis: Three-Way Interaction

The three-way interaction (credibility bias * perceived peer political orientation *prime) coefficient was $\beta=0.703$, $p=0.001$ for liberal-leaning participants, and $\beta=-0.011$, $p=0.899$ for conservative-leaning participants. Therefore, we only plot the three-way interaction for liberal-leaning participants. It is depicted in Figure 5. As shown, line 2 (high perceived peer liberalism and no prime) is the only line with a negative slope. The slope of this line is different from the others (all differences with $p<0.001$), and all other lines have a similar positive slope (all differences with $p>0.142$). It suggests that when peers are liberal-leaning and there is no prime, credibility bias reduces sharing bias. The prime reduces perceived peer effects and increases reliance on one's own biases (lines 1 and 3). Thus, there is a dual contingency effect in liberal-leaning participants—the effect of credibility bias on sharing bias is contingent on their perceived peer political orientation, which is contingent on primed self-objectivity.

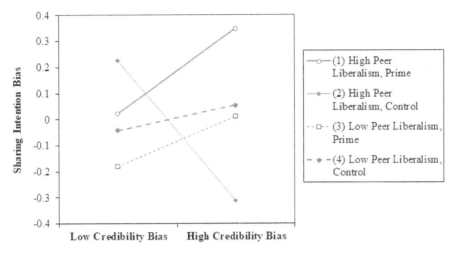

Figure 5. Three-way Interaction Plot for Liberal-leaning Participants

Discussion

This study designed an experiment to examine important overlooked drivers of the consumption and dissemination of fake news on social media from a broad social cognitive perspective. Our first focus was on the biasing effect of users' political beliefs on credibility and sharing biases. Our second focus was on how the social context/environment, manifested in perceived peer political orientation and individual states, specifically primed self-objectivity, influence the translation of credibility bias into sharing bias. The findings indicated that peoples' political orientation increased their credibility and sharing biases in the direction of their political orientation (H1 was supported). In addition, the pilot and main studies consistently showed that people present significantly stronger credibility and sharing biases in the direction of their political orientation, compared to those biases in the other direction. Credibility bias increased sharing bias in conservative-leaning participants but not in liberal-leaning ones (H2 was partially supported). Perceived peer political orientation did not increase users' sharing bias in the direction of their perception of peers' political orientation as hypothesized. Instead, it reduced the sharing bias for conservative-leaning participants (H3a was not supported). However, perceived peer political orientation served as a moderator. It decreased the effect of credibility bias on sharing bias for both liberal and conservative-leaning participants (H3b was supported). Finally, priming a sense of personal objectivity increased the effect of credibility bias on sharing bias in liberal-leaning participants, but not in conservative-leaning participants (H4 was partially supported). These findings inform four key insights.

First, from both consumption and dissemination perspectives, there is evidence of partisanship in how people believe and share news articles on social media. Rather than simply measuring credibility assessments and sharing behaviors, we examined bias toward a political ideology in the credibility and sharing of news articles on social media. The use of "bias" measures can be useful for studying polarization. We show here that credibility bias exists in our sample, and that it predicts political-leaning biases in sharing. More specifically, we found that credibility bias predicted sharing bias for conservative-leaning participants only, which explains evidence from prior research [3,35,76] that shows that conservative-leaning participants are more likely to share news from fake domains than their liberal-leaning counterparts. Consistent with prior research [7], liberal-leaning participants may deliberate the headlines more than their conservative-leaning counterparts before making sharing decisions. Researchers can therefore explore the extent to which cognitive evaluations such as deliberation drive beliefs and dissemination behaviors.

We in essence showed that priming can affect biased decisions. Therefore, future research can use priming and bias measures, like the ones we used here, in IS contexts that serve polarization; social media is an obvious context, but it can also apply, for instance, to biases in information technology personnel hiring and promotion decisions (e.g., a systematic preference toward one group), and information technology project escalation decisions (e.g., a biased systematic preference to keep on investing in information technology projects). These can be fruitful avenues for future research.

Second, we found that the political ideology of peers is an important source of influence on what people share on social media, mostly through its moderating role. Focusing first on its direct effect, our results show that perceived peer political orientation reduced sharing bias in conservative-leaning participants, but not in liberal-leaning participants. The negative effect can be explained by the deliberation effect reported in prior research [7]. Deliberating news headlines in light of how they may be perceived by peers triggers cognitive reflection which has been found to increase the propensity to engage in ideologically motivated reasoning, which has been found to reduce the tendency to share fake news [51,85]. Our results therefore echo the importance of the influence of social context [32] when investigating people's fake news information processing behaviors.

Focusing on the moderating role, our findings show that perceived peer political orientation reduces the effect of credibility bias on sharing bias, in both liberal and conservative-leaning participants. These findings support the importance of social context, as emphasized by social cognitive theory and the identity-based motivation model, and the idea that people, especially on social media, do not function in isolation. Furthermore, our results imply that while users do not need validation to act, they need it for self-affirmation and to build confidence in their in-group identity. Their politics-related actions on social media are, therefore, conditioned on the political stance of their peers. One additional explanation of this result is that in line with prospect theory [52], people may be more sensitive to potential backlash from their in-group when expressing out-group opinions, than to potential benefits of fitting the in-group by expressing in-group opinions. Thus, it is likely that a misfit between own and perceived peer political orientation may hinder reliance on own credibility beliefs and orientations, and drive emphasis on potential damages caused by sharing the information, regardless of its credibility [49]. That is, the objective of avoiding social punishment (e.g., backlash) can guide peoples' actions when their beliefs are not aligned with the beliefs of the group; and in such cases, their decisions may be less influenced by their credibility judgments [16]. Absent measures of backlash concerns, we cannot test this assertion in this study; we hence call for future research to examine this and/or alternative explanations.

Our findings are also consistent with the ideas in the identity-based motivation model [80] because they show that people's decision to share fake news can be influenced by social context factors (social cues from peers), and individual states that can be primed (a sense of self objectivity in our case). Furthermore, we extend the use of the identity-based motivation model from the study of product use and education-related behaviors to the study of political news sharing behaviors.

Third, we examined how personal individual differences in terms of activated perceptions (states) can influence social identity biases in the development of actions. Our findings indicate that the hypothesized influence of credibility bias on sharing bias depends on self-objectivity priming for liberal-leaning participants and not for conservative-leaning participants. A possible explanation of this difference in behavior is that liberal-leaning participants are more likely to practice reflective open-minded thinking [82] which alters their tendency to scrutinize politically sensitive information (i.e., self-objectivity). We realize that other factors can influence social identity, but the focus on self-objectivity is desirable from theoretical and practical perspectives. From a theoretical perspective it is understudied in the IS literature, and especially in studies that focus on biased decisions (e.g., believing and sharing fake news), even though it is an important factor that can influence biased decision making [102]. From a practical standpoint, it adds a layer of understanding of why people believe and share fake news. Based on such insights, information technology can deliver or avoid self-objectivity primes, depending on the objectives of the providers, and through this influence the consumption and dissemination of fake news.

Lastly, people do not exclusively believe and share fake news headlines that are aligned with their political orientation and ignore fake news headlines that are not. Instead, as we show in both the pilot and main studies, they sometimes systematically believe and share news headlines that are inconsistent with their political stance. However, the systematic preference toward believing and sharing fake news headlines that are aligned with their political orientation is significantly larger than this toward fake news headlines that are not aligned with their political orientation.

Research Implications

First, the findings point to the influence of own political orientation on users' credibility and sharing biases. These results provide some perspective for mixed findings reported in prior research. One group of studies report that confirmation bias (i.e., the extent to which news headlines align with political orientation) influences sharing behaviors [55,55,73] whereas other studies consistently show that the decision to share fake news on social media is not related to the extent to which they align with users' political orientation [7,84]. A consistent approach to measuring political alignment in these studies is the use of either a correlation between variables of interest and self-reported political orientation or items that elicited the extent to which headlines aligned with participants' political ideology. However, our conceptualization of bias to study polarization elicits the extent to which a variable of interest (e.g., credibility and sharing behaviors in our case) is viewed in favor of one political orientation over and above a rival political orientation. Measuring bias this way allows for careful deliberation of arguments [7] which has been found to inform believability and sharing behavior decisions. Research is therefore needed to confirm our approach in other contexts including replication of prior studies in the political context.

Second, the findings of the role of perceived peer political orientation in attenuating credibility bias effects underscore the need for IS research to better incorporate contextual factors into IS research models. The reason is that the decisions of many IS users are not done in isolation, and in-group fitting is an important consideration that can motivate people's behaviors across situations [47]. Certainly, our study is not the first one to account for social pressures and influences in IS use contexts [98]. Nevertheless, the role of the specific contextual factor we study here, namely perceived peer political orientation, is novel and can inform research on online politics-related behaviors, and more broadly, sensitive online behaviors, such as discussing hot-button issues. This can be especially true on social media that often present multiple sources of influences that are external to the user and that can influence how people choose to interact with contents they are exposed to on social media platforms. More research is needed to examine how other factors in users' context, such as additional sources of social influence, can predict and/or moderate fake news consumption and dissemination on social media. Ultimately, the findings pave the way for examining the social context in other relevant IT-mediated transactions, such as cyberbullying and sharing private information, in which case what peers think can inform and even guide user behaviors [66].

Third, our results show that priming self-objectivity can influence the mental weight some people give to their own biased beliefs when deciding to share fake news. Since social media platforms are replete with contents from a myriad of sources competing for users' attention, and users can vary in how objective they perceive themselves to be, it is useful to understand when and why users become skeptical of the credibility of those contents. While we found positive effects of such priming on the influence of credibility bias on sharing bias in liberal-oriented participants, it did not affect the relationship for conservative-leaning participants. This can relate to differences in cognitive processing between liberals and conservatives [110]. It implies that it may not be useful to manipulate self-objectivity for having a clear (increase or decrease) effect on fake news consumption by all people, regardless of their political leaning. It suggests, though, that self-objectivity can be an important factor in (a) IT-mediated decision models, at least for some people, and (b) priming experiments. Hence, future research should consider self-objectivity for extending models and theories of IT-mediated decisions, because priming harbors the potential to influence biased IT-mediated decisions, at least in some populations.

Fourth, prior research has pointed to ideological asymmetry in cognitive processing styles between liberal-leaning individuals and conservative-leaning individuals. Findings revealed that liberal-leaning individuals often reflect more on information than conservative-leaning individuals [83], but not always when the information conforms to one's beliefs [25]. Liberal-leaning individuals have also been found to tend to be less rigid and more tolerant of ambiguity, compared to conservative-leaning individuals [50]. Our findings demonstrate several differences between liberal-leaning and conservative-leaning individuals that are consistent with such findings. Specifically, the ability of the prime to influence information processing in liberal-leaning but not in conservative-leaning participants, the more pronounced effects of biased beliefs on willingness to share in conservative-leaning participants, and the more pronounced effect of interest in politics in conservative-leaning participants are all in line with the abovementioned prior findings. As such, our findings reaffirm past findings on ideological asymmetry and extend them to the specific processes we studied, including the processing of political preferences of peers and self-objectivity primes. IS research should further explore ideological asymmetries on online platforms, and find ways to reduce them.

Fifth, from a research design perspective, the observed influence of priming individuals indicates its efficacy in inducing certain behavioral responses from at least some study participants. Researchers should therefore be more critical about where they place scales with a priming potential on surveys to avoid unintended priming effects. Here, these effects were obtained by simply placing survey items in different locations. Hence, future IS research should be mindful of such intended or united priming effects and use counter-balanced designs to avoid them, if such effects are unintended.

Sixth, findings from this study provide support for the core ideas in the theories that inform our hypotheses in the context of fake news on social media. From an interpretation perspective, social identity theory [103] and perceived self-objectivity [102] are useful to explain how users may have been persuaded to share in-group vs. out-group fake news articles. Other persuasion theories such as the identity-based motivation model [80] and the elaboration likelihood model [87] can be employed in future research to extend our findings and to identify and study other mechanisms that explain fake news dissemination on social media.

Lastly, the pilot and main study findings show that while a large portion of people are biased in the direction of their political orientation, there is a smaller portion that are biased in the opposite direction. This suggests that people engage, at least to some extent, but not fully, in motivated reasoning and behaviors related to fake news. The significant preference for believing and sharing fake news headlines that are aligned with one's political orientation supports the idea that fake news behaviors are often (but not always) motivated by confirmation bias [59,76]. There seems to be a minor group of users who systematically prefer political news headlines that are not aligned with their view. These individuals might still be strategic about their choices. They may be alarmed by such news and may want to complain, ridicule the other party, and/or express their concern on social media through sharing such news. Our study did not afford to test such motivations, so this is a fruitful avenue for future research.

Practical Implications

Our results show that social media users filter their sharing of news articles based on the political orientation of their peers. This means that interventions that are presented as opinions of peers can be viable for nudging users to evaluate news articles they consume and share on social media platforms. Social media platforms can contribute to reducing polarization on their platforms by exposing users to related content from other political groups, such that users do not get the impression that their peers have political stances similar to theirs. Our findings also reveal that priming peoples' evaluation objectivity can be dangerous, as it can change their self-objectivity, which can make them less critical of news articles on social media, especially when shared with peers with a similar political stance. Thus, we do not endorse using such tactics to advance fake news in most instances. The findings, nevertheless, suggest that users should be aware of such priming manipulations and their cognitive weaknesses, and through this, question news items. We do, however, see the potential advancement of fake news as reasonable in some instances, though the ethicality of such steps can be debated. For example, using inflated statistics for generating fear and convincing people to wear masks during a pandemic, or inflating smoking damages statistics may convince people to avoid or reduce smoking. In such cases, self-objectivity primes may be used, but only after careful ethical considerations.

Limitations and Future Research Directions

We acknowledge some limitations that may influence the interpretation of results in this study. First, the experimental setting in which the study was conducted may have overlooked other nuances that can influence news consumption and dissemination behaviors. However, self-reported data gathered during the experiments turn out to be strongly correlated to how people share politically charged fake news on social media [73]. Hence, future research can utilize the multi-method approach to combine self-reported data with observational data from crawling social media platforms and experiments to explore nuances not fully captured by any one of these approaches in isolation. Second, the findings reported in this research may be peculiar to the sample of university students in the United States of America that participated in the study (largely liberal-leaning), and to the context of fake news (politics), we focused on. Including other demographic groups may reveal other tendencies that are representative of the user population on social media; and focusing on other areas of fake news (e.g., about the pandemic, or vaccinations) can increase the generalizability of our findings and point to nuanced differences between fake news topics. Lastly, future research can extend our findings to additional contexts in which one's behavior can be socially observed, and the motivation to elaborate depends on the extent to which the person believes he or she is objective (e.g., cyber loafing and cyber security).

Conclusions

This study examined how one's own credibility bias and political orientation translate into biased sharing decisions on social media, and how these processes are influenced by the perceived political orientation of peers on social media and one's self-objectivity. We found that one's political orientation drove credibility and sharing biases, and that credibility bias increased sharing bias for conservatives but not for liberals. We next examined perceived peer political orientation as a social construct and found that while it directly increased sharing bias for only conservatives, it decreased the effects of credibility bias on sharing bias for both liberals and conservatives. Finally, we found support for the effect of priming a sense of personal objectivity on increasing the effect of credibility bias on sharing bias for liberals but not for conservatives. Our findings provide important novel insights into the design of social media to inform how users consume and spread fake news on social media.

Notes

1. Scale direction choice was set for convenience reasons only, and does not reflect the superiority of one orientation over the other.

Disclosure statement

No potential conflict of interest was reported by the author(s).

ORCID

Ofir Turel ⓘD http://orcid.org/0000-0002-6374-6382
Babajide Osatuyi ⓘD http://orcid.org/0000-0001-8859-5536

References

1. Abrams, J.R. and Giles, H. Ethnic Identity Gratifications Selection and Avoidance by African Americans: A Group Vitality and Social Identity Gratifications Perspective. *Media Psychology*, 9, 1 (March 2007), 115–134.
2. Alhabash, S., McAlister, A.R., Lou, C., and Hagerstrom, A. From Clicks to Behaviors: The Mediating Effect of Intentions to Like, Share, and Comment on the Relationship Between Message Evaluations and Offline Behavioral Intentions. *Journal of Interactive Advertising*, 15, 2 (July 2015), 82–96.
3. Allcott, H. and Gentzkow, M. *Social media and fake news in the 2016 election*. National Bureau of Economic Research, 2017.
4. Alós-Ferrer, C. and Granić, D.G. Political space representations with approval data. *Electoral Studies*, 39, (September 2015), 56–71.
5. Arnett, D.B., German, S.D., and Hunt, S.D. The identity salience model of relationship marketing success: The case of nonprofit marketing. *Journal of Marketing 67*, 2003, 89–105.
6. Asch, S.E. Effects of group pressure on the modification and distortion of judgments. In H. Guetzkow, ed., *Groups, leadership and men*. Carnegie Press, Pittsburgh, PA, 1951, pp. 177–190.
7. Bago, B., Rand, D.G., and Pennycook, G. Fake news, fast and slow: Deliberation reduces belief in false (but not true) news headlines. *Journal of Experimental Psychology: General*, 149, 8 (August 2020), 1608–1613.
8. Bakshy, E., Messing, S., and Adamic, L.A. Exposure to ideologically diverse news and opinion on Facebook. *Science, 348*, 6239 (June 2015), 1130–1132.
9. Bandura, A. Social Cognitive Theory of Mass Communication. *Media Psychology*, 3, 3 (2001), 265–299.
10. Bargh, J.A., Chen, M., and Burrows, L. Automaticity of Social Behavior: Direct Effects of Trait Construct and Stereotype Activation on Action. *Journal of Personality and Social Psychology*, 71, 2 (1996), 230–244.
11. Bargh, J.A., Lee-Chai, A., Barndollar, K., Gollwitzer, P.M., and Trötschel, R. The automated will: Nonconscious activation and pursuit of behavioral goals. *Journal of Personality and Social Psychology*, 81, 6 (2001), 1014–1027.

12. Beltramini, R.F. Perceived believability of warning label information presented in cigarette advertising. *Journal of Advertising, 17,* 2 (June 1988), 26–32.

13. Bernard, J.G., Dennis, A.R., Galletta, D.F., Khan, A., and Webster, J. The tangled web: Studying online fake news. In *40th International Conference on Information Systems, ICIS2019.* 2020.

14. Van den Bos, K. and Lind, E.A. On Sense-Making Reactions and Public Inhibition of Benign Social Motives. An Appraisal Model of Prosocial Behavior. In *Advances in Experimental Social Psychology.* Academic Press Inc., 2013, pp. 1–58.

15. Brewer, M.B. Social Identity, Distinctiveness, and In-Group Homogeneity. *Social Cognition, 11,* 1 (March 1993), 150–164.

16. Briley, D.A. and Wyer, R.S. The Effect of Group Membership Salience on the Avoidance of Negative Outcomes: Implications for Social and Consumer Decisions. *Journal of Consumer Research, 29,* 3 (December 2002), 400–415.

17. Brown, S.A., Venkatesh, V., and Goyal, S. Expectation confirmation in technology use. *Information Systems Research, 23,* 2 (2012), 474–487.

18. Carney, D.R., Jost, J.T., Gosling, S.D., and Potter, J. The secret lives of liberals and conservatives: Personality profiles, interaction styles, and the things they leave behind. *Political Psychology, 29,* 6 (December 2008), 807–840.

19. Cheung, C.M.K. and Lee, M.K.O. A theoretical model of intentional social action in online social networks. *Decision Support Systems, 49,* 1 (April 2010), 24–30.

20. Chiu, C.M., Fang, Y.H., and Wang, E.T.G. Building community citizenship behaviors: The relative role of attachment and satisfaction. *Journal of the Association for Information Systems, 16,* 11 (November 2015), 947–979.

21. Colleoni, E., Rozza, A., and Arvidsson, A. Echo Chamber or Public Sphere? Predicting Political Orientation and Measuring Political Homophily in Twitter Using Big Data. *Journal of Communication, 64,* 2 (April 2014), 317–332.

22. Corkalo, D. and Kamenov, Z. National Identity and social distance: Does in-group loyalty lead to outgroup hostility? *Review of Psychology, 10,* 2 (2003), 85–94.

23. Dennis, A.R. and Minas, R.K. Security on autopilot: Why current security theories hijack our thinking and lead us astray. *Data Base for Advances in Information Systems, 49,* s1 (April 2018), 15–37.

24. Deutsch, J.I. Folklore, Politics, and Fake News in the Reception of Rogue One. *New Directions in Folklore, 15,* 1/2 (2018), 109–120.

25. Ditto, P.H., Liu, B.S., Clark, C.J., et al. At Least Bias Is Bipartisan: A Meta-Analytic Comparison of Partisan Bias in Liberals and Conservatives. *Perspectives on Psychological Science, 14,* 2 (March 2019), 273–291.

26. Eckhardt, A., Laumer, S., and Weitzel, T. Who Influences Whom? Analyzing Workplace Referents' Social Influence on it Adoption and Non-Adoption. *Journal of Information Technology, 24,* 1 (March 2009), 11–24.

27. Epley, N. and Dunning, D. Feeling "Holier than thou": Are self-serving assessments produced by errors in self-or social prediction? *Journal of Personality and Social Psychology, 79,* 6 (2000), 861–875.

28. Fareri, D.S. and Delgado, M.R. Social Rewards and Social Networks in the Human Brain. *The Neuroscientist : a review journal bringing neurobiology, neurology and psychiatry, 20,* 4 (August 2014), 387–402.

29. Farivar, S., Turel, O., and Yuan, Y. Skewing users' rational risk considerations in social commerce: An empirical examination of the role of social identification. *Information & Management, 55,* 8 (2018) pp. 1038–1048, doi: https://doi.org/10.1016/j.im.2018.05.008

30. Festinger, L. Cognitive dissonance. *Scientific American, 207,* 4 (1962), 93–106.

31. Flaxman, S., Goel, S., and Rao, J. Filter bubbles, echo chambers, and online news consumption. *Public Opinion Quarterly, 80,* S1 (2016), 298–320.

32. Fuller, M.A., Hardin, A.M., and Davison, R.M. Efficacy in technology-mediated distributed teams. *Journal of Management Information Systems, 23,* 3 (December 2006), 209–235.

33. Gelman, A. *Red state, blue state, rich state, poor state : why Americans vote the way they do.* Princeton University Press, 2010.

34. Gimpel, H., Heger, S., Olenberger, C., and Utz, L. The Effectiveness of Social Norms in Fighting Fake News on Social Media. *Journal of Management Information Systems, 38,* 1 (2021), 196–221.

35. Guess, A., Nagler, J., and Tucker, J. Less than you think: Prevalence and predictors of fake news dissemination on Facebook. *Asian-Australasian Journal of Animal Sciences, 32,* 2 (January 2019), eaau4586.

36. Guess, A.M., Nyhan, B., and Reifler, J. Exposure to untrustworthy websites in the 2016 US election. *Nature Human Behaviour, 4,* 5 (March 2020), 472–480.

37. Guillaume, Y.R.F., Van Knippenberg, D., and Brodbeck, F.C. Nothing succeeds like moderation: A social selfregulation perspective on cultural dissimilarity and performance. *Academy of Management Journal 57,* 2014, 1284–1308.

38. Hackett, J.D. and Hogg, M.A. The diversity paradox: when people who value diversity surround themselves with like-minded others. *Journal of Applied Social Psychology, 44,* 6 (June 2014), 415–422.

39. Hansen, K., Gerbasi, M., Todorov, A., Kruse, E., and Pronin, E. People Claim Objectivity After Knowingly Using Biased Strategies. *Personality & social psychology bulletin, 40,* 6 (June 2014), 691–699.

40. Hertel, G. and Kerr, N.L. Priming in-group favoritism: The impact of normative scripts in the minimal group paradigm. *Journal of Experimental Social Psychology, 37,* 4 (July 2001), 316–324.

41. Higgins, E.T. Knowledge activation: Accessibility, applicability, and salience. In E.T. Higgins and A.W. Kruglanski, eds., *Social psychology: Handbook of basic principles.* The Guilford Press, New York, NY, 1996, pp. 133–168.

42. Hogg, M.A. and Abrams, D. Social Identifications: A Social Psychology of Intergroup Relations and Group Processes. *Choice Reviews Online, 26,* 3 (1988), 26-1826-26-1826.

43. Hogg, M.A., Terry, D.J., and White, K.M. A Tale of Two Theories: A Critical Comparison of Identity Theory with Social Identity Theory. *Social Psychology Quarterly, 58,* 4 (December 1995), 255.

44. Hua, J. and Shaw, R. Corona Virus (COVID-19) "Infodemic" and Emerging Issues through a Data Lens: The Case of China. *International Journal of Environmental Research and Public Health, 17,* 7 (March 2020), 2309.

45. Humprecht, E. Where "fake news" flourishes: a comparison across four Western democracies. *Information, Communication & Society, 22,* 13 (November 2019), 1973–1988.

46. James, T.L., Lowry, P.B., Wallace, L., and Warkentin, M. The Effect of Belongingness on Obsessive-Compulsive Disorder in the Use of Online Social Networks. *Journal of Management Information Systems, 34,* 2 (April 2017), 560–596.

47. Johns, G. The essential impact of context on organizational behavior. *Academy of Management Review, 31,* 2 (April 2006), 386–408.

48. Johnson, T.J. and Kaye, B.K. Reasons to believe: Influence of credibility on motivations for using social networks. *Computers in Human Behavior, 50,* (2015), 544–555.

49. Jones, L.W., Sinclair, R.C., and Courneya, K.S. The Effects of Source Credibility and Message Framing on Exercise Intentions, Behaviors, and Attitudes: An Integration of the Elaboration Likelihood Model and Prospect Theory. *Journal of Applied Social Psychology, 33,* 1 (January 2003), 179–196.

50. Jost, J.T. Ideological Asymmetries and the Essence of Political Psychology. *Political Psychology, 38,* 2 (April 2017), 167–208.

51. Kahan, D.M. Ideology, Motivated Reasoning, and Cognitive Reflection: An Experimental Study. *Judgment and Decision Making, 8,* (December 2013), 407–424.

52. Kahneman, D. and Tversky, A. Prospect Theory: An Analysis of Decision Under Risk. In *Handbook of the Fundamentals of Financial Decision Making,* 2013, pp. 99–127.

53. Karahanna, E., Xu, S.X., Xu, Y., and Zhang, N. The needs-affordances-features perspective for the use of social media. *MIS Quarterly: Management Information Systems, 42,* 3 (January 2018), 737–756.

54. Kenworthy, J.B. and Miller, N. Attributional biases about the origins of attitudes: Externality, emotionality, and rationality. *Journal of Personality and Social Psychology, 82,* 5 (2002), 693–707.

55. Kim, A. and Dennis, A.R. Says Who? The Effects of Presentation Format and Source Rating on Fake News in Social Media. *MIS Quarterly, 43,* 3 (2019), 1025–1039.

56. Kim, A., Moravec, P.L., and Dennis, A.R. Combating Fake News on Social Media with Source Ratings: The Effects of User and Expert Reputation Ratings. *Journal of Management Information Systems, 36,* 3 (July 2019), 931–968.

57. Kim, B. and Kim, Y. Growing as social beings: How social media use for college sports is associated with college students' group identity and collective self-esteem. *Computers in Human Behavior, 97,* (August 2019), 241–249.

58. Kim, Y. The contribution of social network sites to exposure to political difference: The relationships among SNSs, online political messaging, and exposure to cross-cutting perspectives. *Computers in Human Behavior, 27,* 2 (March 2011), 971–977.

59. Knobloch-Westerwick, S. and Meng, J. Looking the other way: Selective exposure to attitude-consistent and counterattitudinal political information. *Communication Research, 36,* 3 (June 2009), 426–448.

60. Kohls, G., Peltzer, J., Herpertz-Dahlmann, B., and Konrad, K. Differential effects of social and non-social reward on response inhibition in children and adolescents. *Developmental Science, 12,* 4 (July 2009), 614–625.

61. Kohls, G., Perino, M.T., Taylor, J.M., et al. The nucleus accumbens is involved in both the pursuit of social reward and the avoidance of social punishment. *Neuropsychologia, 51,* 11 (September 2013), 2062–2069.

62. Kuem, J., Ray, S., Siponen, M., and Kim, S.S. What Leads to Prosocial Behaviors on Social Networking Services: A Tripartite Model. *Journal of Management Information Systems, 34,* 1 (January 2017), 40–70.

63. Laméris, M. *On the Measurement and Validation of Political Ideology.* University of Groningen, Groningen, The Netherlands, 2015.

64. Latane, B. and Darley, J.M. Group inhibition of bystander intervention in emergencies. *Journal of Personality and Social Psychology, 10,* 3 (November 1968), 215–221.

65. Lazer, D.M.J., Baum, M.A., Benkler, Y., et al. The science of fake news: Addressing fake news requires a multidisciplinary effort. *Science, 359,* 6380 (March 2018), 1094–1096.

66. Lazuras, L., Barkoukis, V., Ourda, D., and Tsorbatzoudis, H. A process model of cyberbullying in adolescence. *Computers in Human Behavior, 29,* 3 (May 2013), 881–887.

67. Löhndorf, B. and Diamantopoulos, A. Internal Branding. *Journal of Service Research, 17,* 3 (August 2014), 310–325.

68. London, M. Toward a Theory of Career Motivation. *Academy of Management Review, 8,* 4 (October 1983), 620–630.

69. Lord, C.G., Ross, L., and Lepper, M.R. Biased assimilation and attitude polarization: The effects of prior theories on subsequently considered evidence. *Journal of Personality and Social Psychology, 37,* 11 (November 1979), 2098–2109.

70. McKimmie, B.M., Terry, D.J., and Hogg, M.A. Dissonance Reduction in the Context of Group Membership: The Role of Metaconsistency. *Group Dynamics, 13,* 2 (June 2009), 103–119.

71. Metzger, M.J. and Flanagin, A.J. Credibility and trust of information in online environments: The use of cognitive heuristics. *Journal of Pragmatics, 59,* (December 2013), 210–220.

72. Moravec, P.L., Minas, R.K., and Dennis, A.R. Fake news on social media: People believe what they want to believe when it makes no sense at All. *MIS Quarterly, 43,* 4 (2019), 1343–1360.

73. Mosleh, M., Pennycook, G., and Rand, D.G. Self-reported willingness to share political news articles in online surveys correlates with actual sharing on Twitter. *PLOS ONE, 15,* 2 (February 2020), e0228882.

74. Mullainathan, S. and Washington, E. Sticking with Your Vote: Cognitive Dissonance and Political Attitudes. *American Economic Journal: Applied Economics*, *1*, 1 (January 2009), 86–111.

75. Napper, L. Self-Affirmation and the Processing of Health-Risk Information. *Doctoral Dissertation, University of Sheffield*, (2005).

76. Narayanan, V., Barash, V., Kelly, J., Kollanyi, B., Neudert, L.M., and Howard, P.N. Polarization, partisanship and junk news consumption over social media in the US. *arXiv 6*, 2018.

77. Naranjo-Zolotov M, Turel O, Oliveira T, Lascano JE. Drivers of online social media addiction in the context of public unrest: A sense of virtual community perspective. *Computer in Human Behavior*, *121*, paper 106784 (2021), pp. 1–8

78. Osatuyi, B., Hiltz, S.R., and Passerini, K. Seeing is believing (or at least changing your mind): The influence of visibility and task complexity on preference changes in computer-supported team decision making. *Journal of the Association for Information Science and Technology*, *67*, 9 (2016).

79. Osatuyi, B. and Turel, O. Social motivation for the use of social technologies: An empirical examination of social commerce site users. *Internet Research*, *29*, 1 (February 2019), 24–45.

80. Oyserman, D. Identity-based motivation and consumer behavior. *Journal of Consumer Psychology*, *19*, 3 (July 2009), 276–279.

81. Pan, Z., Lu, Y., Wang, B., and Chau, P.Y.K. Who Do You Think You Are? Common and Differential Effects of Social Self-Identity on Social Media Usage. *Journal of Management Information Systems*, *34*, 1 (January 2017), 71–101.

82. Pennycook, G., Allan Cheyne, J., Barr, N., Koehler, D.J., and Fugelsang $, J.A. *On the reception and detection of pseudo-profound bullshit*. 2015.

83. Pennycook, G. and Rand, D.G. Cognitive Reflection and the 2016 U.S. Presidential Election. *Personality and Social Psychology Bulletin*, *45*, 2 (February 2019), 224–239.

84. Pennycook, G. and Rand, D.G. Lazy, not biased: Susceptibility to partisan fake news is better explained by lack of reasoning than by motivated reasoning. *Cognition*, *188*, (July 2019), 39–50.

85. Pennycook, G. and Rand, D.G. Who falls for fake news? The roles of bullshit receptivity, overclaiming, familiarity, and analytic thinking. *Journal of Personality*, *88*, 2 (April 2020), 185–200.

86. Pérez-Rosas, V., Kleinberg, B., Lefevre, A., and Mihalcea, R. Automatic Detection of Fake News. *arXiv*, (August 2017).

87. Petty, R.E. and Cacioppo, J.T. The elaboration likelihood model of persuasion. *Advances in experimental social psychology*, *19*, (1986), 123–205.

88. Phelan, J.E. and Rudman, L.A. Reactions to ethnic deviance: The role of backlash in racial stereotype maintenance. *Journal of Personality and Social Psychology*, *99*, 2 (August 2010), 265–281.

89. Pronin, E., Gilovich, T., and Ross, L. Objectivity in the eye of the beholder: Divergent perceptions of bias in self versus others. *Psychological Review 111*, 2004, 781–799.

90. Pronin, E., Lin, D.Y., and Ross, L. The Bias Blind Spot: Perceptions of Bias in Self Versus Others. *Personality and Social Psychology Bulletin*, *28*, 3 (March 2002), 369–381.

91. Shearer, E. and Gottfried, J. News Use Across Social Media Platforms 2018. *Pew Research Center, Washington, DC*, 2018, 16.

92. Sherman, D.K. and Cohen, G.L. The Psychology of Self-defense: Self-Affirmation Theory. *Advances in Experimental Social Psychology 38*, 2006, 183–242.

93. Steele, C.M. and Liu, T.J. Dissonance processes as self-affirmation. *Journal of Personality and Social Psychology*, *45*, 1 (July 1983), 5–19.

94. Stets, J.E. and Burke, P.J. Identity theory and social identity theory. *Social Psychology Quarterly*, *63*, 3 (2000), 224–237.

95. Tajfel, H. and Turner, J. The Social Identity Theory of Inter-Group Behavior. In S. Worchel and W. Austin, eds., *Psychology of Intergroup Relations*. Nelson-Hall, Chicago, IL, USA, 1986.

96. Talwar, S., Dhir, A., Kaur, P., Zafar, N., and Alrasheedy, M. Why do people share fake news? Associations between the dark side of social media use and fake news sharing behavior. *Journal of Retailing and Consumer Services*, *51*, (November 2019), 72–82.

97. Toma, C.L. and Hancock, J.T. Toma, Hancock 2013 - Self-Affirmation Underlies Facebook Use. *Personality and Social Psychology Bulletin, 39*, 3 (March 2013), 321–331.

98. Tsai, H.T. and Bagozzi, R.P. Contribution behavior in virtual communities: Cognitive, emotional, and social influences. *MIS Quarterly, 38*, 1 (2014), 143–163.

99. Tucker, J., Guess, A., Barbera, P., et al. Social Media, Political Polarization, and Political Disinformation: A Review of the Scientific Literature. *SSRN Electronic Journal*, (March 2018).

100. Turel, O. Technology-Mediated Dangerous Behaviors as Foraging for Social-Hedonic Rewards: The Role of Implied Inequality.*MIS Quarterly, 45*, 3 (2021):1249–1286. https://doi.org/10.25300/MISQ/2021/16352

101. Turel, O. Untangling the complex role of guilt in rational decisions to discontinue the use of a hedonic Information System. *European Journal of Information Systems, 25*, 5 (2017), 432–447.

102. Turner, J.C. Social influence. In *Mapping social psychology series*. Thomson Brooks/Cole Publishing Co., 1991.

103. Turner, J.C., Hogg, M.A., Oakes, P.J., Reicher, S.D., and Wetherell, M.S. *Rediscovering the Social Group: A Self-Categorization Theory*. New York: Basil Blackwell, 1989.

104. Uhlmann, E.L. and Cohen, G.L. "I think it, therefore it's true": Effects of self-perceived objectivity on hiring discrimination. *Organizational Behavior and Human Decision Processes, 104*, 2 (2007), 207–223.

105. Venkatesh, V. and Morris, M.G. Why don't men ever stop to ask for directions? Gender, social influence, and their role in technology acceptance and usage behavior. *MIS Quarterly, 24*, 1 (2000), 115–139.

106. Verkuyten, M. and Maliepaard, M. A Further Test of the "Party Over Policy" Effect: Political Leadership and Ethnic Minority Policies. *Basic and Applied Social Psychology, 35*, 3 (May 2013), 241–248.

107. Voci, A. The link between identification and in-group favouritism: Effects of threat to social identity and trust-related emotions. *British Journal of Social Psychology 45*, 2006, 265–284.

108. Vosoughi, S., Roy, D., and Aral, S. The spread of true and false news online. *Science, 359*, 6380 (March 2018), 1146–1151.

109. Wang, C., Zhang, X., and Hann, I.H. Socially nudged: A quasi-experimental study of friends' social influence in online product ratings. *Information Systems Research, 29*, 3 (September 2018), 641–655.

110. Wojcik, S.P., Hovasapian, A., Graham, J., Motyl, M., and Ditto, P.H. Conservatives report, but liberals display, greater happiness. *Science, 347*, 6227 (March 2015), 1243–1246.

111. Wong, Q. Fake news is thriving thanks to social media users, study finds. *CNET*, 2019.

112. Xiao, H., Li, W., Cao, X., and Tang, Z. The online social networks on knowledge exchange: Online social identity, social tie and culture orientation. *Journal of Global Information Technology Management, 15*, 2 (2012), 4–24.

113. Yang, S.-U. and Kim, C. Like, comment, and share on Facebook: How each behavior differs from the other. *Public Relations Review, 43*, (2017), 441–449.

114. Yun, D. and Silk, K.J. Social Norms, Self-identity, and Attention to Social Comparison Information in the Context of Exercise and Healthy Diet Behavior. *Health Communication, 26*, 3 (April 2011), 275–285.

115. Zhu, Q., Skoric, M., and Shen, F. I Shield Myself From Thee: Selective Avoidance on Social Media During Political Protests. *Political Communication, 34*, 1 (January 2017), 112–131.

The Effect of the Expressed Anger and Sadness on Online News Believability

Bingjie Deng and Michael Chau

ABSTRACT

Emotional expressions have been widely used in online news. Existing research on the perception of online news has primarily focused on the effect of contextual cues on readers' reasoning and deliberation behavior; the role of discrete emotions such as anger and sadness, however, has been overlooked. This paper addresses this research gap by investigating the influence of angry and sad expressions in online news on readers' perception of the news. Drawing on the emotions as social information (EASI) theory and the appraisal-tendency framework (ATF), we find that expressions of anger in online news decrease its believability. However, sad expressions do not trigger the same effect. A further test reveals that the effect of angry expressions can be explained by the readers' perception of the author's cognitive effort: readers perceive that expressions of anger in the headlines denote a lack of cognitive effort of the author in writing the news, which subsequently lowers the believability of the news. We also show that news believability has downstream implications and can impact various social media behaviors including reading, liking, commenting, and sharing. This research extends current knowledge of the cognitive appraisals and interpersonal effects of discrete emotions (i.e., anger, sadness) on online news. The results also offer practical implications for social media platforms, news aggregators, and regulators that need to manage digital content and control the spread of fake news.

Introduction

Identification of misinformation (e.g., fake news) has become a hot topic for researchers and practitioners alike, arguably because anyone can publish information on social media that may be seen by thousands or even millions of people. Celebrities and social media influencers can also easily dominate social media by using floods of botnet puppeteers and tweet bots. Opinions on social media sites, with some manipulation, can create widespread misinformation [18, 32, 75]. With such power, social media platforms including Facebook, Twitter, YouTube, and Instagram have become a primary medium for spreading fake news [3, 81]. For example, Vosoughi et al. [124] tracked 126,000 stories that were tweeted more than 4.5 million times on Twitter from 2006 to 2017, and showed that false stories were 70% more likely to be shared than the truth, and that it takes true stories about six times longer than fake ones to be tweeted by 1,500 people. With the swift dissemination of fake news via

Access the Support Material: www.routledge.com/ 9781032561127

social media, users are being bombarded with misinformation. The Pew Research Center revealed that 54% of Americans either get their news "sometimes" or "often" from social media [106]. The spread of fake news on social media, therefore, poses a substantial challenge for both individuals and corporations [29, 55, 97].

Given the fast spread of fake news and its harmful downstream effects, researchers have approached the topic in a variety of ways [13]. One widespread field emerges from the information systems (IS) discipline, which identifies the determinants of readers' perceptions of the news—for example, the believability of the news and the readers' subsequent actions vis-à-vis the news article [61, 62, 82, 83]. Believability is an essential quality of a piece of news that influences readers' subsequent behavior. Investigating the elements that make a story trustworthy or not trustworthy can thus enable online news and social media platforms to better understand their readers' perceptions of online news, develop guidelines for content creation, and improve readers' evaluation of their content.

Within this research stream, one overlooked but worthwhile study angle is how discrete emotions, such as anger and sadness, influence news believability. Emotions play a significant role in cognitive, perceptual, and behavioral processes such as information processing and information dissemination [17, 30, 41, 66, 71, 107]. Anger and sadness, two basic negative emotions [36] that are prevalent on social media, have received increasing attention from researchers [12, 76]. For example, Aslam et al. study the news on Covid-19, the main theme of the year 2020-2021, and find that 11% of the news evoke anger, whereas 14% of the news evoke sadness [5]. Moreover, negative information (such as anger and sadness) has been demonstrated to spread faster and, therefore, has a greater impact on society than positive information [19, 24, 25, 39], partly due to human negativity bias in information processing [8, 59, 120]. Furthermore, social media posts with negative emotions are more likely to go viral than those with positive ones [86, 110, 111]. Hence, news stories with typical negative emotions, such as anger or sadness, deserve more attention in IS research.

This paper focuses on the following question: Holding constant the objective content of negative news, whether and how do overt expressions of anger or sadness affect readers' believability of the news and their subsequent social media behavior? For example, while a reader is browsing news on social media, he or she may encounter a piece of news with a headline that highlights negative tones and contains the author's overt expression of anger or sadness toward the issues described in the news. We ask, in this given situation, whether the expression of anger or sadness will impact the extent to which the reader believes the piece of news, and, if so, what the possible underlying psychological mechanism is.

Following van Kleef's theory of emotions as social information (EASI) [118, 119, 121, 122], we propose that expressed anger or sadness influences news perceptions primarily through the inferential processes by which readers form impressions of the author. According to Lerner and Keltner's appraisal-tendency framework (ATF) [71], distinct emotions have specific cognitive appraisals, which can affect judgment and behavior. We argue that readers will interpret the author's anger as a signal of inadequate reasoning, heuristic processing, and a lack of cognitive effort. Therefore, the quality of the writing outcome (i.e., the piece of news) will be questionable and less believable. On the other hand, as sadness relates to appraisals of situational control and systematic thinking, sad expression will not lead to lower believability. Furthermore, as one of the determinants of information diffusion, believability should have a significantly positive effect on social media behaviors such as reading, liking, commenting, and sharing [61, 62, 82, 83].

To answer our research questions, we utilized an experimental method in which participants read and evaluated pieces of online news with the same headlines but vary in expressions of anger or sadness. In doing so, we aim to advance theory regarding perceptions of misinformation, while also offering implications for guiding information management on social media platforms. Our investigation makes three primary contributions. First, we contribute to the news perception studies in IS literature by providing novel perspectives from which to understand news believability determinants. Prior IS research on fake news has examined how the contextual cues (e.g., highlighted source, source rating, fake news flag, social norm messages) influence perceptions of the news via the readers' reasoning and deliberation [47, 61, 62, 83]. To the best of our knowledge, we are among the first studies to explore the effects of discrete emotions, such as anger and sadness, in the textual content on online news perceptions. Moreover, as there is robust existing literature on political news, especially fake news, we pay attention to news topics that have less political relevance and are of general interest (i.e., news related to disease and the environment). Second, previous studies on anger and sadness largely focus on the individual's own emotional states on their cognitive processing, judgment, and behavior [69, 94], but overlook the interpersonal influence of emotions. We, however, use the EASI theory and ATF to provide insights on how the interpersonal inferences of the author's cognitive processing can also affect readers' news believability. Third, we contribute to the affect literature by providing a novel investigation of two distinct emotions, anger and sadness, which are both ubiquitous and substantial in online news but have not yet been adequately studied.

Literature Review and Hypotheses Development

The Discrete Emotions: Anger and Sadness

An emotion is an affective state arising as a reaction to the situational stimulus in one's environment that is relevant to one's concerns. It emphasizes a person's "mental state of readiness that arises from cognitive appraisals of thoughts" [7, p. 184]. The feeling is transient, existing when the supporting perceptions are active and vanishing rapidly when the conditions evaporate [100, 102, 131]. Emotions also serve as a primary predictor of information processing [30] and are associated with specific resulting action tendencies and behaviors [71, 78, 107]. Existing research widely adopt a framework with two dimensions—valence (pleasant vs. unpleasant) and arousal (activated vs. deactivated)—to map emotions [50, 99]. IS literature has also shown that positive and negative emotions influence behavior in a variety of contexts, such as sharing practice [111], stock market prediction [22], usage of websites [34], information seeking [84], and television advertising [88].

This paper goes beyond the two-dimensional framework and focuses on two discrete negative emotions, anger and sadness. Anger represents "a demonstration of displeasure, hostility, frustration, or a dissatisfaction/discrepancy between an ideal and actual outcome" [76, p. 104]. Individuals become angry when they realize that an undesirable event is hampering their goals, and that the event was triggered by another party rather than by themselves or by circumstance [66]. Once they become angry, individuals are motivated to actively oppose the causal party [44]. Consistent with the assertions of negativity bias, anger —as an emotion of negative valence—elicits stronger and faster emotional reactions and behavioral responses than emotions of positive valence, such as joy [8]. Meanwhile, according to Berger and Milkman [12], high-arousal emotions could be more viral. As a high-arousal emotion, anger has been shown to speed up information spread—that is, the number of posts or reposts—on social media [26, 76].

Sadness is another negative emotion that is on the list of universally experienced emotions with a biological basis [36, 89], is regarded as an emotion that should be regulated [38], and is also a widely-used emotion in the online news context. Sadness results from the perception of goal failure, and the impossibility of restoration given one's capability [70]. Sadness has been frequently compared with anger as they both are important negative emotions. For example, studies comparing anger and sadness have examined their effects on social judgment [14, 15, 65, 108, 115], policy preferences and perceptions of corporate crisis [60, 108], neural responses [11], online peer production [49] and the propagation of social media posts [76].

Existing studies on anger and sadness in online content can be classified into two major categories. The first category focuses on how angry or sad the readers feel when they read the online content [80]. The other category concentrates on the anger or sadness that exists in the content. Within the second category, one branch of research adopts machine learning models to classify anger or sadness as a discrete emotion in online content [26, 76, 126] or manually coding anger or sadness in the content [12]. The other branch includes the manipulation of discrete emotions by adding emotional expressions in the given content. For example, studies investigating anger embedded in online reviews manipulate the emotion by adding angry expressions in the review content [127, 129]. The current study contributes to the second branch, since anger and sadness are among the most common expressions embedded in social media news but this is still an understudied topic. Specifically, we manipulate the expressions of anger or sadness by holding the objective content constant in well-controlled experiments (more will be discussed later). In our context, we define *anger-embedded (or sadness-embedded) news* as news posts on social media containing angry (or sad) expressions in their headlines.

Emotions as Social Information (EASI) Theory

Existing research recognizes that emotions play a crucial role in social communication. People may actively share their emotions with others [98] or purposefully express feelings to affect others [40, 43]. Beyond the verbal content of a piece of information, emotional expressions provide a useful message about the information sender's intentions [119], which will affect the observer's judgments and behavior.

> Our primary hypothesis is that angry or sad expressions influence readers' perception of the news through inferences of the authors' cognitive processing. It aligns with the fundamental mechanism proposed in the EASI theory, a framework of emotion and persuasion in social contexts. The premise of the EASI model is that emotional expressions provide observers with information that may influence their behavior [119].

The EASI model is suitable for our research for three reasons. First, this model aims to explain the interpersonal effects of the emotion expressors on the observers. It goes beyond the frameworks that target the intrapersonal effects of emotions, such as the affect infusion model [41] and the "affect-as-a-resource" hypothesis [96]. Therefore, it is appropriate for a context in which readers use emotional expressions in the news as "social information" to draw inferences about the authors. Second, the EASI model fits the context of this study. News authors are typically motivated to vary the nuances of news headlines and content in order to "persuade" readers and attract more attention and exposure as indexed by the metrics of the likes, comments, and shares on social media. The EASI model can thus go beyond traditional persuasion contexts such as negotiation, customer relationship management, and leadership [2, 23, 125], and extend to social media settings to explain the interpersonal inferences. Third, the EASI model has been applied to study the discrete emotion of anger [122, 129]. Thus, we believe that this model can explain the interpersonal effects triggered by anger-embedded or sadness-embedded news when readers view news posts on social media.

The EASI model posits that emotional expressions may affect observers' behavior by two paths: inferential processes (which provide information about the situation) and affective reactions (which affect observers' emotions). The inferential processes assert that observers can often infer information about others' feelings, attitudes, and behavioral intentions based on their emotional expressions [58]. Such inferences may, in turn, affect the observer's behavior. For example, exhibiting sadness will make the observers infer that the actor faces difficulties, leading them to want to provide help to the actor [27]. The affective reactions hold that expressions of emotions can also exert interpersonal influence by evoking affective reactions in observers. This argument is consistent with the propositions of the social-appraisal literature: the other person's emotional reaction will change the individual's own decisions [66]. For example, when individuals observe their friends' excitement about a possible outcome, they may increase their positive assessment of the results because of their own positive feelings [91].

We argue that in the context of social media news, the inferential process plays a more important role than the affective reactions. First, the affective reactions of emotional expressions primarily occur in the context of communal and exchange relationships [28], teamwork [113, 118], and negotiation [117]. Second, studies have also shown how the predictive power of affective reactions depends on the target of emotional expressions. For instance, if someone is the target of the angry or sad expressions, the target may react emotionally; otherwise, he or she may not. In the context of social media news, the story's emotional expressions rarely target a specific reader personally. Meanwhile, most news is posted through an official institutional account (though, indeed, the account can be fake). Even if the news is posted or reposted by an individual, such as a social media influencer or a celebrity, the chance of the reader being the specific target of the news content is low. Therefore, when facing emotional expression in the news on social media, readers are more likely to process the emotions through the inferential processes path, which we are going to focus on in this research.

Anger, Sadness, and Cognitive Effort: The Appraisal-Tendency Framework (ATF)

As discussed, the EASI model posits that emotions expressed in news affect readers' perceptions and behavior. We argue that readers will make inferences about the authors from the emotional expressions, and the inferences will affect the readers' believability of the news. To understand more about the detailed mechanism of this effect for angry and sad expressions, we draw on the appraisal-tendency framework (ATF) [71]. The ATF provides a basis for distinguishing the effects of specific emotions on judgment and decision-making.

Apart from affective outcomes of emotion, the appraisals that define an emotion usually have carry-over effects on perceptions and behavior [37]. According to Han et al. [51], it is crucial to look beyond the valence of emotion and identify the appraisal dimensions and themes of specific emotions. The appraisal dimensions are useful not only because they differentiate emotions in a more fine-grained way than valence approaches, but also because they break feelings down into cognitive dimensions that map emotions onto judgment and decision-making processes. Therefore, this framework is appropriate for our research context focusing on the two discrete emotions.

According to the ATF, "emotions not only arise from but give rise to an implicit cognitive predisposition to appraise future events in line with the central appraisal patterns" [51, p.166]. There are six basic cognitive appraisal patterns of emotions: certainty, pleasantness, attentional activity, control, anticipated effort, and responsibility [109]. Each appraisal pattern relates to specific appraisal tendencies; individuals tend to interpret subsequent events according to the cognitive appraisals characterizing their emotions [71, 72]. In the following, we look into the depth-of-processing induced by the appraisal-tendencies of anger and sadness [51, 73].

Anger is characterized by the appraisal pattern of certainty that arises when an undesirable event motivates individuals to oppose the causal party [51]. As a result, individuals experiencing anger and its certainty appraisal tend to feel certain in subsequent events [85]. Consequently, they are more likely to aim to punish the perceived perpetrator of the event [71, 85, 87], engage in heuristic processing that requires little direct thought [127, 129], and make more biased judgments [71, 72]. For example, angry individuals tend to rely on stereotypes to make inferences and form arguments with insufficient quality [15, 114]. In other words, the angry person relies on trivial cues rather than on deliberate thinking, which leads them to generate perceptions and judgments with lower quality. In the current setting, if the news authors are perceived to experience anger when they write news articles, readers expect them to be thinking heuristically and devoting less cognitive effort to the task.

Sadness relates to the appraisal theme of situational forces beyond anyone's control. Such appraisal themes will trigger appraisal tendencies to perceive situational control in various situations, even in other unrelated domains, such as health outcomes and job performance. Meanwhile, they are expected to evoke an implicit action tendency to change the circumstances that brought about the saddening event. By activating the "goal of reward acquisition," sadness also drives people to repair damage and seek reward [45, 69, 87, 95]. Previous studies have investigated anger and sadness by examining their underlying cognitive processing and their influences on perceptions. However, unlike anger that leads to heuristic processing, sadness results in a more systematic processing [15, 115]. Researchers also find that the differences of depth-of-processing in sadness and anger result in differences in policy preferences and interpretations of corporate crisis [60, 108]. Given that anger biases information processing, it can be assumed that individuals reading an anger-embedded news story will infer that the angry authors wrote the news without depth of thinking or sufficient cognitive effort, thus lowering the believability of the news. In contrast, for sadness-embedded news, sad authors tend to think more systematically and write with effort. As the authors are perceived to write the news with effort, the believability of the news will not be discounted.

Applying the core principles of the EASI theory and ATF to our context, we argue that expressed anger in news headlines influences news believability primarily through interpersonal inferential processes. The expressions of anger first signal to the readers that the author was angry when writing the news article. Readers then make inferences

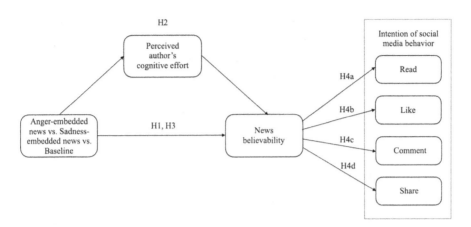

Figure 1. Research model

about the author's cognitive processing in their writing, which influences the readers' believability of the news. To interpret the author's writing, readers rely on the cognitive appraisals and the appraisal tendencies of anger proposed in ATF. Since anger is an incidental emotion associated with certainty appraisals, readers may well interpret angry authors as being less careful, which would impede the author's reasoning and systematic thinking capabilities. Meanwhile, the angry authors were less likely to remove anger from the news item carefully. Therefore, readers interpret overt expressions of anger in the news as a signal of heuristic information processing and the author's lack of cognitive effort in their writing. We emphasize that these arguments do not imply that angry authors must behave less rationally—only that readers *perceive* this to be the case. The inferences regarding the author's cognitive effort should, in turn, influence the believability of the news. When evaluating cognitive performance, observers tend to appreciate the evidence of cognitive efforts and systematic thinking. Observers perceive the judgment guided by systematic reasoning to be credible across various domains [16, 53, 94]. Hence, holding constant the objective content of a news headline, expressions of anger will lead readers to evaluate the news as less believable. To summarize, news that contains expressions of anger will result in a lower perceived level of cognitive effort on the part of the author, which in turn leads to lower news believability from the reader. Our theoretical framework is illustrated in Figure 1, and our first two hypotheses are stated as follows:

H1: Anger-embedded news (vs. baseline) lowers news believability

H2: The effect of anger-embedded news on news believability is mediated by the perceived author's cognitive effort[1]

Following the same logic, readers will also make inferences of the authors based on the expression of sadness in the news. Since sadness is related to situational control and systematic processing, sad authors will be perceived to be deliberate in their writing.

---

[1]The term *perceived author's cognitive effort* refers to the level of cognitive effort of the author as perceived by readers..

Hence, the believability of their news will not be discounted compared with the baseline news, as writing with deliberation should be a default rule in news industry. Therefore, holding constant the objective content of a news headline, expressions of sadness will not lower the news believability. Therefore, our third hypothesis is as follows:

H3: Sadness-embedded news (vs. baseline) does not lower news believability

News Believability and Social Media Behavior

People interact with social media through different kinds of activities. Lee et al. [68] define different consumer engagement levels (e.g., liking, commenting, and sharing) and show how these engagement levels are affected by social media advertising content. People can consume digital content by reading it; they can join the social media community by liking, commenting on, and sharing the digital content; and they can even create their own content by writing or posting [63]. Believability can be a critical determinant of social media usage because, when someone believes the information to be correct, they are more likely to engage with it or encourage its spread by sharing it themselves [57]. Studies on news perceptions have shown that believability affects a variety of social media activities, including reading, liking, commenting, and sharing [61, 62, 83]. Therefore, we further hypothesize that believability influences users' various social media behaviors.

H4a: The believability of the news increases a reader's intention to read the news.

H4b: The believability of the news increases a reader's intention to like the news.

H4c: The believability of the news increases a reader's intention to comment on the news.

H4d: The believability of the news increases a reader's intention to share the news.

Experimental Studies

We conducted two controlled experiments to test the hypotheses we proposed, and collected three rounds of pre-tests before each round of data collection. All these exercises recruited English-speaking U.S. participants from Amazon Mechanical Turk (MTurk). This section discusses the pre-tests and main experiments in detail.

Study 1

Study 1 aimed to provide initial evidence of the relationship between anger-embedded news and news believability and its impact on readers' behavior (H1 and H4) by directly manipulating emotional expressions (i.e., words related to anger) in news headlines. For each news story, participants provided their perceptions of the author's anger, the believability of the news story, and their intention to engage in various social media behaviors. By comparing the readers' perception of the author's anger in different news conditions (anger vs. control), we first demonstrated that our manipulation was successful. We were also able to identify the differential impact of anger by comparing the believability of the news in these two conditions. The details of the study are discussed in the following.

Stimulus materials and pre-tests

Study 1 used disease-related news headlines from news websites as our stimuli, as it is not uncommon for readers to spot disease-related news headlines embedded with anger, and readers have a natural tendency to react quickly to news reporting on social issues such as disease [126]. We conducted three pre-tests to prepare the news stimuli for Study 1. The first pre-test was conducted to see whether the original news headlines were negative in their valence and relatively neutral among basic negative emotions (e.g., anger, fear, sadness). In the beginning, we selected 15 news headlines that were considered neutral in emotions. In the pre-test, 80 participants each read 8 of the 15 news headlines one by one (randomly selected and ordered) and rated their perceptions of the author's emotions (i.e., anger, fear, sadness, happiness). Based on the results, we kept two news headlines. For each of the news headlines, participants' ratings of negative emotions were significantly higher than their ratings of happy ones ($p < .001$), but their perceptions of different negative emotions of the author (i.e., perceived author's anger, perceived author's fear, perceived author's sadness) did not show significant difference ($p > 0.5$).

After selecting the two headlines, we conducted a second pre-test to confirm readers' perceived author's emotions. We recruited another batch of 64 participants who read the two news headlines in a random order. After reading each news headline, participants rated their perceptions of the author's emotions (i.e., anger, fear, sadness, happiness). The result reconfirmed that the participants' ratings of their perception of negative emotions (i.e., anger, fear, sadness) were significantly higher than their ratings of perceived author's happiness ($p < .001$ for both news headlines). Similar to the first pre-test, the participants' rating of the three negative emotions did not show a significant difference ($p > .05$ for both news headlines). The results confirmed that the two news headlines selected had a similar level of negative valence among different negative emotions. Therefore, we were confident that the valence of the selected news is unpleasant, and the basic tone of the emotion in the news does not incline to any particular kind of negative emotions. We could then ensure that the emotion-catching manipulation would be equally consistent with the content of each news headline.

In the third pre-test, we further checked whether adding the angry expression at the beginning of the news headlines triggered different perceptions of the professional quality of the news. We recruited a different sample of 163 participants, randomly assigned them to the control news condition or the anger news condition, and asked them to rate the perceived professionalism of the two news headlines (randomly ordered). The results showed that the perceived professionalism of the news headlines was indifferent between the news with angry expressions and the baseline news ($p > .05$ for both news headlines).

An example of the news stimuli is shown in Figure 2 and more details are provided in Appendix 1.

Procedure of the main experiment

335 U.S. participants (41.19% female, $M_{age}=39$) were recruited from MTurk for a small monetary compensation (see Appendix 2 for details of screening questions and demographics). As a cover story, we asked participants to view some news headlines selected

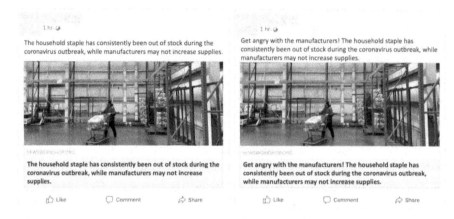

Figure 2. An example of news headline (control vs. anger) in Study 1

from a new social media platform to improve their service. Each participant was randomly assigned to one of two conditions (anger vs. control). The news displays were designed to simulate a regular Facebook post. Following the practices of prior IS studies on news perception [61], we used fabricated news sources such as "Newsworkshop.org" and "Newshour.com" to avoid the potential bias of news sources on the participants' judgment. The news sources were in an inactivated state when we experimented. Meanwhile, the information on the person who posted the news (i.e., the poster) was hidden to prevent any influence brought by perceptions of the poster (see Figure 2). Each participant viewed and read one randomly chosen headline from the two news headlines. After viewing the headline, participants reported how believable they found the news, and their intention to read, like, comment on, and share the news. They were asked to rate their perception of the author's anger, as well as to answer several questions related to the control variables and demographics. At the end of the experiment, we debriefed the participants.

Dependent variables

We measured believability by taking the average of three 7-point items adapted from Kim and Dennis [61]: "How believable do you find this article", "How truthful do you find this article", and "How credible do you find this article". The loadings of the three items were 0.951, 0.958, and 0.958, respectively. The composite reliability of the believability was 0.86. Cronbach's alpha was also adequate (0.95). We measured social media behavior by asking separately which actions the participant would take, including read, like, comment on, and share.

Control variables

Previous studies have examined several variables that affect the believability of a piece of news. Aside from demographics such as age, gender, education, and political affiliation, we controlled social media usage, confirmation bias, familiarity with the news, and general mood.

First, social media usage denotes the frequency of using social media to view news in a typical day [61]. An active user should be more familiar with social media platforms and actively interact with the digital content, whereas an inactive user might be unfamiliar with the platforms and less interested in participating on social media. The believability of news on social media may be different between active and inactive users. We measured *social media usage* by asking: "In a typical day, how often do you check your social media (e.g., Facebook, Twitter, Instagram, Weibo, WeChat, etc.)" with 1 = "Equal to or less than once", 7 = "Always".

Second, confirmation bias is an essential factor in previous fake news studies, especially in the literature on political news [61, 62]. We thus collected the readers' perception of the importance of the news and their position on the news as control variables. We measured the construct *confirmation bias* by multiplying two items, adapted from Kim and Dennis [61]. The first was the perceived importance of the headline ("Do you find the issue described in the article important" with 1 = "Not at all", 7 = "Extremely"). The second was their position on the headline ("What is your position on the headline" with -3 = "Extremely negative", +3 = "Extremely positive).

The third variable is whether the readers' familiarity with the news affects their trust in the story [74, 93, 112]. Previous studies have demonstrated that prior exposure to news content may cause "illusory truth" [92]—that is, readers tend to believe the news when they have been exposed to similar news content several times. Therefore, we controlled the participants' *familiarity with the news* in this study by measuring the construct on a 7-point scale ranging from "definitely not heard before" to "definitely heard before," which we adapted from Swire et al. [112].

The fourth variable is the participants' general mood when they read the news, which may affect their judgments. In contrast to emotion, which is intense, context-specific, intentional, and temporary, mood refers to a nonspecific feeling state that is usually mild, aimless, and long-lasting [10, 31, 36]. Mood is also considered a powerful motivation for judgment and behavior [35, 42, 51, 104, 105]. Previous studies have explored the roles of general mood in technology acceptance behavior and online trust formation [123, 132]. Moreover, mood affects people's behavior by reorganizing their cognitive states [103], such as by occupying cognitive resources [96]. Therefore, in this study, mood may occupy some cognitive resources and affect a reader's information processing of news headlines. In keeping with existing research, we measured participants' *general mood* by first classifying moods into positive and negative ones. Then, we took the difference of the average of the six items of positive feelings and the average of the six items of negative moods, adapted from Aaker et al. [1]. The details of the variables in the experiments can be found in Appendix 3.

Results

We first checked our manipulation of angry expressions. As expected, the results showed that news in the anger condition triggered a significantly higher level of the perceived author's anger than that of the control condition ($t = 8.94$, $p < .001$).

Table 1. Means and standard deviations of the variables in the two conditions in Study 1

	Baseline news (N=171)	Anger-embedded news (N=164)
Believability	4.43 (1.69)	3.70 (1.80)
Read	4.49 (1.94)	3.99 (2.15)
Like	2.50 (1.87)	2.37 (1.89)
Comment on	2.46 (1.87)	2.41 (1.98)
Share	2.32 (1.89)	2.32 (1.94)
Social media usage	4.39 (1.88)	4.76 (1.90)
Confirmation bias	-5.53 (8.93)	-4.87 (9.60)
Familiarity with the news	3.39 (1.39)	3.04 (1.45)
General mood	1.91 (2.32)	1.80 (2.48)
Age	38.09 (12.53)	39.95 (12.37)
Gender	0.63 (0.49)	0.55 (0.50)
Education	3.84 (0.87)	3.76 (0.96)
Political affiliation	2.33 (1.21)	2.26 (1.23)

Note: Standard deviations are in parentheses.

Our primary research question concerned whether the believability of news varied between anger-embedded news and baseline news. The summary of the results can be found in Table 1. Our data showed that, when compared with the baseline news, news embedded with anger leads to significantly lower believability (M_{anger} = 3.70, SD = 1.80, vs. $M_{control}$ = 4.43, SD =1.69; t = -3.79, $p < .001$), which supports H1.

As a robustness check, we conducted additional ANCOVA analysis with the inclusion of news topics, social media usage, confirmation bias, familiarity with the news, general mood, and participants' demographic variables (age, gender, education, political affiliation) as covariates. Preliminary analyses were conducted to confirm that the assumptions of normality and homogeneity of variables were met. The ANCOVA analysis confirmed the focal finding that angry expressions significantly reduced the believability of news on social media still holds when taking the above variables into account (F (1, 319) = 12.02, $p < .001$; post-hoc, t = -3.47, $p < .001$). The details of the results can be found in Appendix 4.

Finally, our analysis also showed that believability had downstream consequences and impacted users' actions on social media. Consistent with existing literature [61, 62, 83], we found that users were more likely to read, like, comment on, and share articles when they believed the news ($p < .001$ for all four cases). The results still held when taking all the control variables into account, which supported H4a to H4d. The details of the analysis can be found in Appendix 5.

Discussion

By leveraging a well-controlled experimental approach, Study 1 provided initial causal evidence for our hypotheses H1 and H4. The design of Study 1 enabled us to avoid potential confounds and further clarify the effect of anger. Pre-tests and manipulation check confirmed the effectiveness of our manipulations. This study also demonstrated that news believability has a positive effect on readers' intention to read, like, comment on, or share the news.

Study 1 leaves several questions unaddressed. First, we did not directly examine the underlying mechanism of our main effect. We speculated that, as anger acted as social information, a higher recognized level of the author's anger gave readers inferences about the author's cognitive information processing. When authors were perceived to be angry, they were expected to think heuristically and put less cognitive effort into their writing. Therefore, the perceived author's cognitive effort may explain the effect we found in Study 1. Second, we did not address the hypothesis of the sadness-embedded news in this study. Third, it is unclear whether the effect is still robust after expanding news topics and headlines, as well as controlling more relevant variables, such as the consumption frequency of relevant news topics, the personal relevance of the news, and the perceived political connection of the news. We conducted Study 2 in order to address these questions.

Study 2

Study 2 has three primary goals. First, we explore the underlying mechanism of the effect of anger-embedded news on news believability. We expected that the perceived author's cognitive effort would explain this effect, as angry authors may be perceived to lack the depth of thinking and write the news article using less cognitive effort, which makes the news less believable (H2). Second, we aim to understand the effect of the sadness-embedded news on news believability. As we proposed, sadness-embedded news (vs. baseline news) does not lower news believability as anger-embedded news does (H3). Third, we test the robustness of our findings in Study 1 by expanding the news topics to include both disease-related news and environment-related news, and by including the additional control variables of news topic consumption, personal relevance of the news, and political connections of the news.

Stimulus materials and pre-tests

To enhance the external validity of the effect, we expanded the news topics from Study 1 and selected one disease-related news headline and one environment-related news headline for this study (see Appendix 1). Both of these news topics are natural to anger and sadness emotions and are commonly found to contain emotional expressions. We followed the pre-tests used in Study 1 to prepare the stimulus materials.

In the first pre-test, we examined 12 disease-related news headlines and 12 environment-related news headlines from real news websites. The news headlines were relatively neutral in emotions and the content was reasonable for adding angry or sad expressions. We recruited 439 participants, each read four news headlines randomly selected and ordered from the 24 news headlines. We selected one piece of disease-related news and one piece of environment-related news, for which the participants' ratings of their perception of negative emotions (i.e., anger, fear, sadness) were significantly higher than their ratings of perceived author's happiness ($p < .001$ for both news headlines). In terms of the perceived author's emotions, the participants' rating of the three negative emotions did not show significant difference ($p > .05$ for both news headlines).

We conducted the second pre-test to confirm the emotions in the two selected news headlines. We recruited 64 participants to read two news headlines in a random order. The results were similar to those in the first pre-test and reconfirmed that the participants' ratings of their perception of negative emotions (i.e., anger, fear, sadness) were significantly higher than their ratings of perceived author's happiness ($p < .001$ for both news headlines). For the perceived author's emotions, the participants' rating of the three negative emotions did not show significant difference ($p > .05$ for both news headlines).

After adding the angry expressions or sad expressions at the beginning of the news headlines, we recruited a different sample of 246 participants, randomly assigned to one of the three conditions (anger vs. sadness vs. control), and asked them to rate their perceived professionalism of two news headlines (randomly ordered). The results showed that the perceived professionalism of the news headlines was indifferent among anger-embedded news, sadness-embedded news, and the baseline news ($p > .05$ for both news headlines). Therefore, we were confident that the emotional valences of the two news headlines were negative, the basic tone of the emotion in the news did not incline toward any basic negative emotions, and the perceived professionalism did not vary among treatment conditions and the control condition.

Procedure of the main experiment

Study 2 used the same procedure as Study 1. Each participant was randomly assigned to one of the conditions (anger vs. sadness vs. control) and read one randomly chosen news headline (either the disease-related news or the environment-related news). We used the fabricated news sources from Study 1 and hid the poster's information to avoid their potential influence on the participants' judgment. 633 U.S. participants (56.87% female, $M_{age} = 40.08$) were recruited from MTurk for a small monetary compensation for further analysis (see Appendix 2 for details of the screening questions and demographics). We also ensured that the people recruited had not participated in Study 1.

Dependent variables

We used the same dependent variables as for Study 1, asking participants about their believability of the news headline and their intention to read, like, comment on, and share the news.

Mediator

To uncover the underlying mechanism of the effect, we tested *the perceived author's cognitive effort* by taking the average of three 7-point items: "In your opinion, how much effort had the author put into writing this news"; "In your opinion, how much thought had the author given to the above news when he/she wrote it"; and "In your opinion, how much time did the author spent writing this news" with 1= "Not at all" and 7= "Very much."

Control variables

In addition to the control variables used in Study 1, we used more control variables in this study to improve the robustness of our results. The additional variables that may influence the news believability include news topic consumption, personal relevance of the news, and political connections.

First, if the readers frequently browse certain types of news in a certain period, their consumption of the news topics may affect their judgment and behavior toward news about that topic. Therefore, we controlled the news topic consumption for the corresponding news and measured it by asking, "In a typical day, how often do you browse/search disease-related (environment-related) news" with 1 = "Equal to or less than once" and 7 = "Always."

Second, people often exchange information with those with like-minded thinking. On social media, people may be more likely to believe and share information from similar people or people with shared interests [17]. In this case, people may think that information from similar people is more relevant to themselves, so they are more likely to believe the news. Therefore, we controlled the *personal relevance of the news* in this study, measuring this variable by a 7-point scale question adapted from Celsi et al. [20]: "Do you find the news is of personal importance to you" with 1 = "Not at all" and 7 = "Very much."

Third, considering that participants on the Amazon Mechanical Turk platform might evaluate content related to the pandemic or environmental issues as being politicized, we added the *political connections of the news* as a control variable. We measured this variable by asking, "To what extent do you connect the news headlines to political conditions" with 1= "Not at all" and 7 = "Very much" (see Appendix 3 for details on the variables in the experiments).

Results

To check our manipulation, we measured the perceived author's anger/sadness by asking: "In your opinion, to what extent does angry/sad describe how the author felt when he/she wrote the above news" with 1 = "Not at all" and 7 = "Very much," adapted from Yin et al. [127]. The results showed that news in the anger condition triggered a significantly higher level of the perceived author's anger than that in the control condition ($t = 9.39; p < .001$). In contrast, news in the sadness condition induces a significantly higher level of the perceived author's sadness than in the control condition ($t = 4.91; p < .001$). In summary, the results showed that our manipulation was successful.

The summary of variables in the three news conditions is shown in Table 2. We carried out an ANOVA test to examine the news believability of anger-embedded news, sadness-embedded news, and baseline news. Additional tests were also conducted to demonstrate the reliability and validity of our measurements in this study (see Appendix 6). The results showed that there was a main effect of news conditions on believability ($F (2, 630) =7.93, p < .001$). Corroborating the results of Study 1, news believability was significantly lower in the anger-embedded news than

Table 2. Means and standard deviations of variables in the three conditions in Study 2

	Baseline news (N=216)	Anger-embedded news (N=206)	Sadness-embedded news (N=211)
Believability	4.31 (1.58)	3.71 (1.65)	4.19 (1.64)
Read	4.62 (1.86)	4.18 (2.08)	4.45 (1.98)
Like	2.67 (1.82)	2.37 (1.66)	2.47 (1.82)
Comment on	2.39 (1.92)	2.09 (1.54)	2.28 (1.69)
Share	2.43 (1.92)	2.01 (1.53)	2.27 (1.84)
Social media usage	4.81 (1.85)	4.61 (1.94)	4.36 (2.04)
Confirmation bias	-2.63 (8.59)	-3.21 (7.57)	-3.86 (8.29)
Familiarity with the news	2.18 (1.74)	1.71 (1.40)	2.10 (1.69)
General mood	1.53 (2.76)	1.91 (2.55)	1.73 (2.62)
News topic consumption	2.84 (1.73)	2.67 (1.74)	2.59 (1.68)
Personal relevance of the news	4.01 (1.90)	3.49 (1.94)	3.59 (1.94)
Political connection of the news	2.84 (1.83)	3.07 (1.93)	3.07 (2.00)
Age	39.84 (12.68)	39.49 (12.05)	40.89 (12.36)
Gender	0.46 (0.50)	0.42 (0.49)	0.41 (0.49)
Education	2.90 (0.73)	2.85 (0.66)	2.76 (0.67)
Political affiliation	2.06 (1.12)	2.14 (1.15)	2.21 (1.23)

Note: Standard deviations are in parentheses.

the baseline news (M_{anger} = 3.71, SD =1.65, vs. $M_{control}$ = 4.31, SD =1.58; post-hoc, t = -3.77, p < .001), which was in line with H1. Additionally, news believability did not show significant difference between the sadness-embedded news and the baseline news ($M_{sadness}$ = 4.19, SD =1.64, vs. $M_{control}$ = 4.31, SD =1.58; post-hoc, t = -.73, p = .75), supporting H3. Moreover, we found that news believability in the anger condition was significantly lower than that in the sadness condition (M_{anger} = 3.71, SD =1.65, vs. $M_{sadness}$ = 4.19, SD =1.64; post-hoc, t = -3.03, p < .01). The result is charted in Figure 3.

To examine the proposed mechanism, we formally tested whether the perception of the author's cognitive effort could explain and mediate the effect of anger-embedded news on news believability. A PROCESS Model 4 mediation analysis [52] with 5,000 bootstrapping samples confirmed that the effect of anger-embedded news on news believability could be explained by a lower level of the perceived author's cognitive effort (95% CI: [-.43, -.03]). The results supported H2 and the details of the mediation analysis can be found in Appendix 7.

Next, we performed ANCOVA to examine the news believability of anger-embedded news and sadness-embedded news while controlling for the effect of covariates such as news topics, social media usage, confirmation bias, familiarity with the news, news topic consumption, personal relevance of the news, political connections of the news, general mood, and participants' demographic variables (age, gender, education, and political affiliation). Replicating the results of the Study 1, news believability was significantly different among the three conditions (F (2, 614) = 5.43, p < .01). Post-hoc analysis showed that news believability was significantly lower in the anger-embedded news than in the baseline news (t = -2.67, p = .02) and in the sadness-embedded news (t = -3.01, p < .01). Meanwhile, news believability is indifferent between the sadness-embedded news and the baseline news (t = -.34, p = .94). The details of the results can be found in Appendix 4.

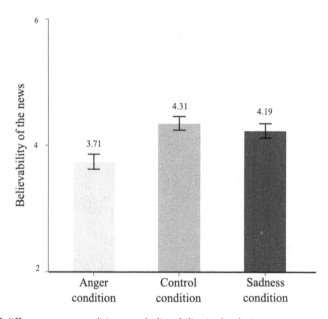

Figure 3. Plots of different news conditions on believability in Study 2

The results replicated the findings of Study 1 that believability influences users' intentions of social media behavior. Users were more likely to read, like, comment on, and share articles when they believed the news ($p < .001$ for all cases). The results still held when taking into account all of the control variables, which provided additional evidence for H4a to H4d. Details can be found in Appendix 5.

Discussion

Study 2 corroborated the findings of Study 1 that anger-embedded news would lower news believability, and also examined its underlying mechanism and confirmed that the perceived author's cognitive effort could explain the main effect. As discussed in the ATF, anger is a discrete emotion associated with the cognitive appraisal of certainty, which is closely related to the lack of thought and heuristic processing. Therefore, the expressed anger serves to signal a lack of cognitive effort in the news writing. According to the EASI theory, expressed emotions affect the recipient's perception primarily through an interpersonal inferential process, in which readers make inferences about the author's cognitive processing during their writing (i.e., the perceived author's cognitive effort) through the expressed anger. Readers will infer the expressed anger as a lack of cognitive effort for the author's writing; thus, they are less likely to believe the news.

This study also demonstrated that sad expressions in the news would not lead to lower news believability, suggesting that the effect of anger cannot be easily extended to other negative emotions. Based on the ATF, sadness is related to the appraisal tendencies of situational control and systematic information processing. Following the logic of the EASI model and the ATF, once readers observe sad authors, they may infer that sad authors think systematically and put in sufficient cognitive effort when they wrote the news article. In the default mode, news authors are supposed to write the news systematically; such inferences about sad authors will not lower readers' believability of the news. Thus, our findings echoed prior studies comparing anger and sadness, which demonstrated that angry subjects render more stereotypical judgments in social perception than sad subjects, who do not differ from those with neutral emotions [14, 15].

This study also addressed several issues remained from Study 1. First, we used shorter news headlines adapted from real news articles in this study to improve the realism of the news articles. Second, to address the fact that disease-related news may be highly impacted by context and timing, we expanded our news topics to include environment-related news. Environment-related news is another news topic that contains negative valence and can be manipulated with different negative emotions, and it is less impacted by context and timing. In this study, we tested both news topics. Compared with Study 1, the salience of the disease-related news varied at the two different time points of our data collection. By directly controlling the participants' consumption of disease-related news and environment-related news, the effect of anger-embedded news on news believability still held. Together with the findings of Study 1, we alleviated the concerns about the context and timing issue of news consumption. Third, we showed that the effect still holds even after controlling for more variables that may affect readers' believability toward the news in real life—news topic consumption, personal relevance of the news, and political connections of the news.

General Discussion

Discussion of Results

The results of our experiments support our hypotheses and provide insights into the mechanism of the effect of anger-embedded and sadness-embedded news on news believability. First, anger-embedded news headlines (vs. headlines without anger expression) lowered news believability. We draw on the EASI theory and ATF to explain this effect. Anger, as social information, can trigger interpersonal inferences and readers can infer the authors' cognition from their expressions of anger in the news article. Readers perceive the authors of anger-embedded news as lacking sufficient cognitive effort in their writing. Such inferences about the authors reduce readers' perceptions on the believability of anger-embedded news. Second, we demonstrated that sadness-embedded news would not lower news believability. We argued that, because sadness is related to the appraisals of situational control and the tendencies of systematic thinking, it will not affect readers' perception of the author's cognitive effort, since news writing is supposed to be deliberate. Third, this study cross-validated prior findings that news believability positively affects readers' intention to read, like, comment on, or share it. This effect was still robust after adding control variables. Supplementary analyses of the direct effect of anger-embedded news on readers' intention to read, like, comment on, or share it are provided in Appendix 8. By applying the EASI theory and the ATF to the social media context, we were able to go above and beyond the relationship between an individual's emotions and information processing to uncover an interpersonal effect triggered by the discrete emotion of anger or sadness on news perceptions.

One possible alternative explanation regarding the interpersonal effects of emotions is that observing an actor expressing emotion may result in observers experiencing emotion themselves through an automatic process such as emotional contagion, which affects their judgment and behavior [91]. In the context of this research, the lower believability of anger-embedded news may be explained by the reader's anger triggered by the author's anger. If the readers become angry, they may tend to think heuristically, which affects their judgment. A similar explanation may be offered for the effect of sadness-embedded news. To further rule out this alternative explanation, we checked whether the readers' feelings of anger or sadness differed between treatment groups and the control group after reading each news headline. Our results showed that anger-embedded news (vs. baseline news) did not bring a higher level of anger to the readers themselves (Study 1: $t = .26$, $p = .79$; Study 2: $t = 1.37$, $p = .17$). Meanwhile, sadness-embedded news in Study 2 did not bring a higher level of sadness to the readers themselves, compared to the baseline news ($t = .56$, $p = .58$). These results supported our claim that the emotional expressions would successfully trigger the readers' perception of the author's feeling of anger or sadness, but not the reader's own anger or sadness toward the news. We can thus rule out the alternative explanation. In other words, our results suggest that emotional expressions in the news can trigger interpersonal influence (i.e., readers' perception of the authors) through the inferential path rather than the affective path.

One may suggest that the interpersonal inferences proposed by the EASI model may not fit with the current research, as it requires readers to think systematically about their reading. In our experiment setting, we explicitly asked participants to rate their believability of the news right after reading, following the design of similar studies (e.g., [61, 83]). By asking them to make a judgment, they had to deliberately think about it. Therefore, we believe the interpersonal inference of the EASI model is suitable and reasonable for our context. Furthermore, in practice, although people on social media have a hedonic mindset in general [61], social media content has a better chance of fitting to the users' interests. When the content fits the users' needs better, the users will read the news content more deliberately.

Moreover, unlike other fake news studies examining actual fake news, our study used news headlines from real news websites which were not reported to be fake. However, whether the original news we used is true should not affect the robustness of our findings. First, although the original news was not reported as fake news by fact-checking websites, it was not perceived to be true without any doubt. We looked into the details of the reported believability of the baseline news we used in our studies. In Study 1, 30.99% of the participants rated the believability lower than 4 out of 7; 9.36% of them rated it as neutral, while 59.65% of them rated higher than 4. In Study 2, 32.41% of the participants reported relatively lower believability (i.e., lower than 4 out of 7); 11.11% showed neutral perception, while 56.48% tended to believe the news (i.e., rated more than 4 out of 7). The results showed that the news headlines were not believed by many people. Second, the news headlines we used could be fake depending on some investigation. For example, the phrase "has consistently been out of stock" in the news headline used in Study 1 (as shown in Figure 2) could be untrue. The authors might have just observed the situation once or twice but framed it as "consistently". Third, since we manipulated the characteristics of the headlines (e.g., adding angry or sad expression in the front) in our well-controlled experiments, we were exploring the relative believability of the treatment news and the baseline news. Hence, the truth of the headlines was not an issue in this study.

Implications for Research

This paper provides important theoretical contributions by integrating the emotion as social information theory and the appraisal-tendency framework in the context of social media. In doing so, we provide novel insights into the perception of online news by assessing the impact of anger-embedded news and sadness-embedded news on news believability. First, this study contributes to news perception studies by exploring the anger and sadness embedded in the content of different news topics. Prior studies on perceptions of news, especially of fake news, largely focus on the news sources, news ratings, social norms, and other observable news or interface characteristics [47, 61, 62, 82, 83]. However, the emotions embedded in the news content have been understudied. This paper addressed this gap and contributed to this research by showing that the anger and sadness embedded in the news has influences on how the news is perceived and evaluated. Furthermore, previous studies on fake news have concentrated on political news because the threat of fake news is particularly prevalent and salient in the political arena [67, 124]. Beyond political news, Xiong et al. [126] have found that users react most quickly to news reporting on "social issues" such as diseases, crises, or natural disasters. In the domain of fake news, it is worthwhile to know people's perceptions of stories in areas other than political news. Thus, this study focused on disease-related news and environment-related news. Anger and sadness are prevalent in these two news topics. Our results show that, for these two news topics, angry expressions may harm users' believability toward the news, whereas sad expressions do not.

Second, this research provides a more comprehensive understanding of the effect of anger and sadness on judgment and behavior by applying the EASI model and the ATF to the social media context. There has been extensive research in psychology examining the relationship between emotions and cognition. These studies largely focus on the individual's own emotions on their cognitive processing, judgment, and behavior [69, 94], but overlook the interpersonal influence of emotions. Our study investigates the interpersonal effects of anger and sadness in the news content on the reader's believability by combining the inferential processes of the EASI model and the cognitive appraisals introduced by the ATF. Specifically, our findings show that, when asked to make a judgment on the news, individuals on social media can infer from the authors' anger and its underlying cognitive appraisals that the authors wrote the news with heuristic processing and less cognitive effort, which in turn lowers the individuals' believability of a piece of news. However, the expressions of sadness will not lower news believability, since the inferences of sad authors are related to the systematic thinking in their writing. Hence, the news believability will not be affected.

Third, this paper contributes to the literature on affect and its relationship with online behavior. Affect has attracted increasing attention from scholars in organizational behavior and marketing [4, 31]. In a recent study, news items with the five basic emotions of anger, disgust, joy, sadness, and fear [36] have been found to cover 87.1% of news items on social media [26]. Scholars in the IS field have promoted investigating the role of emotions as well [131]. Prior research has investigated the role of general emotions in various IS-related topics, such as website design, online trust formation, technology acceptance behavior, technology-related overload, financial decision-making, e-loyalty, online community contribution, perceived helpfulness of online reviews, perceived credibility of online reviewers, as well as attitude and intention in group buying [67, 34, 48, 54, 56, 64, 79, 101, 116, 132]. However, merely classifying emotions into positive and negative is insufficient. Even if emotions are in the same valence and arousal domains, they can induce different perceptions and behaviors [127]. Therefore, some researchers in IS have examined the role of distinct emotions on IT-related perceptions and decisions, such as frustration and behavioral beliefs [33], regret and IT real options decision making [90], detection of people with emotional distress [21], emotional trust and the use of health infomediaries [130], anxiety and technology acceptance [123], as well as discrete emotions in technology use [9]. Research also investigates how anger or fear that is embedded in the reviews affects perceived helpfulness of online reviews [127–129]. Our paper contributes to the IS research on emotions and extends the current research by investigating how the discrete emotion of anger and sadness embedded in the news content affects online news believability. Despite being the most commonly expressed emotions in social media, the impact of anger and sadness have so far received little scholarly attention in IS research. Our paper addresses this gap by examining the influences of expressions of anger and sadness in the news on online news perceptions and providing insights on critical issues concerning the spread of online news. Our research asserts that, holding the negative valence and the text of the news constant, angry impressions in the news evoke different perceptions of the authors' cognitive processing. The perception of the authors' anger would allow readers to make inferences about the authors' information processing and cognitive efforts, which subsequently affects the readers' judgment of the news. We also demonstrate that this effect does not exist for sadness-embedded news, which is in line with the EASI model and the appraisal tendencies of sadness suggested by the ATF. The findings further validate ATF by indicating that discrete emotions, such as anger and sadness, will have differential effects on information processing, perceptions and judgement.

Implications for Practice

Although news authors and digital content creators have various goals when writing an article, an important desire is to spread information. Compared with positive news, negative news has a higher potential to influence social media users' perceptions and behaviors of reading, liking, commenting, and sharing. The believability of the news acts as an antecedent of news spread. We found that angry expressions might backfire by making users less likely to believe the news. Our results suggest that using angry expressions to capture readers' attention might be a questionable strategy under certain circumstances. Indeed, when asking readers about their judgment, angry expressions in the news reduce its believability as well as the reader's intentions of reading, liking, commenting, and sharing on social media. However, sad expression may not be a big issue, in terms of the perceived believability of the digital content and the downstream social media behaviors.

Social media platforms might use our findings to develop writing or posting guidelines to encourage more trustworthy content and improve the quality of their online community, since emotional content in the form of angry expressions may reduce users' trust and, in turn, the spread of the news. A healthy news-spreading system should focus on how to promote credible news and minimize the spread of fake news. If news articles use angry expressions, readers may have a lower believability in the news and become less likely to read, like, comment on, and share the news. Therefore, platforms should suggest that credible authors and posters carefully express their feelings and mind the tone of their words. Moreover, if the signals of anger and sadness are detected in the news, social media platforms can adjust their recommendation strategy accordingly. Our findings can be extended to other digital content contexts beyond online news, such as to online advertising and user-generated content. Information containing emotions that indicate the author's heuristic information processing may not help obtain the trust of consumers and users, especially in settings where the information recipients need to judge the quality of the information.

Limitations and Future Research

The present study has a few unaddressed limitations that offer useful insights for avenues of future research. First, as an attempt to check the EASI model and the ATF, our study examined two discrete negative emotions, anger and sadness. Since our findings provide insights into examining the influence of discrete emotions on perceptions of online news, one potential direction for future studies is to investigate the effect of other discrete emotions on individuals' perceptions. Research has explored the role of happiness in live streaming engagement [77]. In the context of online news perception, negative emotions such as disgust and fear and positive emotions such as joy and excitement would be well worth considering. Another potential direction is to compare mixed emotions in different contexts. For instance, anger and happiness are both attributed to a high level of certainty in the appraisal-tendency framework, despite their opposite valences. Therefore, people encountering these two discrete emotions may tend to process information heuristically [51]. It would be interesting to observe whether the presence of either emotion in the news generates similar consequences on the perceptions of the users.

Second, unlike prior empirical studies using behavior-level data, which assert that emotional information spreads faster [12, 26, 76, 126], our study finds that angry expressions lead to lower news believability, resulting in lower intentions to read, like, comment on, or share the news. In terms of the "share" behavior, the results from this study seem inconsistent with the results of existing research. One explanation for this inconsistency is that sharing is not equivalent to sharing intention. Nowadays, social media users may not read an article before they share it—on Twitter, 59% of shared links are not clicked on first [46]. This suggests that users might share a piece of information without reading or making a careful judgment on it. Such judgment would, in certain cases, change their intention to share the news. For instance, people may share a news post with angry expressions simply because it is eye-catching. However, if they make careful judgments of the news first, they may find the news to be less believable, and thus will not share it. Future studies may consider whether an intervention asking people to make a judgment on news believability before taking action would mitigate the negative consequence of emotional expression. Another explanation is that discrete emotions may have different effects. In empirical studies using large-scale dataset, their conclusion is based on the analysis of a bunch of different emotions, or simply news with positive or negative emotions. Our study, however, focuses on anger and sadness. It might be that anger and sadness trigger particular effects. It inspires us to further investigate the effect of discrete emotions on news perceptions and social media behaviors.

Third, according to Brady et al. [17], news spread on social media might be the consequence of echo chambers, as individuals are likely to believe and share information from people with similar interests and mindsets. Consequently, social media users are more likely to believe or share information with those to whom they feel similar, such as their friends and other users in the same groups. Because of this, it may be worthwhile to study the posters of the news or the news sources in terms of users' perceptions and behavior toward the news. Our study used inactive news sources and hid the poster's information, but it may be hard for the participants to identify whether news items are posted from similar people or groups. Future studies may consider directly manipulating the similarity issues (e.g., news posts from friends vs. strangers, news posted by a person within an interest group vs. not) and examine how these factors may interplay with the effect of anger expression.

Finally, this study focused on only two news topics and used a limited number of news headlines in order to control the experiment design, while using the control variables of confirmation bias, personal relevance of the news, and news topic consumption to attenuate the effects brought about by different news topics and news content. However, if certain news or expressions tend to appear frequently in the media, it is unclear whether this effect will be attenuated or strengthened. To fully address this concern, further studies may examine a greater variety of news topics and news stories. Another possibility is to examine the effects of a discrete emotion as it manifests in different news topics. The effectiveness of one discrete emotion may vary among different news topics. For example, it may not be important whether an entertainment news author uses heuristic processing in writing, in contrast to finance news, science news, or technology news. The effects of anger or happiness in relation to heuristic information processing may be weakened for the entertainment news. Additionally, future research may investigate the effect of anger-embedded content in other contexts, such as online advertising and negotiation.

Conclusion

Anger and sadness, as universally experienced emotions, affect people's perceptions and behaviors. Given the fast spread of fake news on social media, it is worth studying how angry and sad expressions in the news affect users' perceptions of its believability and their subsequent social media behavior. Using two experiments, we found that angry expressions in news headlines lead to lower news believability. Using the appraisal-tendency framework and the emotion as social information theory, we argued that the perception of the author's anger helps the readers infer that the authors wrote the news with less cognitive effort. A lower level of perception of the author's cognitive effort decreases the readers' perceptions of the believability of the news. We also found that sadness does not affect news believability. This study cross-validates prior findings that the believability of the news positively affects readers' intention to read, like, comment on, or share it. The findings of this study advance our understanding of theories regarding the emotion as a social information model, the appraisal-tendency framework, and studies of fake news, while also providing insights to practitioners and regulators on how to manage information perception and diffusion on social media.

Acknowledgements

We are extremely grateful to the guest editors and the anonymous reviewers for their invaluable comments and suggestions throughout the review process. We also thank all participants of the experiments.

Disclosure statement

No potential conflict of interest was reported by the author(s).

References

1. Aaker, J.; Drolet, A.; and Griffin, D. (2008). Recalling mixed emotions. Journal of Consumer Research, 35, 2 (2008), 268–278.
2. Adam, H.; and Shirako, A. Not all anger is created equal: The impact of the expresser's culture on the social effects of anger in negotiations. Journal of Applied Psychology, 98, 5 (2013), 785–798.
3. Anderson, M.; and Jiang, J. Teens, social media & technology 2018. Pew Research Center, 31, (2018), 1673-1689.
4. Ashkanasy, N.M.; Härtel, C.E.; and Daus, C.S. Diversity and emotion: The new frontiers in organizational behavior research. Journal of Management, 28, 3 (2002), 307–338.
5. Aslam, F.; Awan, T.M.; Syed, J.H.; Kashif, A.; and Parveen, M. Sentiments and emotions evoked by news headlines of coronavirus disease (COVID-19) outbreak. Humanities and Social Sciences Communications, 7, 1 (2020), 1–9.
6. Astor, P.J.; Adam, M.T.; Jerčić, P.; Schaaff, K.; and Weinhardt, C. Integrating biosignals into information systems: A NeuroIS tool for improving emotion regulation. Journal of Management Information Systems, 30, 3 (2013), 247–278.
7. Bagozzi, R.P.; Gopinath, M.; and Nyer, P.U. The role of emotions in marketing. Journal of the Academy of Marketing Science, 27, 2 (1999), 184–206.
8. Baumeister, R.F.; Bratslavsky, E.; Finkenauer, C.; and Vohs, K.D. Bad is stronger than good. Review of General Psychology, 5, 4 (2001), 323–370.
9. Beaudry, A.; and Pinsonneault, A. The other side of acceptance: Studying the direct and indirect effects of emotions on information technology use. MIS Quarterly, 34, 4 (2010), 689–710.
10. Beedie, C.; Terry, P.; and Lane, A. Distinctions between emotion and mood. Cognition & Emotion, 19, 6 (2005), 847–878.
11. Blair, R.J.R.; Morris, J.S.; Frith, C.D.; Perrett, D.I.; and Dolan, R.J. Dissociable neural responses to facial expressions of sadness and anger. Brain, 122, 5 (1999), 883–893.
12. Berger, J.; and Milkman, K.L. What makes online content viral? Journal of Marketing Research, 49, 2 (2012), 192–205.
13. Bernard, J.G., Dennis, A., Galletta, D., Khan, A., & Webster, J. (2019). The tangled web: Studying online fake news, in Proceedings of the International Conference on Information Systems (ICIS 2019), Munich, Germany.
14. Bodenhausen, G.V.; Kramer, G.P.; and Süsser, K. Happiness and stereotypic thinking in social judgment. Journal of Personality & Social Psychology, 66, 4 (1994a), 621.
15. Bodenhausen, G.V.; Sheppard, L.A.; and Kramer, G.P. Negative affect and social judgment: The differential impact of anger and sadness. European Journal of Social Psychology, 24, 1 (1994b), 45–62.
16. Bond, S.D.; Bettman, J.R.; and Luce, M.F. Consumer judgment from a dual-systems perspective: Recent evidence and emerging issues. In Malhotra, N.K. (ed.), Review of Marketing Research. New York, New York, USA: Routledge, 2017, pp. 3–37.
17. Brady, W.J.; Wills, J.A.; Jost, J.T.; Tucker, J.A.; and van Bavel, J.J. Emotion shapes the diffusion of moralized content in social networks. Proceedings of the National Academy of Sciences, 114, 28 (2017), 7313–7318.
18. Bu, Z.; Xia, Z.; and Wang, J. A sock puppet detection algorithm on virtual spaces. Knowledge-Based Systems, 37, (2013), 366–377.
19. Castillo, C.; Mendoza, M.; and Poblete, B. Information credibility on Twitter. In Proceedings of the 20th International Conference on World Wide Web, (2011), 675–684.
20. Celsi, R.L.; Chow, S.; Olson, J.C.; and Walker, B.A. The construct validity of intrinsic sources of personal relevance: An intra-individual source of felt involvement. Journal of Business Research, 25, 2 (1992), 165–185.
21. Chau, M.; Li, T.M.; Wong, P.W.; Xu, J.J.; Yip, P.S.; and Chen, H. Finding People with Emotional Distress in Online Social Media: A Design Combining Machine Learning and Rule-Based Classification. MIS Quarterly, 44, 2 (2020).

22. Chen, H.; De, P.; Hu, Y.J.; and Hwang, B.H. Wisdom of crowds: The value of stock opinions transmitted through social media. The Review of Financial Studies, 27, 5 (2014), 1367–1403.

23. Cheshin, A.; Amit, A.; and van Kleef, G.A. The interpersonal effects of emotion intensity in customer service: Perceived appropriateness and authenticity of attendants' emotional displays shape customer trust and satisfaction. Organizational Behavior and Human Decision Processes, 144, (2018), 97–111.

24. Cheung, C.M.; and Lee, M.K. Online consumer reviews: Does negative electronic word-of-mouth hurt more? AMCIS 2008 Proceedings, (2008), 143.

25. Cheung, C.M.; and Thadani, D.R. The impact of electronic word-of-mouth communication: A literature analysis and integrative model. Decision Support Systems, 54, 1 (2012), 461–470.

26. Chuai, Y.; and Zhao, J. Anger makes fake news viral online. arXiv preprint arXiv:2004.10399, (2020).

27. Clark, M.S.; Pataki, S.P.; and Carver, V.H. Some thoughts and findings on self-presentation of emotions in relationships. Knowledge Structures in Close Relationships: A Social Psychological Approach, (1996), 247–274.

28. Clark, M.S.; and Taraban, C. Reactions to and willingness to express emotion in communal and exchange relationships. Journal of Experimental Social Psychology, 27, 4 (1991), 324–336.

29. Clarke, J.; Chen, H.; Du, D.; and Hu, Y.J. Fake news, investor attention, and market reaction. Information Systems Research, 32, 1 (2021), 35–52.

30. Clore, G.L.; Schwarz, N.; and Conway, M. Affective causes and consequences of social information processing. In R. S. Wyer, Jr. and T. K. Srull (eds.), Handbook of social cognition: Basic processes; Applications. Mahwah, New Jersey, USA: Lawrence Erlbaum Associates, Inc., 1994, pp. 323–417.

31. Cohen, J.B.; Pham, M.T.; and Andrade, E.B. The nature and role of affect in consumer behavior. Handbook of Consumer Psychology, 4, (2008), 297–348.

32. Cook, E.J.; Randhawa, G.; Sharp, C.; Ali, N.; Guppy, A.; Barton, G.; . . . and Crawford-White, J. Exploring the factors that influence the decision to adopt and engage with an integrated assistive telehealth and telecare service in Cambridgeshire, UK: A nested qualitative study of patient 'users' and 'non-users'. BMC Health Services Research, 16, 1 (2016), 137.

33. de Guinea, A.O.; Titah, R.; and Léger, P.M. Explicit and implicit antecedents of users' behavioral beliefs in information systems: A neuropsychological investigation. Journal of Management Information Systems, 30, 4 (2014), 179–210.

34. Deng, L.Q.; and Poole, M.S. Affect in web interfaces: A study of the impacts of web page visual complexity and order. MIS Quarterly, 34, 4 (2010), 711–730.

35. Ekkekakis, P. The measurement of affect, mood, and emotion: A guide for health-behavioral research. Cambridge University Press, 2013.

36. Ekman, P. Are there basic emotions? Psychological Review, 99, 3 (1992), 550–553.

37. Ellsworth, P.; and Scherer, K. R. Appraisal processes in emotion. Oxford University Press, 2003.

38. Erber, R.; and Erber, M.W. The self-regulation of moods: Second thoughts on the importance of happiness in everyday life. Psychological Inquiry, 11, (2000), 142–148.

39. Fiske, S.T. Attention and weight in person perception: The impact of negative and extreme behavior. Journal of Personality and Social Psychology, 38, 6 (1980), 889–906.

40. Fitness, J. Anger in the workplace: An emotion script approach to anger episodes between workers and their superiors, co-workers and subordinates. Journal of Organizational Behavior, 21, 2 (2000), 147–162.

41. Forgas, J.P. Mood and judgment: The affect infusion model (AIM). Psychological Bulletin, 117, 1 (1995), 39.

42. Forgas, J.P. On being happy and mistaken: Mood effects on the fundamental attribution error. Journal of Personality & Social Psychology, 75, 2 (1998), 318.

43. Frank, R.H. Passions within reason: The strategic role of the emotions. Norton, 1988.

44. Frijda, N.H. Emotion, cognitive structure, and action tendency. Cognition and Emotion, 1, 2 (1987), 115–143.
45. Frijda, N. Emotion experience. Cognition & Emotion, 19, 4 (2005), 473–497.
46. Gabielkov, M.; Ramachandran, A.; Chaintreau, A.; and Legout, A. Social clicks: What and who gets read on Twitter? In Proceedings of the 2016 ACM SIGMETRICS International Conference on Measurement and Modeling of Computer Science, 2016, pp. 179–192.
47. Gimpel, H.; Heger, S.; Olenberger, C.; and Utz, L. The effectiveness of social norms in fighting fake news on social media. Journal of Management Information Systems, 38, 1 (2021), 196–221.
48. Gregor, S.; Lin, A.C.; Gedeon, T.; Riaz, A.; and Zhu, D. Neuroscience and a nomological network for the understanding and assessment of emotions in information systems research. Journal of Management Information Systems, 30, 4 (2014), 13–48.
49. Greving, H.; Kimmerle, J.; Oeberst, A.; and Cress, U. Emotions in Wikipedia: The role of intended negative events in the expression of sadness and anger in online peer production. Behaviour & Information Technology, 38, 8 (2019), 796–806.
50. Halberstadt, J.; Winkielman, P.; Niedenthal, P.M.; and Dalle, N. Emotional conception: How embodied emotion concepts guide perception and facial action. Psychological Science, 20, 10 (2009), 1254–1261.
51. Han, S.; Lerner, J.S.; and Keltner, D. Feelings and consumer decision making: The appraisal-tendency framework. Journal of Consumer Psychology, 17, 3 (2007), 158–168.
52. Hayes, A.F. Introduction to mediation, moderation, and conditional process analysis: A regression-based approach. Guilford publications, 2017.
53. Hsee, C.K.; Zhang, J.; Yu, F.; and Xi, Y. Lay rationalism and inconsistency between predicted experience and decision. Journal of Behavioral Decision Making, 16, 4 (2003), 257–272.
54. Hwang, Y.J.; and Kim, D.J. Customer self-service systems: The effects of perceived web quality with service contents on enjoyment, anxiety, and e-trust. Decision Support Systems, 43, 3 (2007), 746–760.
55. Jang, S.M.; and Kim, J.K. Third person effects of fake news: Fake news regulation and media literacy interventions. Computers in Human Behavior, 80, (2018), 295–302.
56. Jensen, M.L.; Averbeck, J.M.; Zhang, Z.; and Wright, K.B. Credibility of anonymous online product reviews: A language expectancy perspective. Journal of Management Information Systems, 30, 1 (2013), 293–324.
57. Johnson, T.J.; and Kaye, B.K. Reasons to believe: Influence of credibility on motivations for using social networks. Computers in Human Behavior, 50, (2015), 544–555.
58. Keltner, D.; and Haidt, J. Social functions of emotions at four levels of analysis. Cognition and Emotion, 13, 5 (1999), 505–521.
59. Kensinger, E.A.; and Corkin, S. Effect of negative emotional content on working memory and long-term memory. Emotion, 3, 4 (2003), 378.
60. Kim, H.J.; and Cameron, G.T. Emotions matter in crisis: The role of anger and sadness in the publics' response to crisis news framing and corporate crisis response. Communication Research, 38, 6 (2011), 826–855.
61. Kim, A.; and Dennis, A.R. Says who? The effects of presentation format and source rating on fake news in social media. MIS Quarterly, 43, 3 (2019), 1025–1039.
62. Kim, A.; Moravec, P.L.; and Dennis, A.R. Combating fake news on social media with source ratings: The effects of user and expert reputation ratings. Journal of Management Information Systems, 36, 3 (2019), 931–968.
63. Kim, C.; and Yang, S.U. Like, comment, and share on Facebook: How each behavior differs from the other. Public Relations Review, 43, 2 (2017), 441–449.
64. Kuan, K.K.; Zhong, Y.; and Chau, P.Y. Informational and normative social influence in group-buying: Evidence from self-reported and EEG data. Journal of Management Information Systems, 30, 4 (2014), 151–178.
65. Kühne, R.; and Schemer, C. The emotional effects of news frames on information processing and opinion formation. Communication Research, 42, 3 (2015), 387–407.
66. Lazarus, R.S. Emotion and adaptation. Oxford, 1991.

67. Lazer, D.M.; Baum, M.A.; Benkler, Y.; Berinsky, A.J.; Greenhill, K.M.; Menczer, F.; . . . and Schudson, M. The science of fake news. Science, 359, 6380 (2018), 1094–1096.

68. Lee, D.; Hosanagar, K.; and Nair, H.S. Advertising content and consumer engagement on social media: Evidence from Facebook. Management Science, 64, 11 (2018), 5105–5131.

69. Lench, H.C.; Flores, S.A.; and Bench, S.W. Discrete emotions predict changes in cognition, judgment, experience, behavior, and physiology: a meta-analysis of experimental emotion elicitations. Psychological Bulletin, 137, 5 (2011), 834.

70. Lench, H.C.; Tibbett, T.P.; and Bench, S.W. Exploring the toolkit of emotion: What do sadness and anger do for us? Social and Personality Psychology Compass, 10, 1 (2016), 11–25.

71. Lerner, J.S.; and Keltner, D. Beyond valence: Toward a model of emotion-specific influences on judgement and choice. Cognition & Emotion, 14, 4 (2000), 473–493.

72. Lerner, J.S.; and Keltner, D. Fear, anger, and risk. Journal of Personality and Social Psychology, 81, 1 (2001), 146.

73. Lerner, J.S; and Tiedens, L.Z. Portrait of the angry decision maker: How appraisal tendencies shape anger's influence on cognition. Journal of Behavioral Decision Making, 19, 2 (2006), 115–137.

74. Lewandowsky, S.; Ecker, U.K.; and Cook, J. Beyond misinformation: Understanding and coping with the "post-truth" era. Journal of Applied Research in Memory and Cognition, 6, 4 (2017), 353–369.

75. Lewandowsky, S. Working memory capacity and categorization: Individual differences and modeling. Journal of Experimental Psychology: Learning, Memory, and Cognition, 37, 3 (2011), 720.

76. Li, L.F.; Wang, Z.Q.; Zhang, Q.; and Wen, H. Effect of anger, anxiety, and sadness on the propagation scale of social media posts after natural disasters. Information Processing & Management, 57, 6 (2020), 102–313.

77. Lin, Y.; Yao, D.; and Chen, X. Happiness begets money: Emotion and engagement in live streaming. Journal of Marketing Research, 58, 3 (2021), 417–438.

78. Mackie, D.M.; Devos, T.; and Smith, E.R. Intergroup emotions: Explaining offensive action tendencies in an intergroup context. Journal of Personality and Social Psychology, 79, 4 (2000), 602.

79. Malik, M.S.I.; and Hussain, A. Helpfulness of product reviews as a function of discrete positive and negative emotions. Computers in Human Behavior, 73, (2017), 290–302.

80. Martel, C.; Pennycook, G.; and Rand, D.G. Reliance on emotion promotes belief in fake news. Cognitive research: principles and implications, 5, 1 (2020), 1–20.

81. Mihailidis, P.; and Viotty, S. Spreadable spectacle in digital culture: Civic expression, fake news, and the role of media literacies in "post-fact" society. American Behavioral Scientist, 61, 4 (2017), 441–454.

82. Moravec, P.L.; Kim, A.; and Dennis, A.R. Appealing to sense and sensibility: System 1 and system 2 interventions for fake news on social media. Information Systems Research, 31, 3 (2020), 987–1006.

83. Moravec, P.; Minas, R.; and Dennis, A.R. Fake news on social media: People believe what they want to believe when it makes no sense at all. MIS Quarterly, 43, 4 (2019), 18–87.

84. Myrick, J.G. The role of emotions and social cognitive variables in online health information seeking processes and effects. Computers in Human Behavior, 68, (2017), 422–433.

85. Nabi, R.L. Exploring the framing effects of emotion: Do discrete emotions differentially influence information accessibility, information seeking, and policy preference? Communication Research, 30, 2 (2003), 224–247.

86. Naveed, N.; Gottron, T.; Kunegis, J.; and Alhadi, A.C. Bad news travel fast: A content-based analysis of interestingness on twitter. In Proceedings of the 3rd international web science conference. New York, New York, USA: 2011, pp. 1–7.

87. Nerb, J.; and Spada, H. Evaluation of environmental problems: A coherence model of cognition and emotion. Cognition & Emotion, 15, (2001), 521–551.

88. Nian, T.; Hu, Y.; and Chen, C. Examining the Impact of Television-Program-Induced Emotions on Online Word-of-Mouth Toward Television Advertising. Information Systems Research, 32, 2 (2021), 605–632.

89. Panksepp, J. The basic emotional circuits of mammalian brains: Do animals have affective lives?. Neuroscience & Biobehavioral Reviews, 35, 9 (2011), 1791–1804.

90. Park, E.H.; Ramesh, B.; and Cao, L. Emotion in IT investment decision making with a real options perspective: The intertwining of cognition and regret. Journal of Management Information Systems, 33, 3 (2016), 652–683.

91. Parkinson, B.; and Simons, G. Affecting others: Social appraisal and emotion contagion in everyday decision making. Personality and Social Psychology Bulletin, 35, 8 (2009), 1071–1084.

92. Pennycook, G.; Bear, A.; Collins, E.T.; and Rand, D.G. The implied truth effect: Attaching warnings to a subset of fake news headlines increases perceived accuracy of headlines without warnings. Management Science, 66, 11 (2020), 4944–4957.

93. Pennycook, G.; Cannon, T.D.; and Rand, D.G. Prior exposure increases perceived accuracy of fake news. Journal of Experimental Psychology: General, 147, 12 (2018), 1865.

94. Pham, M.T. Emotion and rationality: A critical review and interpretation of empirical evidence. Review of General Psychology, 11, 2 (2007), 155–178.

95. Raghunathan, R.; and Pham, M.T. All negative moods are not equal: Motivational influences of anxiety and sadness on decision making. Organizational Behavior & Human Decision Processes, 79, 1 (1999), 56–77.

96. Raghunathan, R.; and Trope, Y. Walking the tightrope between feeling good and being accurate: Mood as a resource in processing persuasive messages. Journal of Personality and Social Psychology, 83, 3 (2002), 510.

97. Rapp, D.N.; and Salovich, N.A. Can't we just disregard fake news? The consequences of exposure to inaccurate information. Policy Insights from the Behavioral and Brain Sciences, 5, 2 (2018), 232–239.

98. Rimé, B.; Mesquita, B.; Philippot, P.; and Boca, S. Beyond the emotional event: Six studies on the social sharing of emotion. Cognition and Emotion, 5, 5–6 (1991), 435–465.

99. Russell, J.A. A circumplex model of affect. Journal of Personality and Social Psychology, 39, 6 (1980), 1161.

100. Russell, J.A. Core affect and the psychological construction of emotion. Psychological Review, 110, 1 (2003), 145.

101. Saunders, C.; Wiener, M.; Klett, S.; and Sprenger, S. The impact of mental representations on ICT-related overload in the use of mobile phones. Journal of Management Information Systems, 34, 3 (2017), 803–825.

102. Scherer, K.R. What are emotions? And how can they be measured? Social Science Information, 44, 4 (2005), 695–729.

103. Schuch, S.; and Koch, I. Mood states influence cognitive control: The case of conflict adaptation. Psychological Research, 79, 5 (2015), 759–772.

104. Schwarz, N. Feelings as information: Moods influence judgment and processing strategies. In T. Gilovich; D. Griffin; and D. Kahneman (eds.), Heuristics and biases: The psychology of intuitive judgment. New York, New York, USA: Cambridge University Press, 2002, pp. 534–547.

105. Schwarz, N.; and Clore, G.L. Mood as information: 20 years later. Psychological Inquiry, 14, 3–4 (2003), 294–301.

106. Shearer, E.; and Grieco, E. Americans are wary of the role social media sites play in delivering the news. Pew Research Center, 2, (2019).

107. Shoss, M.K.; Jundt, D.K.; Kobler, A.; and Reynolds, C. Doing bad to feel better? An investigation of within- and between-person perceptions of counterproductive work behavior as a coping tactic. Journal of Business Ethics, 137, 3 (2016), 571–587.

108. Small, D.A.; and Lerner, J.S. Emotional policy: Personal sadness and anger shape judgments about a welfare case. Political Psychology, 29, 2 (2008), 149–168.

109. Smith, C.A.; and Ellsworth, P.C. Patterns of cognitive appraisal in emotion. Journal of Personality and Social Psychology, 48, 4 (1985), 813.

110. Soroka, S.; Young, L.; and Balmas, M. Bad news or mad news? Sentiment scoring of negativity, fear, and anger in news content. The Annals of the American Academy of Political and Social Science, 659, 1 (2015), 108–121.

111. Stieglitz, S.; and Dang-Xuan, L. Emotions and information diffusion in social media sentiment of microblogs and sharing behavior. Journal of Management InformationSystems, 29, 4 (2013), 217–248.

112. Swire, B.; Ecker, U.K.; and Lewandowsky, S. The role of familiarity in correcting inaccurate information. Journal of Experimental Psychology: Learning, Memory, and Cognition, 43, 12 (2017), 1948-1961.

113. Sy, T.; Côté, S.; and Saavedra, R. The contagious leader: Impact of the leader's mood on the mood of group members, group affective tone, and group processes. Journal of Applied Psychology, 90, 2 (2005), 295.

114. Tiedens, L.Z. The effect of anger on the hostile inferences of aggressive and nonaggressive people: Specific emotions, cognitive processing, and chronic accessibility. Motivation and Emotion, 25, 3 (2001), 233–251.

115. Tiedens, L.Z.; and Linton, S. Judgment under emotional certainty and uncertainty: The effects of specific emotions on information processing. Journal of Personality & Social Psychology, 81, 6 (2001), 973–988.

116. Tsai, H.T.; and Bagozzi, R.P. Contribution behavior in virtual communities: Cognitive, emotional, and social influences. MIS Quarterly, 38, 1 (2014), 143–164.

117. van Beest, I.; van Kleef, G.A.; and van Dijk, E. Get angry, get out: The interpersonal effects of anger communication in multiparty negotiation. Journal of Experimental Social Psychology, 44, 4 (2008), 993–1002.

118. van Kleef, G.A. How emotions regulate social life: The emotions as social information (EASI) model. Current Directions in Psychological Science, 18, 3 (2009), 184–188.

119. van Kleef, G.A. The emerging view of emotion as social information. Social and Personality Psychology Compass, 4, 5 (2010), 331–343.

120. van Kleef, G.A.; de Dreu, C.K.W.; and Manstead, A.S.R. The interpersonal effects of anger and happiness in negotiations. Journal of Personality and Social Psychology, 86, 1 (2004), 57.

121. van Kleef, G.A.; Homan, A.C.; Beersma, B.; van Knippenberg, D.; van Knippenberg, B.; and Damen, F. Searing sentiment or cold calculation? The effects of leader emotional displays on team performance depend on follower epistemic motivation. Academy of Management Journal, 52, 3 (2009), 562–580.

122. van Kleef, G.A.; Homan, A.C.; and Cheshin, A. Emotional influence at work: Take it EASI. Organizational Psychology Review, 2, 4 (2012), 311–339.

123. Venkatesh, V. Determinants of perceived ease of use: Integrating control, intrinsic motivation, and emotion into the technology acceptance model. Information Systems Research, 11, 4 (2000), 342–365.

124. Vosoughi, S.; Roy, D.; and Aral, S. The spread of true and false news o online. Science, 359, 6380 (2018), 1146–1151.

125. Wang, L.; Restubog, S.; Shao, B.; Lu, V.; and van Kleef, G. A. Does anger expression help or harm leader effectiveness? The role of competence-based versus integrity-based violations and abusive supervision. Academy of Management Journal, 61, 3 (2018), 1050–1072.

126. Xiong, X.; Zhou, G.; Huang, Y.; Chen, H.; and Xu, K. Dynamic evolution of collective emotions in social networks: A case study of Sina Weibo. Science China Information Sciences, 56, 7 (2013), 1–18.

127. Yin, D.; Bond, S.D.; and Zhang, H. Anxious or angry? Effects of discrete emotions on the perceived helpfulness of online reviews. MIS Quarterly, 38, 2 (2014), 539–560.

128. Yin, D.; Bond, S.D.; and Zhang, H. Keep your cool or let it out: Nonlinear effects of expressed arousal on perceptions of consumer reviews. Journal of Marketing Research, 54, 3 (2017), 447–463.

129. Yin, D.; Bond, S.D.; and Zhang, H. Anger in consumer reviews: Unhelpful but persuasive? MIS Quarterly, forthcoming, (2021).

130. Zahedi, F.M.; and Song, J. Dynamics of trust revision: Using health infomediaries. Journal of Management Information Systems, 24, 4 (2008), 225–248.

131. Zhang, P. The affective response model: A theoretical framework of affective concepts and their relationships in the ICT context. MIS Quarterly, 37, 1 (2013), 247–274.

132. Zhang, P.; and Li, N. The importance of affective quality. Communications of the ACM, 48, 9 (2005), 105–108.

Dynamic Effects of Falsehoods and Corrections on Social Media: A Theoretical Modeling and Empirical Evidence

Kelvin K. King(iD), Bin Wang(iD), Diego Escobari(iD), and Tamer Oraby(iD)

ABSTRACT
Government agencies and fact-checking websites have been combating the spread of falsehoods on social media by issuing correction messages. There has been, however, no research on the effectiveness of correction messages on falsehoods and their dynamic interaction. We develop a theoretical model of the competition between falsehoods and correction messages on Twitter and show different interventions under which falsehoods could be hampered. Moreover, we use panel vector autoregressive models and machine learning techniques to empirically investigate the dynamic interactions between falsehoods and correction messages through a unique longitudinal dataset of 279,597 tweets. We find that correction messages cause an increase in the propagation of falsehoods on social media if their use is not optimized. This study highlights the importance of having government agencies, fact-checking websites, and social media platforms work together to optimize effective correction messages. We argue such an effort will counter the spread of falsehoods.

Introduction

A vast majority of Americans are easily deceived by false news, with 50% of the American public willingly endorsing at least one conspiracy theory [47] and up to 75% believing false news headlines [52]. Online social networks propagate misinformation [30] due to the dynamic nature of the content and the reliance of the public on microblogging sites such as Twitter for news and information [45].

In recent years, information systems (IS) researchers have investigated the concept of misinformation [3, 21, 28, 35, 46] and have suggested ways of combating this and other related phenomena [19, 37, 54]. One such proposed method is the use of correction messages to mitigate potentially disruptive rumors. However, such proposed methods may be ineffective or even counterproductive if they cause blowbacks [40]. In recognition of the need to address this issue, the Department of Homeland Security (DHS) recently established a 25-member agency, the Social Media Working Group (SMWG) for Emergency Services and Disaster Management; the Federal Emergency Management Agency (FEMA) is a member to help provide recommendations to curb the menace. The agency published a set of guidelines for dispelling

Access the Support Material: www.routledge.com/ 9781032561127

rumors in 2018 but noted that correction messages may not always be effective and even have the potential to make the spread of falsehoods worse [16]. Results from prior studies have not only been fragmented, inconsistent, and inconclusive but have also primarily relied on surveys [17, 28, 37, 43, 47].

In this study, we investigate the dynamic interaction between falsehoods and correction messages both theoretically and empirically using panel data. Our research questions are as follows:

(1) Are there bidirectional relationships between the diffusion of falsehoods and correction messages on Twitter during shock events?
(2) What are the effects of correction messages on falsehoods and vice versa?

To address these questions and advance our knowledge of this crucial yet intricate relationship, we first develop a theoretical (mechanistic) model depicting the diffusion of both falsehoods and correction messages on Twitter and their mutual relationship. We show the conditions under which they can both cease to propagate, both continue to propagate, or only one continues to propagate. Additionally, we use a unique panel dataset containing 279,597 social media interactions during Hurricane Harvey in 2017 and Hurricane Florence in 2018 to empirically examine the bidirectional relationships between the diffusion of falsehoods and their correction messages through the structural panel vector autoregression (PVAR) methodology.

Our study has the following contributions to the literature on information diffusion, misinformation, and rumors. First, our research holistically examines the diffusion of both falsehoods and correction messages, thus achieving a better understanding of how falsehoods and correction messages co-diffuse – as well as reinforce and compete with each other – rather than just examining the diffusion of each type of message on its own. Second, the use of a theoretical model coupled with empirical evidence allows us to identify scenarios under which each type of message continues or ceases to propagate. We then empirically examine the dynamic relationships using real Twitter data during Hurricanes Harvey and Florence. Third, we derive three possible outcomes through a theoretical and mechanistic model: (1) The numbers of tweets for falsehoods and correction messages both diminish (2) One message (either falsehood or correction) stops spreading and the other one continues to propagate; and (3) Both falsehoods and correction messages continue to diffuse. The outcome where falsehoods cease to spread and correction messages continue is the ideal outcome. Fourth, our empirical results using Twitter data show robust evidence that falsehoods cause an increase in correction messages. Counterintuitively, correction messages have a positive effect on the propagation of falsehoods, suggesting that the current state of correction messages is neither optimal nor effective. These results highlight the importance for policy makers, social media administrators, and developers of emergency warning systems to design more effective correction messages and coordinate to effectively combat the propagation of falsehoods while improving the diffusion of correction messages.

Related Literature

Recent Proposed Solutions

There have been several major proposals for curbing misinformation. For example, researchers have recommended the use of detection [33, 34, 40] to target falsehoods and automated entities on social media in order to prevent the spread of falsehoods. However, several studies using large datasets have shown that falsehoods are not primarily shared by automated entities but rather by humans [19, 54]. Others have proposed the use of source credibility as a solution to this phenomenon [3]. However, the results of these studies have proven to be quite inconsistent. For example, [46] showed that credible sources may be able to lower anxiety and be more successful in suppressing falsehoods, while a more recent study [40] revealed that appealing to coherence was more successful in reducing falsehoods. Finally, two recent studies [31, 32] proposed the use of source rating and presentation in suppressing falsehoods and nudging users toward rethinking and believing a story. Using a survey instrument, the authors found that presenting news in a story format with source ratings may cause users to evaluate the veracity of the news content more critically. However, this solution is mostly used in the retail domain, where users rate credible buyers and sellers and may be vulnerable to manipulations that are difficult to detect [27, 29, 58, 37].

Information Correction

IS researchers have examined information correction using predictions [25] and inoculation theories [44]. In recent times, government agencies created rumor control mechanisms and aimed to identify, investigate, and mitigate potentially disruptive rumors, especially during extreme events, such as during the aftermath of the great East Japan Earthquake on March 11, 2011 [54]. While results on their effectiveness have been mixed and inconclusive, questions have been raised regarding ideal ways to create and deploy effective correction mechanisms to combat falsehoods. For example, some studies showed that including both facts as well as the falsehood in the same message causes engagement and leads to an overall increase in the knowledge about the falsehood [10]. However, using qualitative studies and reviews from previous studies [50] showed that repeating falsehoods could be detrimental to the overall correction efforts because receivers of the messages may not be able to differentiate facts from falsehoods and may misremember the message. Quite recently, using a meta-analysis of several studies [59] showed that corrections may reduce misinformation across diverse audiences and may be more successful in informing the receivers. Their study was partially supported by findings from [26], whose results showed that corrections reduce people's beliefs in specific rumor content, but the senders of the messages were often unable to recover the trust that was lost due to the falsehood. Other studies have introduced factors such as source credibility and coherence in tackling against misinformation correction. For example, [40] showed that when sending a correction message, appealing to coherence was more successful at minimizing the influence of misinformation than using fact checking and source credibility. This occurrence is in direct contrast to [46], who showed that using reliable information with credible sources can lower anxiety and be much more successful in suppressing falsehoods. Another method currently used by rumor control mills is the pairing of correction messages with warnings, which leads to reduced rumor spread [49]. However, this study is the first of its kind to use Twitter data prior to, during, and after shock events that captures in its entirety the interactions between a government agency, fact-checking organizations, and their responses to falsehoods.

In summary, our review of prior research reveals the following gaps in the extant literature:

(1) Due to the fragmented and inconsistent findings, our understanding of the intricate relationship between correction messages and falsehoods is limited with the empirical findings often being contradictory [e.g., 16, 27, 36].

(2) Several prior studies on correction messages have been based on rumors [e.g., 45], which showed that when correction messages are paired with warning messages, rumors tend to reduce in their dissemination. Rumors are social in nature and can be either true or false. It is therefore necessary to investigate the propagation of verifiable false and correction messages.

(3) Findings from prior research have favored the use of small and individual survey samples [e.g., 10, 24] and may lack generalizability to other contexts.

(4) Existing studies did not treat the diffusion of both falsehoods and correction messages as endogenous that have feedback loops. Furthermore, none have attempted to investigate the potential for causal inference. As a result, the endogeneity and possible causal relationship between both variables need to be further investigated.

(5) None of the studies have presented a solution supported by theory to mitigate the flow of falsehoods while improving the efficacy of correction messages. Our research examining the co-diffusion of falsehoods and corrections will help us better understand how the two affect each other in the diffusion process and allow us to design better counter mechanisms.

Our goal is to address these research gaps using a theoretical study supplemented by an empirical analysis using two Twitter datasets.

Influence of Falsehoods on Correction Messages and Vice Versa

As suggested by previous studies, falsehoods tend to be resilient [19], and the format and presentation of the message may have an impact on their believability [32]. While most studies have centered correction messages as a general topic, none of the studies have investigated this phenomenon using real datasets nor has any attempted to infer causality. A recent study using simulations and networks showed how rumors and correction messages diffuse independently through the same users [54]. While several studies have shown that correction messages can be very effective in addressing misinformation on social media by reducing the credibility of the refuted contents and as such are shared more [12, 25], other studies have also pointed out that even after the rebuttals, falsehoods continually influence memory and reasoning even if the retraction is recalled [18]. The study further noted that even after the retraction of false information and specific warnings were combined with an explanation of the misinformation, users still remembered and were influenced significantly by falsehoods. One study further noted that in some cases even though corrections reduce beliefs in the misinformation, the trust may be lost [26].

A recent study [49] argued that when combating falsehoods, presenting warning messages may reduce their propagation and thus improve the quality of information that is being shared in online social networks. This analogy does not state that the news ultimately dies but that it counterbalances the information flow. We therefore argue that once the correction message is introduced and people see the message, some may refrain from resharing the false messages while others may engage the correction message. These actions will slow the rate of the diffusion of falsehoods but increase the diffusion of correction messages over time.

Theoretical Model and Analysis

We develop a mathematical mechanistic model that describes the diffusion of a falsehood topic and its corresponding correction messages on Twitter. In contrast to the Bass diffusion model [6] that describes the spread of an innovation, our model describes the competition between the two messages besides their spread. Our model originates in the literature of mathematical ecology as a model of competitive exclusion [20]. We extend the model based on the literature to include mutual reinforcement of each message to the other. The model is comprised of a system of ordinary differential equations and implemented via numerical simulations and stability analysis. The model depicts the competition of these two falsehood and correction messages.

Let M_t be the number of tweets and retweets of falsehood F_t and correction C_t messages at hour t. The system of differential equations:

$$\frac{dF_t}{dt} = r_F F_t \left[\left(1 - \frac{F_t}{K} \right) - \beta_F \frac{C_t}{K} \right] - \mu_F F_t + \gamma_F C_t \tag{1}$$

and

$$\frac{dC_t}{dt} = r_C C_t \left[\left(1 - \frac{C_t}{K} \right) - \beta_C \frac{F_t}{K} \right] - \mu_C C_t + \gamma_C F_t \tag{2}$$

depict the rate of change in the numbers of tweets or retweets of the falsehood and correction messages at time t, respectively. The first components in both equations $r_M M_t \left[(1 - M_t/K) - \beta_M M_t'/K \right]$ capture the growth rate of the message M_t (where $M_t = F_t$ or C_t; and $M_t' = C_t$ or F_t, respectively) with a maximum capacity to tweet/retweet, as well as the negative impact (competition effect) of the other message M' on the diffusion of M. K, measured on the same scale as F_t and C_t, is the capacity (e.g., number of Twitter user or bot accounts) to tweet or retweet, r_M (units: hour^{-1}) is the per-tweet retweet rate of message M, and μ_M (units: hour^{-1}) captures the loss of interest among Twitter users of the falsehood or correction message M, β_M (unitless) is the aggressiveness of the message M' in its interaction with message $M(M, M' = F, C; M \neq M')$ and captures the reputation of the issuer of the message as well as the effectiveness or structure of the message. The parameter γ_M (units: hour^{-1}) is the rate at which the other message M' is reinforcing the growth of message M. Despite the common conception that correction messages reduce the spread of

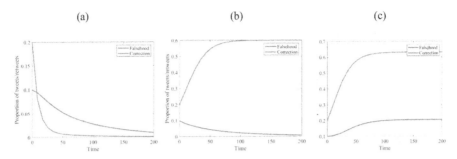

Figure 1. Possible Outcomes of Interaction Between Falsehood (F) and Correction (C) Tweets.

falsehoods, academic research has shown the opposite may happen due to how correction messages are interpreted and used to reinforce beliefs of falsehoods [22]. Hence, we use $\gamma_M M_t'$ to capture such possible positive impacts (reinforcement) of falsehoods and correction messages on each other's diffusion. All the parameters in this model are positive.

We provide the complete details on the stability analysis in the online supplemental Appendix A. In summary, the underlying system of equations has the following possible equilibria:

(1) $F^* = 0$, and $C^* = 0$;

(2) $F^* = 0$, and $C^* = K(1 - \mu_C/r_C)$, which exists only if $\gamma_F = \gamma_C = 0$ and $\mu_C < r_C$;

(3) $F^* = K(1 - \mu_F/r_F)$, and $C^* = 0$, which exists only if $\gamma_F = \gamma_C = 0$ and $\mu_F < r_F$;

(4) If $\gamma_F = \gamma_C = 0$, $F^* = K((1 - \mu_F/r_F) - \beta_F(1 - \mu_C/r_C))/(1 - \beta_F\beta_C)$, and $C^* = K((1 - \mu_C/r_C) - \beta_C(1 - \mu_F/r_F))/(1 - \beta_F\beta_C)$, which exists only when $0 \leq F^*, C^* \leq K$. If, $\gamma_F, \gamma_C \neq 0$, the fourth equilibrium point is more complicated to be presented here, and it will be handled numerically. In that case there are only two equilibria, (1) and (4).

Figure 1 provides a visual illustration of the possible outcomes. Figure 1(a) shows the scenario where eventually both falsehood and correction messages stop spreading under the appropriate conditions. Figure 1(b) shows a situation where tweets containing falsehoods stop spreading, while correction tweets continue to propagate. This scenario is ideal in the fight against misinformation. We can reduce and eliminate falsehoods while ensuring that correction messages continue spreading. In this simulation, we show that correction messages eliminate falsehoods while increasing in tweet/retweets. This model can be interchanged to ensure that the opposite happens: falsehoods continue to spread by eliminating correction messages. Figure 1(c) shows a scenario in which both falsehood and correction messages continue.

The mathematical model in Equations (1-2) can be linearized to create a panel vector autoregression model with p lags. The derivation of the empirical model based on the theoretical model can be found in the online supplemental Appendix B.

Empirical Evidence

Data

Our data consist of verified false tweets and their correction tweets during Hurricane Harvey in 2017 and Hurricane Florence in 2018. We selected these two extreme events because studies have shown that misinformation propagates the most "during events that have importance in the lives of individuals and when the news received about them is either lacking or subjectively ambiguous" [4]. Hurricanes match these descriptions because they create public safety concerns and are quite unpredictable. Furthermore, hurricanes allow researchers to accurately record exactly when the rumor associated with the shock event begins and ends. As a result, we can measure the beginning and ending of the shock event (a hurricane), which cannot be said for other crisis scenarios. For example, unlike hurricanes, it is not easy to predict when an earthquake or other natural disasters occur. Hence, when we capture data after a shock event occurs, it may lead to not only data with missing information but also endogeneity.

Our data collection steps were as follows: First, we identified and collected all tweets during Hurricane Harvey, from August 18 to September 22, 2017, and Hurricane Florence, from September 5 to October 3, 2018, using the Twitter stream API in real time. We used keywords and hashtags related to the hurricanes and the ensuing flooding, such as "#Harvey," "Hurricane Harvey," "Gulf Coast Hurricane Harvey," "#HoustonFlood," "#HoustonFlooding," "#Florence," "Hurricane Florence," "#FlorenceNC," "#FlorenceFlood," and "#FlorenceFlooding." This resulted in 12,357,530 tweets and retweets during the two extreme events with data on the content of each tweet, user metadata that includes information about the post, the author, a snapshot of the author's profile, and other related images at the time the tweet was posted. We performed standard text preprocessing on the tweet corpus, including converting all characters to lower cases, tokenization, text normalization and removing stop words.

Next, we identified 21 falsehood stories during the two hurricanes, either from FEMA's rumor control page and their Twitter timelines within those periods or from verified fake stories by at least four out of five independent fact-checking websites: Snopes, Factcheck.org, PolitiFact, Truth or Fiction and BS Detector. The use of these fact-checking websites similar to [57] allows us to ensure the accuracy of the veracity of the news. We obtained a total of 21 verified falsehoods topics as a result. An example of a false tweet on a shark on the freeway in Houston during Hurricane Harvey, an ensuing correction message, a rebuttal of the correction message, and another subsequent correction tweet are shown in Table 1.

As the number of keywords from each verified false tweet topic from FEMA and fact-checking websites was limited and would not allow us to identify all related tweets from our sample, we next used topic modeling technique Latent Dirichlet allocation (LDA) to

Table 1. Sample False and Correction Tweets.

Tweet Type	Tweet Content
Original falsehood	"Believe it or not, this is a shark on the freeway in Houston, Texas. #HurricaneHarvy"
Correction message	"Harvey Hoax: There are no sharks on Houston's flooded freeways http://dlvr.it/PjCr91"
Rebuttal of correction message	"That ain't what I heard"
Additional correction message	"Fact check: A shark in the street, and other Hurricane Harvey rumors you shouldn't believe"

Table 2. Descriptive Statistics of Falsehoods and Correction Messages.

Topic	Falsehoods			Corrections		
	Obs.	Mean	Std. Dev.	Obs.	Mean	Std. Dev.
Black Lives Matter and emergency response	10	0.08	0.40	9,651	72.56	140.90
Donation to Clinton foundation	10,130	25.33	59.41	500	1.25	6.20
Georgia mosque relief effort	793	8.62	13.61	45	0.49	2.89
FEMA hiring	6	0.02	0.15	755	2.71	14.57
Prince Harry's donation	8,433	32.31	68.57	5	0.02	0.14
Harvey shark	2,787	6.88	7.90	1,562	3.86	12.74
Florence shark	42,197	126.34	231.72	40,182	120.31	439.22
Texas mosque relief effort	10	0.04	0.22	357	1.47	4.24
Underwater planes	33	0.41	0.92	141	1.74	3.38
Brunswick nuclear plant	13,559	39.53	55.32	694	2.02	4.72
Diverted funds	12,043	35.84	128.32	45	0.13	0.50
FEMA budget	4,824	8.82	45.79	191	0.35	4.44
Tetanus due to flooding	106,748	207.68	113.26	65	0.13	0.72
Environmental Protection Agency	31	0.10	0.47	10	0.03	0.24
Navy destroyer	3	0.14	0.47	25	1.14	4.89
Mayweather donation	716	3.20	9.80	248	1.11	3.55
Category 6 hurricane	87	0.34	0.92	72	0.28	1.15
Manny donation	195	1.08	2.52	5	0.03	0.20
Pets and service animals	14	0.04	0.24	127	0.34	1.22
Immigration law enforcement	8,461	23.31	126.18	13,755	37.89	132.98
Prince William's donation	80	0.12	0.85	2	0.003	0.06
Total	211,160	33.29	99.56	68,437	10.79	111.44

identify a more comprehensive list of keywords associated with each topic. This process was done by running the LDA separately for each of the 21 tweet topics by trying different numbers of subtopics, reviewing the resulting subtopics and keywords associated with each subtopic, and identifying all relevant keywords. This generative modeling technique exposes and identifies underlying topics in text documents and their similarities between them [8]. An example would be identifying "fish" as an additional keyword based on the LDA results for the fake shark story during the hurricanes, as using "shark" only would leave out relevant tweets including "fish" in the tweets. We used this more comprehensive list of keywords to filter our tweet sample and removed all irrelevant or duplicate tweets. At the end, we obtained 279,597 tweets and retweets on the 21 verified falsehoods and their correction message topics during the two hurricanes. We then hand-coded each tweet as either a falsehood or a correction message. Tweets that repeat, corroborate, or cite verified falsehoods were coded as falsehoods, while tweets debunking or citing those rebutting the falsehoods were coded as correction messages.

In order to obtain the diffusion count data, we kept track of tweets and retweets by hour for each falsehood and correction topic over the duration of the data collection period and obtained a minimum of 22 and a maximum of 648 hours of tweets for every falsehood and correction topic. This tally ultimately resulted in 6,343 hourly observations for 21 topics. Table 2 summarizes the descriptive statistics of the counts of the tweets and retweets by veracity and topic. The correlation coefficient between the hourly tweet counts of falsehoods and correction messages was 0.41.

Empirical Model Specification

Based on our simulation results, we next conducted an empirical analysis using time series and PVAR models [1, 41] to characterize the dynamic relationships between falsehoods and correction messages. Vector autoregression (VAR) is a stochastic process model commonly used in economics to capture the linear relationships among multiple time series variables [1, 30]. It has a robust framework that can be easily verified and replicated. In addition, it addresses biases that might arise due to auto-correlations, endogeneity and causal inferences [42]. In IS research, it has been applied to examine the relationships between sentiments from microblogs and stock returns [15] as well as the existence of several patterns of supply-side technology relationships in the context of wireless networking [2]. In this research, we use it to examine how the diffusion of falsehoods and correction messages unfold as a result of falsehood and correction message tweets in the past. The framework allows us to treat both false-hoods and correction message tweets as endogenous, predict them using their lags, and capture the feedback loops among them [1]. For example, falsehoods in the current period may influence the number of correction messages in the next period, which may cause a change in the following period's falsehoods.

Building on a structural VAR, we analyze the dynamic effects between false tweets and their correction messages during Hurricanes Harvey and Florence based on [1]. We empirically estimate the diffusion between falsehoods F_t and correction messages C_t based on their past diffusion histories. We model both as endogenous in the (2 x 1) vector $M_{it} = (F_{it}, C_{it})$, where we now include subscript i as we have data on 21 different topics $i \in (1, 2, \ldots, 21)$ at every hour $t \in (1, 2, \ldots, T_i)$. Due to the non-stationarity nature of our sample and excessive zeros, we follow [2] and transform both messages by taking natural logarithm plus 0.5 of the variables. Dickey Fuller and the Fisher type unit root tests [11] for non-strongly balanced data sets show that the transformations are stationary.

To capture the dynamics between falsehoods and correction messages we estimate the following:

$$M_{it} = M_{i,t-1}A_1 + M_{(i,t-2)}A_2 + \cdots + M_{i,t-p}A_p + \eta_{it}\theta_1 + h_{it}\theta_2 + u_i + \varepsilon_{it}, \quad (3)$$

where the (2×2) matrices A_1, A_2, ..., A_p along with the vectors θ_1 and θ_2 are the parameters to be estimated. Moreover, η_{it} is a (1×2) vector of exogenous dummy variables representing the year and h_{it} is the matrix of exogenous dummy variables that captures the hour of the day. The lag order p is determined empirically from the data. In addition, u_i and ε_{it} are (1×2) vectors of dependent variable-specific panel fixed effect and idiosyncratic errors, respectively.

In the online supplemental Appendix B, Equation 3 follows from Equations 1 and 2, where we approximate the continuous changes in falsehoods and corrections with discrete changes at the hourly level. The structure in Equation 3 is a panel version of [53] that allows a flexible approach to model dynamics between falsehoods and corrections. The assumptions on the innovations are $E(\varepsilon_{it}) = 0$, $E(\varepsilon_{it}{}^T \varepsilon_{it}) = \Sigma$, and $E(\varepsilon_{it}{}^T \varepsilon_{is}) = 0$ for all $t > s$, which is a white noise multivariate process of our two variables. Following studies by [24], we assume that the topics (i.e., cross-sectional units) share the same underlying data

Table 3. Estimates of Dynamic Effects Between Falsehoods and Corrections.

	(1)	(2)	(3)	(4)	(5)	(6)
	All Topics		Florence		Harvey	
Variables:	F_{it}	C_{it}	F_{it}	C_{it}	F_{it}	C_{it}
$F_{i,t-1}$	0.504***	0.027**	0.491***	0.042**	0.02	0.004
	(0.021)	(0.015)	(0.028	(0.016)	(0.023)	(0.032)
$F_{i,t-2}$	0.243***	0.032**	0.211***	0.007	0.01	0.078**
	(0.022)	(0.017)	(0.028	(0.018)	(0.020)	(0.034)
$F_{i,t-3}$	0.169***	-0.018	0.169***	-0.02	0.003	-0.032
	(0.019)	(0.015)	(0.024	(0.017)	(0.022)	(0. 028)
$C_{i,t-1}$	0.042***	0.538***	0.494***	0.534***	0.070***	0.527***
	(0.016)	(0.027)	(0.036	(0.034)	(0.021)	(0.039)
$C_{i,t-2}$	0.001	0.218***	0.288***	0.232***	-0.021	0.205***
	(0.014)	(0.024)	(0.035	(0.030)	(0.021)	(0.039)
$C_{i,t-3}$	0.008	0.153***	0.155***	0.131***	0.015	0.169***
	(0.016)	(0.021)	(0.031)	(0.026)	(0.020)	(0.033)
Topic FE [a]	Yes		Yes		Yes	
Year FE	Yes		No		No	
Hour FE	Yes		Yes		Yes	
Obs.	5,997		3,870		2,127	

Notes: Robust standard errors in parentheses. * p<0.1; ** p<0.05; ***p<0.01. [a] Controls for topic, year, and hour fixed effects.

generating process, with common parameters $A_1, A_2, \ldots, A_p$. We use Equation 3 to test for the existence of dynamic relationships between the number of falsehood tweets and correction tweets. The time period is from 0 to 313 hours.

Empirical Results

We estimate different versions of Equation 3 using the generalized method of moments (GMM) estimators described in [1]. Our baseline model pools data from all topics, while our second and third models use only the topics for Florence and Harvey, respectively. We select the optimal lag p for each of the models based on a multivariate version of the Bayesian information criteria as recommended in [5].[1] For our three models $p = 3$ had the best performance. To improve efficiency, we included longer sets of lags as instruments as recommended by [1]. This approach has the unattractive property of reducing observations, especially with unbalanced panels and those with missing data because past realizations are not included. A proposed solution recommended by [24] is to use the method of moments in the estimation, which substitutes missing observations with zeros, but this solution does not solve the reduced observation problem associated with unbalanced panels. Hence, we used the first to fourth lags as instruments.

The coefficients in A_1, A_2, and A_3 from the estimation of Equation 3 for the first three models are reported in Table 3. The numbers in parentheses are robust standard errors. All specifications include topic and hour dummies to control for unobserved differences between topics as well as factors that might change during the day. In addition, the first model includes a year fixed effect to control for differences across hurricanes. We observe that across all models most of the coefficients on the lagged falsehoods and corrections are statistically significant in both the falsehood and correction equations. The positive

---

[1]The Bayesian information criteria, along with the Akaike information criteria, and the Hannan–Quinn information criteria are among the most commonly used model selection criteria [1, 30]. Using Akaike or Hannan–Quinn rendered similar results.

coefficients show that lagged falsehood and correction tweets not only contribute to more of their own tweets in subsequent hours but also reinforce subsequent tweets of the opposite message type. This evidence supports the existence of dynamics between F_{it} and C_{it}, and it is consistent with the predictive causality tests between F_{it} and C_{it} reported in the online supplemental Appendix C.

All the statistically significant point estimates reported in Table 3 are positive, suggesting a direct bidirectional relationship between F_{it} and C_{it}. To be able to better assess the relationship between the two, we focus on the analysis of the results using the vector moving average representation of Equation 3. Hence, in Figure 2 we plot the impulse response functions to capture the dynamic effects of an exogenous variation in corrections on falsehoods (left-hand side), and of falsehoods on corrections (right-hand side), with all other effects held constant [1, 38]. The shaded areas correspond to the 95% confidence intervals based on 200 Monte Carlo simulations using the Gaussian approximation.

The plot on the left-hand side of Figure 2 shows how a one standard deviation positive shock in C_{it} has a positive and statistically significant effect on F_{it} that lasts for over 48 hours. Note that the response in the Y-axis is measured in number of falsehoods. The effect is quite surprising, as it illustrates how corrections actually increase falsehoods. It is reasonable to argue that FEMA is likely to pursue the opposite effect when trying to correct false messages. That is, the organization probably expects that the competition effect, captured by β_F in Equation 1, dominates the reinforcement effect γ_F. This interpretation is consistent with the existing literature that documents policies that obtain results that are the opposite of the expected results as originally intended [23], with our estimates suggesting that correction tweets increase the awareness of or strengthen prior beliefs of falsehoods, thus intensifying the spread of falsehoods. Note that the contemporaneous response is constrained to zero due to the ordering of the endogenous variables in the Cholesky decomposition. The Cholesky decomposition, originally proposed by [50], imposes identification restrictions, and in our case, we impose the restriction that falsehoods occur first. This makes sense because corrections can only exist if there has been a falsehood.

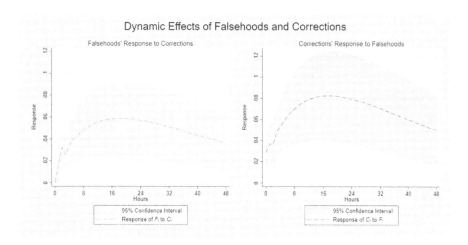

Figure 2. Impulse Response Functions for All Topics.

The plot on the right-hand side shows how a one standard deviation exogenous increase in falsehoods increases corrections, where the response in the Y-axis is measured in number of corrections. The effect is statistically significant at the 95% level for at least 48 hours. This result is expected where the relative importance of γ_C is greater than β_C .

The results on the left-hand side of Figure 3 illustrate how an exogenous increase in F_{it} leads to more falsehood messages in the following two days, with the effect being statistically significant at the 95% level. Note that the marginal effect is relatively larger during the first few hours and drops relatively fast and monotonically. This positive effect shows how the natural growth rate of falsehoods r_F is dominating the loss of interest μ_F, signaling the existence of herding effects [60]. A similar story holds for corrections on the right-hand side of the figure, where it is worth noting the similarity between both sides.

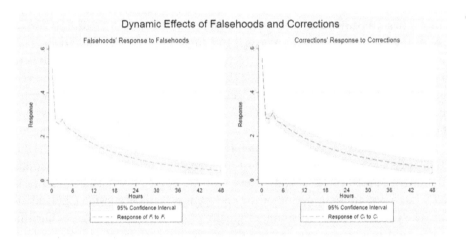

Figure 3. Impulse Response Functions for All Topics.

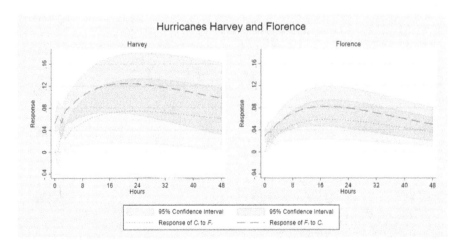

Figure 4. Impulse Response Functions at the Hurricane Level.

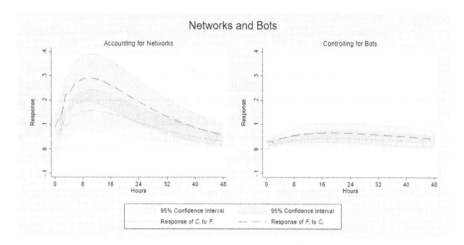

Figure 5. Impulse Response Functions When Controlling for Networks and Bots.

We plot the impulse response functions for falsehoods and corrections on each other separately for Hurricanes Harvey and Florence in Figure 4. The results are similar across the two hurricanes and are consistent with those in Figure 2, where positive reinforcement effects of falsehoods exist on both correction tweets and on correction tweets of falsehoods.

Robustness Checks

We performed multiple robustness checks to verify our empirical results under different scenarios. First, we calculated bi-hourly tweet counts instead of hourly counts for our main empirical analyses. The optimal lag of the bihourly model was two, consistent with the lag of three for the hourly tweet count model of data from both hurricanes. We also obtained consistent results of the dynamic effects where correction tweets caused falsehoods to increase and falsehoods also caused corrections to increase.

Second, we controlled for the networks of the accounts responsible for tweets and retweets in terms of the numbers of followers and obtained similar results. We achieved this outcome by multiplying each tweeted or retweeted message by the account's total number of followers. This new measure is likely to be a good approximation of the number of people who see the message. The resulting impulse response functions are plotted on the left-hand side of Figure 5. Consistent with previous results, the responses of falsehoods and corrections to one another are both positive and statistically significant, with effects that last for over two days. The most striking difference is on the magnitude of the coefficients as on average the responses are at least twice as large as before. Moreover, the marginal effects peak at about 10 hours after the original message versus the 18 hours found earlier. It makes sense to observe these larger effects as messages from accounts with more followers are more likely to have larger impacts.

Third, we controlled for bots on Twitter. A Twitter bot performs automated actions such as tweeting or retweeting which have been pre-programmed by a user on an account. In this research, we are interested in modeling the dynamics between falsehood and correction messages, including the participation of bots because users experience it. However, we also assessed whether our results change after controlling for bots, as some bots might be aimed at reproducing falsehoods. Leveraging the Botometer bot detection algorithm [13], we calculated the likelihood of each Twitter account in our sample being a bot based on the account profile and tweet/retweet history. Accounts with likelihoods less than .5 were labeled as humans and those with .5 or higher were labeled as bots. We then aggregated the total number of tweets/retweets per hour in our dataset for bots and non-bots separately. The impulse response functions on the right-hand side of Figure 5 control for bots by estimating an augmented version of Equation 3 using $M_{it} = (F_{ij}^{NB}, F_{ij}^{B}, C_{ij}^{NB}, C_{ij}^{B})$ to model the dynamics of messages from bots (F_{ij}^{B} and C_{ij}^{B}) and non-bots (F_{ij}^{NB} and C_{ij}^{NB}) as four endogenous variables.[2] The results mirror the previous results in statistical significance and magnitude.

Fourth, we controlled for the fact that different topics have different total numbers of messages. We reran the analysis after dropping 11 topics that had less than 1,000 observations between falsehoods and corrections and another analysis using the total number of messages as weights. This process is similar to running weighted least squares to correct for heteroscedasticity and account for the possibility that topics with more messages might be measured with more precision. The results showed to be consistent across all these robustness checks.[3]

Fifth, we ran separate analyses after classifying topics under environmental news and under social news. The results were consistent with positive reinforcements between falsehoods and correction messages on Twitter.

Discussion

The current research examines the dynamic effects between the diffusion of falsehoods and correction messages on social media during shock events. We model falsehoods and corrections as two competing messages on Twitter and develop a theoretical model that illustrates different scenarios under which only one type of message survives, both survive, or both die off. We further provide empirical evidence supporting our theoretical modeling results using tweets data collected from Hurricanes Harvey and Florence. Our study has the following theoretical contribution and practical implications.

Theoretical Contributions

First, we contribute to the literature on information diffusion, rumors, misinformation and correction and bridge the gaps in literature by investigating the bidirectional relationships between both falsehoods and correction messages and how each affects the other in the Twittersphere. Previous studies have examined the effects of either falsehoods or correction messages on human behavior [17, 18, 28] or the lasting effects of misinformation on the behavior of humans after exposure to falsehoods [26]. Some studies have also proposed methods to effectively debunk misinformation and present correction messages [31, 37, 46]. Our study is the first to examine both simultaneously and how falsehoods and correction

---

[2]Note that $F_{ij} = F_{ij}^{NB} + F_{ij}^{B}$ and $C_{ij} = C_{ij}^{NB} + C_{ij}^{B}$. Moreover, the order of the variables in the Cholesky decomposition is as presented in M_{it}, with falsehoods modeled first. Within falsehoods and within corrections, whether bots or non-bots were ordered first, the results were qualitatively the same.

[3]All additional results are available upon request.

messages affect each other's diffusion on social media. As a result, our research provides a more holistic picture of the different scenarios under which each type of message propagates or is eliminated, how falsehoods and correction messages co-diffuse on social media, and how one affects the other's tweet count. Furthermore, we show how user networks and automated entities such as bots play a role in the nomology of things.

Second, we develop a theoretical model of the diffusion using ordinary differential equations. The model takes into consideration the fact that when both falsehoods and correction messages coexist dependently of each other, they vie for users' attention. Our model allows us to capture the competition between falsehoods and correction messages, their reinforcement of each other, and the loss of interest among Twitter users for either type of messages during their diffusion. Our analysis shows three possible outcomes. First, the more dominant message eliminates the weaker. In our model, we posit that the ideal or optimal scenario (Figure 1(b)) occurs when we observe falsehoods die off because their per-tweet retweet rate is considerably lower than users' interest in the message and correction messages prevail with a per-tweet retweet rate that is higher than users' loss of interest in the correction message. This occurrence happens when Twitter users share the correction messages more than falsehoods when they find these correction tweets to be more novel, newsworthy, or awe-inspiring. In contrast, when users find falsehoods to be more appealing, newsworthy, or believable, they share them more than correction tweets, leading to the scenario when falsehoods prevail, and correction messages die off. Second, our theoretical model shows that under certain conditions both falsehood and correction messages "survive" (Figure 1(c)). This behavior was noted in a recent study by [57] that showed that sometimes messages may survive at lower frequencies only to resurface and flare up once the conditions are appropriate. An example is the shark story during both hurricanes that resurfaced several times in the past years. This falsehood may thus become quite harmless, receive less tweets and shares, and its target audience also changes. This finding is supported by empirical evidence that suggests when tension from those messages dissolves, it resurfaces by repackaging itself as a different news story to attract a different audience [51]. Third, falsehoods and correction messages may both die off (Figure 1(a)). On Twitter, this occurrence happens when the users do not find the news or messages appealing enough to share. Studies have shown that falsehoods usually contain less information but aim for novelty and some awe-inspiring effect on users [48]. Previous studies further corroborated this theory by showing that novel and awe-inspiring news stories go viral more than news stories that are not [7, 26].

Third, we provide empirical analyses using data of falsehood and correction tweets collected during Hurricanes Harvey and Florence. Our results are consistent across both hurricanes and are robust in additional analyses that control for the networks, bots, number of messages on the topic, and news category. Our empirical results reveal that the third outcome of our theoretical model where both types of messages survive (Figure 1(c)) to be the case, rather than the optimal scenario where correction messages eliminate falsehoods (Figure 1(b)). Specifically, we find that correction messages from FEMA and other fact-checking organizations are not only ineffective but also help in spreading falsehoods on social media. The results may be indicative of the flaws that can be attributed to FEMA and other fact-checking organizations' responses to falsehoods on social media. Our result further contradicts those from studies on the effectiveness of using correction messages. For example, prior research [25, 46, 56] suggests that exposing users to correction information that refutes falsehood reduces its spread. In contrast, our results indicate that the reinforcement effect (γ) dominates the competition effect (β) where correction messages create awareness or reinforce users' prior beliefs of falsehoods, thus leading to a wider spread of falsehoods. We propose increasing the per-tweet retweet rate of correction messages in order to overwhelm falsehoods or not issuing corrections at all. Our results indicate that currently leaving falsehoods to run their course may be even more effective than the current correction approaches, as results indicate they cause blowbacks. This phenomenon can be attributed to falsehoods losing their novelty over time if left alone. Prior studies have shown that the spread of falsehoods on social media is affected by its novelty, such that falsehoods are more novel than real news stories and disseminate faster [57]. Moreover, studies on message framing showed that humans behaved consistently irrationally, relying on several mental shortcuts to speed up reasoning, which can make people remarkably sensitive to how events are framed [56]. Recent studies have shown that humans may be reinforcing beliefs when they attempt to warn of inherent misinformation, such as during political elections without framing the correction accurately [39]. This notion can also be attributed to the presentation and format of the news item, as espoused by a recent study [24] that revealed certain changes in the way information is presented influences how users perceive and behave on the information.

Finally, our theoretical results show how the diffusion of falsehoods can eventually be reduced and removed by making the per-tweet retweet rate of correction greater than the rate of the loss in interest in it. An alternative is to make the correction message aggressive enough to discredit the falsehood and establish the facts correctly. Even though the ideal scenarios from our theoretical model suggest that one message will survive while the other one dies off, our empirical results suggest falsehoods and correction messages feed off each other on Twitter and each lead to more of the other. Hence, the current state of correction messages has not reached the equilibrium state of reducing and eventually eliminating falsehoods. Given the ineffectiveness of the correction messages in reducing falsehoods, our theoretical modeling results show the conditions under which correction messages can effectively eliminate falsehoods. For instance, when there is no reinforcement, when the per-tweet retweet rate of correction messages are greater than its loss of interest rate, correction messages will expel falsehoods and prevail on Twitter.

Practical Implications

This study has the following practical implications for government agencies and social media platforms. First, the results from our study can inform government agencies such as FEMA and policy makers on the ineffectiveness of current rebuttals and correction messages on social media and help them understand the relationships between falsehoods and correction messages and the impact of framing correction messages. For example, repeating the same falsehood message "shark on the freeway in Houston" when debunking the falsehoods on shark sightings might not be the best approach and might reinforce the belief in the falsehood. This procedure may also encourage people to look for and reshare those false messages, as research has shown that falsehoods tend to contain less information and instead rely on "catchy" headlines meant to attract users [48]. This change in procedure can go a long way in helping government agencies design more effective correction messages in the fight against misinformation. For example, rather than simply refuting the Hurricane

Harvey shark story as false, correction tweets with more supporting evidence, such as Google reverse image search results showing a date earlier than Hurricane Harvey or the original image where the photoshopped Houston freeway shark image came from, may provide a more convincing rebuttal of the falsehood. Such messages with more clear evidence may be perceived as more novel and garner more per-tweet retweets, thus curbing the diffusion of falsehoods.

Second, the findings from this study can assist government agencies and administrators in the design of effective emergency warning systems that can safeguard lives during emergencies and crises situations, such as earthquakes and hurricanes. Studies have shown that during emergency situations people are susceptible and fall prey to falsehoods [52]. Hence, we propose a few actionable recommendations. For government agencies to effectively succeed in their combat against falsehoods on social media, we suggest they first increase the per-tweet retweet rates (sharing) of correction messages. This action may be achieved by restructuring and strategizing on their social media presence. Studies have shown that the majority of US citizens use social media for news [45]. Government agencies should consider increasing their social media presence, for example, in every state. In addition, they can consider having their social media presence interconnected with other federal and state agencies across the country. These government agencies (federal and state) may then mirror rebuttals and corrections where appropriate. For example, a recent study on the analysis of cascades suggests that while diffusion is inhibited when similar content from competing cascades diffuse in tandem, similar content from parallel cascades tend to amplify each other [61]. Thus, if such agencies work in unison, the per-tweet retweet rate for correction messages can substantially increase. Moreover, government agencies may need to create incentives, such as tax benefits for private entities and independent fact-checking organizations to encourage fact checking. Government agencies may also form partnerships with fact-checking organizations and exchange information with each other when important falsehoods emerge. These collaborations ensure that shared knowledge can flow more freely, and the response time to debunk falsehoods is improved. It also provides a single voice in the fight against misinformation.

Third, the results from this study can help social media platforms in understanding the diffusion of falsehoods and correction messages and in combating the spread of the former. In order to reduce the per-tweet retweet rate of falsehoods, social media platforms can use more efficient automated detection technology to flag suspicious messages based on a combination of user, textual content, and network features. The use of these methods as a first line of defense may drastically reduce the total number of falsehoods being spread. In addition, empirical evidence suggests that bots are also responsible for sharing falsehoods though not significantly higher than humans [57]. Hence, it is important for social media platforms to effectively detect, thwart, and remove automated malicious entities [36]. The adoption of such technologies can considerably reduce the per-tweet retweet rate of falsehoods by automated entities and ultimately reduce the spread and per-tweet retweet rate of falsehoods.

Finally, government agencies and fact-checking organizations can use the empirical framework presented in this research to further understand the bidirectional relationships between additional falsehoods and corrections. As our results show evidence of heterogeneities in the responses (e.g., when controlling for bots), we understand that further heterogeneities can exist when considering falsehoods beyond the extreme events we have in our sample. As more data become available, government agencies and fact-checking organizations can use our proposed framework to learn more about the types of falsehoods and test the effectiveness of different corrections. They can fine-tune their correction messages and respond even more selectively than they currently do, depending on the nature of the falsehood and its potential to become viral. Being more selective may be the most efficient approach given the large volume, variety, and velocity of falsehoods (a characteristic of social media) and the differences in the severity of falsehoods. Responding selectively can help establish and increase the issuer's reputation, which in turn can further help the effectiveness of correction messages.

While the empirical results show that for our sample of falsehoods, government agencies and fact-checking organizations should not intervene as corrective tweets can spur more false tweets, we acknowledge that they might have additional objectives and priorities. However, we believe that selectively responding to falsehoods both in frequency and quality is the most effective approach.

Conclusion and Limitations

We examine the bidirectional relationship between falsehoods and correction messages on social media. Our theoretical model and empirical evidence show the scenarios under which each type of message survives or dies off and their impacts on each other. Our study has several limitations. First, we had to aggregate our tweet data at the hourly level to obtain the counts, which may cause loss of information at the granular level. Second, we only analyzed tweets during two crisis events from two periods. Future studies can investigate other news stories from other social media platforms to cross-validate our results. Third, we only included verifiable false news and correction messages. Future studies may examine other types of news, such as rumors, urban legends, and conspiracy theories. Fourth, as a study on the dynamics between falsehoods and correction messages on social media, we examine their diffusion at the hourly and topic levels. Studies have shown that cognitive and behavioral factors such as cognitive ability, expert sources, and clearly phrased messages affect the effectiveness of correction messages on falsehoods [9, 14, 55]. Future research can examine the issue at a more granular level and the impacts of factors such as user cognition, sentiment of the tweet, and source of the tweet using other research designs, such as surveys and experiments. Furthermore, future research may also investigate other factors that may contribute to the in/effectiveness of correction messages on falsehoods, such as message framing, timing of the correction message, tone, emotions and textual similarities between both falsehoods and correction messages. Fifth, even though we showed the bidirectional relationships between falsehoods and correction messages, we were unable to show why they happened. Future studies may employ surveys or experiments to examine why correction messages are ineffective and identify the optimal timing to correct falsehoods. Finally, a full sensitivity analysis can be beneficial to understand the degrees of change of the quantitative outcomes of the model in response to slight changes in the parameters. While that analysis was partially done here for some parameters, it will be useful to rank those parameters' influence on the quantitative and qualitative results of the model.

Disclosure statement

No potential conflict of interest was reported by the author(s).

ORCID

Kelvin K. King http://orcid.org/0000-0002-8774-1148
Bin Wang http://orcid.org/0000-0002-4479-2500
Diego Escobari http://orcid.org/0000-0003-4532-8563
Tamer Oraby http://orcid.org/0000-0002-8176-1324

References

1. Abrigo, M.R.M. and Love, I. Estimation of panel vector autoregression in Stata. *The Stata Journal: Promoting Communications on Statistics and Stata, 16*, 3 (September 2016), 778–804.
2. Adomavicius, G., Bockstedt, J., and Gupta, A. Modeling supply-side dynamics of IT components, products, and infrastructure: An empirical analysis using vector autoregression. *Information Systems Research, 23*, 2 (June 2012), 397–417.
3. Agrawal, M., Rao, H.R., and Oh, O. Community intelligence and social media services: A rumor theoretic analysis of tweets during social crises. *MIS Quarterly, 37*, 2 (February 2013), 407–426.

4. Allport, G.W. and Postman, L. An analysis of rumor. *Public Opinion Quarterly*, *10*, 4 (Winter 1946), 501–517.

5. Andrews, D.W.K. and Lu, B. Consistent model and moment selection procedures for GMM estimation with application to dynamic panel data models. *Journal of Econometrics*, *101*, 1 (March 2001), 123–164.

6. Bass, F.M. A new product growth for model consumer durables. *Management Science*, *15*, 5 (January 1969), 215–227.

7. Berger, J. and Milkman, K.L. What makes online content viral? *Journal of Marketing Research*, *49*, 2 (April 2012), 192–205.

8. Blei, D.M., Ng, A.Y., and Jordan, M.I. Latent Dirichlet Allocation. *The Journal of Machine Learning Research*, *3*, (January 2003), 993–1022.

9. Bode, L. and Vraga, E.K. See something, say something: Correction of global health misinformation on social media. *Health Communication*, *33*, 9 (September 2018), 1131–1140.

10. Cameron, K., Rooff, M., Friesema, E., et al.Patient knowledge and recall of health information following exposure to "facts and myths" message format variations. *Patient Education and Counseling*, *92*, 3 (September 2013), 381–387.

11. Choi, I. Unit root tests for panel data. *Journal of International Money and Finance*, *20*, 2 (April 2001), 249–272.

12. Chua, A.Y.K., Tee, C.-Y., Pang, A., and Lim, E.-P. The retransmission of rumor and rumor correction messages on Twitter. *American Behavioral Scientist*, *61*, 7 (June 2017), 707–723.

13. Davis, C.A., Varol, O., Ferrara, E., Flammini, A., and Menczer, F. BotOrNot: A system to evaluate social bots. In *Proceedings of the 25th International Conference Companion on World Wide Web - WWW'16 Companion*. ACM Press, Montreal, Quebec, Canada, 2016, pp. 273–274.

14. De Keersmaecker, J. and Roets, A. "Fake news": Incorrect, but hard to correct. The role of cognitive ability on the impact of false information on social impressions. *Intelligence*, *65*, (November 2017), 107–110.

15. Deng, S., Huang, Z.J., Zhao, H., and Sinha, A. The interaction between microblog sentiment and stock returns: An empirical examination. *MIS Quarterly*, *42*, 3 (March 2018), 895–918.

16. Department of Homeland Security. Countering false information on social media in disasters and emergencies. 2018. https://www.dhs.gov/publication/st-frg-countering-false-information-social-media-disasters-and-emergencies.

17. Ecker, U.K.H., Lewandowsky, S., and Apai, J. Terrorists brought down the plane!—No, actually it was a technical fault: Processing corrections of emotive information. *Experimental Psychology*, *64*, 2 (February 2011), 283–310.

18. Ecker, U.K.H., Lewandowsky, S., and Tang, D.T.W. Explicit warnings reduce but do not eliminate the continued influence of misinformation. *Memory & Cognition*, *38*, 8 (December 2010), 1087–1100.

19. Friggeri, A., Adamic, L., Eckles, D., and Cheng, J. Rumor cascades. In *Proceedings of the Eighth International AAAI Conference on Weblogs and Social Media*. AAAI Publications, 2014, pp. 101–110.

20. Gause, G.F. Experimental studies on the struggle for existence. *Journal of Experimental Biology*, *9*, 1 (April 1932), 389–402.

21. Gimpel, H., Heger, S., Olenberger, C., and Utz, L. The effectiveness of social norms in fighting fake news on social media. *Journal of Management Information Systems*, *38*, 1 (January 2021), 196–221.

22. Glaeser, E. and Sunstein, C.R. Does more speech correct falsehoods? *The Journal of Legal Studies*, *43*, 1 (January 2014), 65–93.

23. Hoekstra, M., Puller, S.L., and West, J. Cash for Corollas: When stimulus reduces spending. *American Economic Journal: Applied Economics*, *9*, 3 (July 2017), 1–35.

24. Holtz-Eakin, D., Newey, W., and Rosen, H.S. Estimating vector autoregressions with panel data. *Econometrica*, 56, 6 (November 1988), 1371–1395.
25. Hovland, C. Reconciling conflicting results derived from experimental and survey studies of attitude change. *American Psychologist*, 14, 1 (1959), 8–17.
26. Huang, H. A war of (mis)Information: The political effects of rumors and rumor rebuttals in an authoritarian country. *British Journal of Political Science*, 47, 2 (April 2017), 283–311.
27. Itti, L. and Baldi, P. Bayesian surprise attracts human attention. *Vision Research*, 49, 10 (June 2009), 1295–1306.
28. Jindal, N., Liu, B., and Lim, E.-P. Finding unusual review patterns using unexpected rules. In *Proceedings of the 19th ACM International Conference on Information and Knowledge Management - CIKM '10*. ACM Press, Toronto, ON, Canada, 2010, pp. 1549.
29. Jolley, D. and Douglas, K.M. The effects of anti-vaccine conspiracy theories on vaccination intentions. *PLoS ONE*, 9, 2 (February 2014), 1–9 e89177.
30. Kazienko, P. and Chawla, N. *Applications of Social Media and Social Network Analysis*. Springer, Cham, Switzerland, 2015.
31. Killins, R.N., Egly, P.V., and Escobari, D. The impact of oil shocks on the housing market: Evidence from Canada and U.S. *Journal of Economics and Business*, 93, (September 2017), 15–28.
32. Kim, A. and Dennis, A.R. Says Who? The effects of presentation format and source rating on fake news in social media. *MIS Quarterly*, 43, 3 (March 2019), 1025–1040.
33. Kim, A., Moravec, P.L., and Dennis, A.R. Combating fake news on social media with source ratings: The effects of user and expert reputation ratings. *Journal of Management Information Systems*, 36, 3 (July 2019), 931–968.
34. King, K. The gray side of fake news: A multiclass approach to detecting fake news, real news and everything else in between. In *The 26th Americas Conference on Information Systems.*, AIS Electronic Library, Utah 2020, pp. 1–10.
35. King, K., Wang, B., and Escobari, D. Effects of Sentiments on the morphing of falsehoods and correction messages on social media. In *Proceedings of the 54th Hawaii International Conference on System Sciences*. Hawaii, 2021, pp. 6563–6572.
36. King, K.K. and Sun, J. Catch bots with a bot: An automated approach to misinformation detection. In *4th International Conference on Design Science Research in Information* Systems *and* Technology</i>. Springer, Worcester, MA, 2019, pp. 1–6.
37. Kumar, N., Venugopal, D., Qiu, L., and Kumar, S. Detecting review manipulation on online platforms with hierarchical supervised learning. *Journal of Management Information Systems*, 35, 1 (January 2018), 350–380.
38. Kwon, H.E., Oh, W., and Kim, T. Platform structures, homing preferences, and homophilous propensities in online social networks. *Journal of Management Information Systems*, 34, 3 (July 2017), 768–802.
39. Lakoff, G., Dean, H., and Hazen, D. *George Lakoff -The Essential Guide for Progressives*. Chelsea Green Publishing, White River Junction, Vermont, 2004.
40. Lewandowsky, S., Ecker, U.K.H., Seifert, C.M., Schwarz, N., and Cook, J. Misinformation and its correction: Continued influence and successful debiasing. *Psychological Science in the Public Interest*, 13, 3 (December 2012), 106–131.
41. Love, I. and Zicchino, L. Financial development and dynamic investment behavior: Evidence from panel VAR. *The Quarterly Review of Economics and Finance*, 46, 2 (May 2006), 190–210.
42. Luo, X., Zhang, J., and Duan, W. Social media and firm equity value. *Information Systems Research*, 24, 1 (March 2013), 146–163.
43. Ma, J., Gao, W., Mitra, P., et al. Detecting rumors from microblogs with recurrent neural networks. In *Proceedings of the Twenty-Fifth International Joint Conference on Artificial Intelligence (IJCAI-16)*. New York, USA, 2016, pp. 3818–3824.
44. McGuire, W.J. Inducing resistance to persuasion. Some contemporary approaches. *Advances in Experimental Social Psychology*, 1, (1964), 191–229.

45. Moon, A. Most American adults get news from social media. *Media and Telecoms*, 2017. https://www.reuters.com/article/us-usa-internet-socialmedia-idUSKCN1BJ2A8.

46. Oh, O., Kwon, K.H., and Rao, H.R. An exploration of social media in extreme events: Rumor theory and Twitter during the Haiti earthquake 2010. In the *Thirty-First International Conference on Information Systems*. AIS Electronic Library, St. Louis, Missouri, USA, 2010, pp. 1–13.

47. Oliver, J.E. and Wood, T.J. Conspiracy theories and the paranoid style(s) of mass opinion. *American Journal of Political Science*, 58, 4 (October 2014), 952–966.

48. Osatuyi, B. and Hughes, J. A tale of two internet news platforms-real vs. fake: An elaboration likelihood model perspective. In *Proceedings of the 51st Hawaii International Conference on System Sciences*. Hawaii, 2018, pp.3986–3994.

49. Ozturk, P., Li, H., and Sakamoto, Y. Combating rumor spread on social media: The effectiveness of refutation and warning. In *Proceedings of the 48th Hawaii International Conference on System Sciences*. IEEE, HI, USA, 2015, pp. 2406–2414.

50. Schwarz, N., Sanna, L.J., Skurnik, I., and Yoon, C. Metacognitive experiences and the intricacies of setting people straight: Implications for debiasing and public information campaigns. In *Advances in Experimental Social Psychology*. Elsevier, 2007, pp. 127–161.

51. Shin, J., Jian, L., Driscoll, K., and Bar, F. The diffusion of misinformation on social media: Temporal pattern, message, and source. *Computers in Human Behavior*, 83, 6 (June 2018), 278–287.

52. Silverman, C. and Singer-Vine, J. Most Americans who see fake news believe it, new survey says. *BuzzFeed News*, 2016. https://www.buzzfeednews.com/article/craigsilverman/fake-news-survey#.hjpN2eMqqg.

53. Sims, C.A. Macroeconomics and reality. *Econometrica*, 48, 1 (January 1980), 1–48.

54. Takayasu, M., Sato, K., Sano, Y., Yamada, K., Miura, W., and Takayasu, H. Rumor diffusion and convergence during the 3.11 Earthquake: A Twitter case study. *PLoS ONE*, 10, 4 (April2015), 1–18 e0121443.

55. Torres, R.R., Gerhart, N., and Negahban, A. Combating fake news: An investigation of information verification behaviors on social networking sites. In *The 51st Hawaii International Conference on System Sciences*. Hawaii, 2018, pp. 3976–3985.

56. Tversky, A. and Kahneman, D. Rational choice and the framing of decisions. *The Journal of Business*, 59, 4 Part 2: The Behavioral Foundations of Economic Theory (October 1986), S251–S278.

57. Vosoughi, S., Roy, D., and Aral, S. The spread of true and false news online. *Science*, 359, 6380 (March 2018), 1146–1151.

58. Vraga, E.K. and Bode, L. Using expert sources to correct health misinformation in social media. *Science Communication*, 39, 5 (October 2017), 621–645.

59. Walter, N. and Murphy, S.T. How to unring the bell: A meta-analytic approach to correction of misinformation. *Communication Monographs*, 85, 3 (July 2018), 423–441.

60. Xitong Li and Lynn Wu. Herding and social media word-of-mouth: Evidence from Groupon. *MIS Quarterly*, 42, 4 (December 2018), 1331–1351.

61. Yoo, E., Gu, B., and Rabinovich, E. Diffusion on social media platforms: A point process model for interaction among similar content. *Journal of Management Information Systems*, 36, 4 (October 2019), 1105–1141.

Cure or Poison? Identity Verification and the Posting of Fake News on Social Media

Shuting (Ada) Wang, Min-Seok Pang, and Paul A. Pavlou

ABSTRACT

The proliferation of fake news on social media has become a major societal and political problem. Meanwhile, social media platforms have started to require identity verification from users and label the verified users with a verification badge, making users more responsible for their online behavior. In this study, we empirically investigate two research questions: 1) What is the impact of identity verification on users' propensity to post fake news? and 2) How does a verification badge moderate the impact of identity verification? Results suggest that while identity verification without a verification badge has a negative impact on users' posting of fake news, this impact is significantly weakened when users are granted a verification badge after identity verification. Given the criticisms on identity verification policies, these findings underscore both the potential upsides and risks for social media platforms seeking to combat fake news through identity verification techniques.

Introduction

Fake news, as its name indicates, is news that is completely fabricated or partially distorted to mislead audiences [45]. Although it has been used as a propaganda tool throughout human history [45], the Internet and social media have provided fertile soil for its wide proliferation [56]. The ever-increasing availability of the Internet, as well as the sheer quantity of news stories available on social media, can easily lead to information overload that impairs people's ability to discern between the authentic and the fake. When a piece of fake news spreads widely, it can alter public perceptions and inflame societal problems, often for the worse [10]. For example, the anti-vaccine movement has spread fake news on social media, resulting in many unvaccinated children. Even after being disproved by science, anti-vaccine fake news continues to spread, putting public health and safety in grave danger (*The Washington Post* 2019).

Given the ability and incentive to post fake news on social media, the source of fake news has shifted from official media to a much broader, and often anonymous, population – social media users [70]. Historically, publishing news has been exclusively controlled by

Access the Support Material: www.routledge.com/ 9781032561127

official news media, such as newspapers or TV news stations, and the public read that official news. Unofficial news was often regarded as urban legends or rumors, the circulation of which was often limited. Today, however, nameless social media users can post content and share news with each other. Some users intentionally post fake news with eye-catching headlines or entirely fabricated information to gain attention ("clicks") for political and monetary gain [45]. For example, during the 2016 U.S. Presidential Election, many anonymous users posted fake news on Facebook and Twitter, attracting millions of page views to their websites, thereby misleading millions of viewers while gaining substantial revenues from advertisements (*NBC News* 2016). Many others unintentionally repeat or (re)post fake news that they encounter online when they themselves are misled by the false content. The resulted influx of "newsbreakers" makes it hard for any social media platforms to implement the gatekeeping process of news production [71].

Additionally, the anonymity of social media further fuels the proliferation of fake news by allowing people to hide behind aliases [54]. While anonymity in cyberspace is important for free speech and privacy, it may have negative consequences [1]. For example, anonymity makes social media users less responsible for cyber-misconduct such as intentionally spreading fake news [58], as anonymity makes it costly for individual users, platforms, or law enforcement to target offenders. The perceived lower risk of being caught and penalized adds another catalyst to fake news proliferation [52]. With the speed of exchange and circulation of information on social media, fake news spreads at a massive scale, leading to serious implications for the society at large [4].

Concerned that fake news may threaten their long-term viability [47], many social media platforms have attempted to mitigate fake news with *identity verification policies*. These policies require users to verify their accounts with personally identifiable information, such as phone numbers or official government-issued photo identifications (IDs). The idea is that after disclosing such information, users would lose their anonymity to the platform and become more disciplined with their online behavior. It is not surprising that users do not welcome such a move. Identity verification policies have faced much criticism and resistance [17]. As a result, rather than instituting identity verification as a universal compulsory requirement, platforms have experimented with introducing identify verification policies in different ways. These experimental policies differ in whether identity verification is mandatory or voluntary and whether a verified user can get a verification badge.[1] Yet, to the best of our knowledge, how effective identity verification policies are in deterring fake news and whether a verification badge affects the effectiveness remain unanswered.

In this study, we break open the black box by examining the impact of identity verification policies on users' posting of fake news. When posting fake news, a user assumes authorship, taking responsibility for and lending her own reputation to the credibility of the post. Compared to sharing a post of fake news, where the user merely exhibits herself as a reader or information consumer of other users' posts and thus takes less responsibility, posting of fake news is subject to more scrutiny and restrictions, especially when identity verification raises the user's risks of being caught and even punished. Above all, posting behavior is the starting point of the proliferation of fake news on social media. As such, we

---

[1] For example, Twitter has adopted four policies: mandatory verification with no verification badges for certain users (e.g., suspicious users), voluntary verification with no verification badges in certain cases (e.g., account security), mandatory verification with a verification badge for accounts that are considered to be influential, and voluntary verification with a verification badge if a user opts to do so. (https://help.twitter.com/en/managing-your-account/twitter-verified-accounts)

limit the scope of our study to the posting of fake news and explore two research questions: 1) What is the impact of identity verification (without a verification badge) on users' propensity to post fake news on social media? and 2) Does this impact of identity verification vary if users are granted a verification badge after identity verification?

We empirically investigate our research questions using a dataset from Weibo, a leading social media platform and an equivalent of Twitter in China. This is an ideal setting for this study for several reasons. First of all, Weibo actively classifies different types of misbehavior (e.g., fake news, privacy invasion, personal attack, and plagiarism) on the platform and clearly defines fake news in line with the general definition used in academia and practice [45, 70]. Second, Weibo actively investigates the posts of fake news reported by other users, along with the evidence provided by the accusers and the author, and discloses the results, which gives us an official way to label fake news. Although we recognize that not all fake news is detected, the fake news disclosed on the website should be largely accurately labeled due to the public scrutiny. We further confirmed this with a manual check of a random sample. Third, in October 2011, Weibo implemented a policy change in which it mandated identity verification from its users. This policy serves as an exogenous shock that allows us to cautiously estimate the impact of identity verification. Fourth, the context of Weibo allows us to compare the effects of two designs in identity verification systems, viz. with and without a verification badge, making our findings generalizable to other settings.

Our study yields several interesting findings. First, results suggest that identity verification (without a verification badge) has a negative impact on users' propensity to post fake news. Second, a verification badge negatively moderates the impact of identity verification. Specifically, if users are granted a verification badge after verification, the impact of identity verification on their propensity to post fake news is insignificant. This finding indicates that if not designed appropriately, identity verification policies may not help reduce the posting of fake news on social media platforms. More interestingly, results indicate that users post more fake news after voluntarily choosing to undergo identity verification with a verification badge. This finding underscores the potential risks when platforms openly disclose users' verified status. Theoretical and practical implications for designing effective identity verification systems are discussed.

Prior Work and Hypotheses Development

Prior Work

"Fake news" is fabricated or false information that mimics news media content, typically with the intent to mislead people, damage an agency, entity, or person, and/or obtain financial or political gain [46, 70]. Historically, only journalists from traditional news media published news to mass audiences, but the rise of social media has enabled anyone to produce news stories, including fake news [50, 62]. Due to the negative impact of fake news on political systems [4, 36, 46] as well as peoples' social lives [16, 76], many scholars have begun to investigate interventions to deter the spread of fake news [5, 33, 41, 42, 46, 59].

Lazer et al. (2018) posit that the most common approaches to combatting fake news are to encourage the audience—the readers or recipients of fake news—to disprove fake news or require platforms to detect and prevent fake news exposure. Specifically, the audience can disprove fake news using external and internal information. External information includes books, other news, posts from official accounts, and results from search engines [73, 77], whereas internal clues include the titles and sources of the social media posts, platform design attributes (e.g., design features, depth of content, site complexity), and the characteristics of the posts' authors (e.g., gender) [6, 27, 41, 49]. Simultaneously, platforms can detect fake news using linguistic cue approaches (e.g., machine learning) and network analysis methods [32, 35, 63, 65]. Our study explores the platform side, specifically examining how to design an information system to address this issue before it happens.

Identity verification relates to the literature on online anonymity. There are generally two types of online anonymity: (i) anonymity to other users and (ii) anonymity to the authorities. Our study on identity verification polices relates to the latter. By definition, anonymity to the authorities means that the acting person is unidentifiable to the government or law enforcement [28, 38, 55]. Proponents of online anonymity argue that anonymity is pivotal for freedom of speech and democratic values, while critics claim that anonymity leads to a lack of accountability [20, 28, 57]. Recent investigations have showed that such anonymity is often related to hate speech, child pornography, fraud, and cyber-stalking [1]. It may also cause offensive communications, such as insulting language and threats [37, 60, 61].

Studies have found that online anonymity is a key enabler of the massive spread of fake news in the online environment because it lowers the risk of punishment for misbehavior (i.e., posting of fake news) [2, 53]. Concomitantly, recent studies have examined how identity verification, a practice to remove users' online anonymity, affects users' behavior on social media [15, 19, 25]. For example, Cho et al. (2012) and Fu et al. (2013), based on data from South Korea and China, respectively, found that identity verification disciplines online communications and reduces offensive speech and discussions of sensitive subjects by social media users. Edwards and McAuley (2013), examining the identity disclosure policies on Google+ and Facebook, argued that identity verification helps deter undesirable communication behaviors by making it easier for these platforms to go after offenders.

Despite existing work (as summarized in Table 1), a notable literature gap presents an opportunity for our study. First, although prior studies have investigated how audiences and platforms detect fake news after it is posted [13, 45, 63], few studies, if any, have examined interventions that can prevent the posting of fake news. Second, although the literature suggests that online anonymity is one of the root causes of fake news proliferation, and that identity verification helps reduce online anonymity, few studies have empirically examined how identity verification influences the spread of fake news. Third, extant research has explored the impact of identity verification [25, 46], but verification badges, a key component in the design of identity verification policies, have received little attention. This design has been widely adopted by social media platforms, and investigating its role is crucial to designing a more effective identity verification system.

Hypotheses Development

Impact of Identity Verification without A Verification Badge

Rational choice theory in social behavior suggests that a user decides whether to post fake news by weighing the benefits of committing the act, the costs of the expected penalty, and the chances of being caught [21]. If the user perceives the payoff as too small, costs as too

Table 1. Summary of the Related Literature

Selected Paper	Outlet	Main Findings
A. The spread and impact of fake news over social media		
A1. Political fake news		
Allcott and Gentzkow (2017)	*Journal of Economic Perspectives*	Fake news circulated largely through social media and might have impacted the 2016 U.S. presidential election.
Grinberg, et al. (2019)	*Science*	Engagement with fake news was highly concentrated. Individuals who are conservative leaning, older, and highly engaged with political news are most likely to engage with fake news.
A2. Societal fake news		
Chiou and Tucker (2018)	*National Bureau of Economic Research*	Anti-vaccine Facebook groups actively spread false stories over the platform. Yet, after Facebook banned advertising by fake news sites, the number of fake news articles shared by these groups significantly dropped.
Waszak, et al.(2018)	*Health Policy and Technology*	40% of the most frequently shared medical news are fake.
B. Interventions for deterring fake news		
B1. Audience-based detection and interventions		
Flanagin and Metzger (2007)	*New Media & Society*	Users' credibility assessments of websites are influenced by website attributes (e.g. design features, depth of content) rather than users' familiarity with website sponsors.
Armstrong and McAdams (2009)	*Journal of Computer-Mediated Communication*	Male weblog authors are considered more credible than female authors.
Kim and Dennis (2019)	*MIS Quarterly*	Highlighting the source of an article affects its believability and social media users' engagement with the article.
Moravec et al. (2020)	*Information Systems Research*	Flags of fake news affect social media users' beliefs of news articles, as well as their engagement with the articles.
B2. Platform-based detection and interventions		
Gilda (2017)	*2017 IEEE 15th Student Conference on Research and Development (SCOReD)*	Natural language processing (NLP) techniques can be used for detecting fake news.
Granik and Mesyura (2017)	*2017 IEEE First Ukraine Conference on Electrical and Computer Engineering (UKRCON)*	Naive Bayes classifier can be used for detecting fake news.
Shu et al. (2019)	*Proceedings of the Twelfth ACM International Conference on Web Search and Data Mining*	The inherent tri-relationship, among publishers, news pieces and users, can be leveraged to improve fake news detection.
Shu et al. (2020)	*Proceedings of the International AAAI Conference on Web and Social Media*	Hierarchical propagation networks, both local and global pattern of information diffusion, can help improve the detection of fake news.
C. Online anonymity and identity verification		
Albright and Communication (2017)	*Media and Communication*	Online anonymity is a key enabler of the spread of fake news over social media.
Cho et al. (2015)	*Computers in Human Behavior*	Anonymity control mechanisms help improve the quality of online discussions by making users more responsible for their online behavior.
D. Gaps in the literature that this paper aims to fill		1)No studies have examined the potential inventions that can prevent the spread of fake news from the starting point, viz. the posting of fake news. 2)Few studies have empirically examined the potential of using identity verification to combat fake news. 3)The role of verification badges has received little attention.

high, or the act as too risky, then she would choose not to post fake news [23, 51]. We explicitly discuss the benefits, costs, and chances of being caught for posting fake news as follows.

In general, the benefits gained by posting any content on social media can be placed into three categories: *psychological* gain (e.g., attention from peers [8]), *political* gain (e.g., propaganda [45]), and *financial* gain (e.g., monetary profits from click traffic and ads on their websites [4]). While prior studies have extensively discussed psychological and political gain [70], financial gain has fueled the recent rise of the misinformation-for-profit industry [69]. The magnitude of these benefits depends on how many people see and engage with the post, thereby incentivizing users to post stories characterized by click-bait and eye-catching titles that are more likely to go viral [74]. Although fake news usually has such characteristics, most users are reluctant to post fake news or suspicious news that might be fake because posting fake news incurs costs.

When a user directly posts a piece of news from her account, her authorship of the post lends her reputation to its credibility and implies responsibility for its accuracy.[2] As such, posting fake news could result in damage to her reputation, account restrictions imposed by the platforms, lawsuits by victims, or even prosecution by the government depending on the extent of violation of the law.[3] For example, a Chinese law illegalizes disseminating fake news as a crime punishable by up to seven years in prison,[4] while users in the United States can face defamation lawsuits for posting false facts that cause material damage to another person.[5] Because of these costs, social media users evaluate every piece of news they intend to post. Any suspicion about the credibility of the content could remind them of the costly consequence, preventing them from posting [23].

Intuitively, identity verification without a verification badge would hardly influence users' benefits or costs of posting fake news. Yet, it can significantly increase the third factor– the chances of being caught. Traditionally, users can retain anonymity on social media by not disclosing their real names or identities to the platform. The ability to remain anonymous enables online users to escape the costs of posting fake news. However, when platforms such as Facebook and Twitter implement identity verification policies, verified users can easily be targeted for misconducts. Specifically, while allowing users to use aliases and remain anonymous to other users, these policies typically require users to disclose identifiable information (e.g., phone numbers or IDs) to the platform. By doing so, the platforms can collect information to discover verified users' real identities, so that the platforms, victims, or the government can go after offenders hidden behind the aliases. For these reasons, identity verification increases users' risk of being caught and punished for misconduct over the platform, leading to more disciplined online behavior. Given that posting fake news is an improper behavior that may incur punishment, identity verification should also encourage users to validate the credibility of any news they want to post from their accounts and discourage users from posting suspicious news, leading to a lower chance of posting fake news [14]. Therefore, we propose the following hypothesis for testing

---

[2]Although sometimes a user often merely copies a message from other sources, we still consider this behavior as "posting" in our study if the post appears as stand-alone without citing another source. Our rationale is that in this case, the user presents herself to other users as the author who originally creates the post, taking the same level of responsibility as the original creator and a similar risk of unwanted consequences.

[3]https://www.poynter.org/ifcn/anti-misinformation-actions/

[4]https://www.bloomberg.com/news/articles/2017-10-10/china-s-google-checks-3-billion-fake-news-claims-every-year

[5]https://www.legalzoom.com/articles/fake-news-what-laws-are-designed-to-protect

H1: *Identity verification without a verification badge is negatively associated with users'
propensity to post fake news on social media.*

Impact of Identity Verification with A Verification Badge

We next consider the moderating role of a verification badge. After a user verifies her
identity, her verified status is not always known to other users. Some platforms explicitly
disclose users' verified status to the public (e.g., Facebook and Twitter give verified users
a blue tick after verification), whereas many other platforms do not. We ask a crucial
question: will the impact of identity verification on the posting of fake news be different if
users are granted a verification badge after identity verification?

As mentioned earlier, a user decides whether to post fake news by weighing the benefits,
the costs, and the chances of being caught [21]. Despite increasing the risk of being caught,
identity verification with a verification badge also increases the benefit of posting fake news
as well. In most cases, more engagement means greater benefits from posting, such as
additional psychological attainment, amplified political influence, or increased advertising
revenues from click traffic [4, 8, 67]. Most audiences prefer not to engage with fake news on
social media because their engagement (e.g., liking, commenting, or sharing) shapes others'
perceptions of themselves (e.g., knowing their personality and behavioral characteristics)
[30, 44, 75], and engaging with fake news could harm their image as being credible or
intelligent [75]. Thus, users generally assess the credibility of posts before engaging with
them, especially when the posts are characterized by sensational content that raises suspicion [64].

Signaling theory suggests that a verification badge increases the perceived credibility of
posts (e.g., fake news posts) to audiences and facilitates engagement with the posts [44, 75].
A signal is an indicator of desirable personal qualities or resources. Effective signals are
sufficiently costly to obtain so that only individuals of high quality can afford the costs [22].
As discussed in H1, identity verification increases users' risks of being punished for posting
fake news. Therefore, a verification badge conveys a costly signal for the users' credibility on
the platform [34]. Although some people may hold pre-existing cognitive bias that may
make them easily buy certain fake news stories [36], many others do not blindly follow their
pre-existing beliefs. Instead, they use heuristic thinking or leverage the internal and external
cues (e.g. a verification badge) to evaluate the credibility of a news post [6, 27, 41, 49]. From
this aspect, a verification badge explicitly exhibited on users' profile is likely to be used as
a signal for credibility and lower the audience's susceptibility to fake news posts from the
verified users, especially when the verified user presents herself as the author who takes
responsibility for the post content [24]. Hence, users who intend to post fake or suspicious
news would expect less suspicion and more engagement with their posts and, as a result,
greater benefits of doing so, with a verification badge [31]. Such increased benefits would
weaken the impact of identity verification on reducing users' posting of fake news by
increasing verified users' willingness to take the risk of being caught. Therefore, we posit
the following hypothesis for testing:

H2: *The negative association between identity verification and users' propensity to post fake
news would be weakened if users are granted a verification badge after identity verification.*

Context and Data

Context

To empirically test our hypotheses, we utilize data from Weibo, a major social media platform in China that began its service in 2009. "Weibo" stands for a "microblog" in Chinese. The platform has many features similar to those on Twitter, including the 140-character length limit, short messages, private messaging, commenting, and sharing. Weibo users can follow other users' posts, mention or talk to other users using a "@UserName" format, add a hashtag, and share others' posts in a way similar to Twitter's retweet function. As of the first quarter of 2017, Weibo had 340 million active monthly users, overtaking the number of Twitter users (328 million) [9]. In addition to its scale and resemblance to Twitter, Weibo is an ideal setting for this study because of its generalizable definition of fake news, its evidence-based approach for determining fake news, and its verification methods that are similar to other social media platforms. In addition, we take advantage of an exogenous shock to users' verification decisions to address potential self-selection bias, which we elaborate below.

Definition of Fake News

Weibo defines and judges fake news in a manner consistent with the common definition by academia and other social media platforms [45, 70], making the definition of fake news in our study generalizable to other contexts and countries. Specifically, Weibo's definition of fake news includes: 1) the overall false: the event itself is non-existent; 2) fabricated details: fabricated details making the whole event distorted; 3) graphic discrepancy: through the graphic and text mismatch errors to mislead others; 4) exaggerated: being exaggerated in the description of the facts, misleading others; 5) outdated information: misrepresent news in the past as recent event; 6) incomplete information: hide some of the facts, and use the incomplete information to mislead others; 7) take out of context: to publish partial facts along with some speculation as fact.[6] In this study, we focus on fake news that have been determined and announced on Weibo's website according to this definition. We recognize that not all fake news can be detected and publicized, but the fake news disclosed on the website should be largely accurately labeled due to the public scrutiny, as we elaborate below.

Identifying Fake News Posts

The platform provides us with an official source to collect a record of fake news circulated on the platform. On Weibo, users can report any plausibly fake post to a Weibo administrator, with evidence and detailed information (e.g., creator, time, and content) of the post. Upon receiving a report, the administrator contacts the author of the post and requires her to submit evidence for the authenticity of the accused post. If she responds, the administrator forwards her response to the accuser, requesting more counterevidence. In the end, the administrator decides whether the post is fake news based on the evidence provided by both the accuser and the accused. When Weibo determines the post as fake, it flags the post

---

[6]http://service.account.weibo.com

on the poster's page. The post is also listed on Weibo's website in the category of "fake news," along with the detailed information on the author, time of posting, content, time of reporting, and the evidence from both the accuser and the accused. As all information throughout this process is accessible to the public, we believe that transparency and public scrutiny largely ensure Weibo's accuracy in adjudicating fake news, although there may not be a perfectly unbiased way to adjudicate fake news.

One concern is that the accuracy of fake news announcements could be biased if Weibo has any political or commercial motivation to mischaracterize a legitimate post as fake news. Yet, as Weibo is a public platform open to the world, we believe that the incidence of mistreatment of an authentic post should be rare and limited. Moreover, regardless of Weibo's determination of a post as fake or true, the user who posts the news has the right to retain the post on her page, further limiting the likelihood of misjudging any post by Weibo. To check the validity of the fake news in our sample, we randomly selected 200 fake posts from our sample. We manually validated them by investigating the legitimacy of the evidence provided by the accusers of each fake news post. Except for a few posts about personal affairs that we could not validate with external sources, all other posts were confirmed as fake. We do recognize, however, that perfect accuracy is impossible to achieve in practice. To further reduce bias due to potential inaccuracy in Weibo's determination of fake news, we include time-fixed effects in our model as detection inaccuracy across the platform should be universal at each time point at the platform level.

Table 2. Comparison of the Identity Verification with and without A Verification Badge

	Identity Verification without A Verification Badge	Identity Verification with A Verification Badge
Introduction time	2010	2012
Badge name	*Rulaishenzhen* Badge, meaning a "movement" in Chinese martial arts	*Micro Identity* Badge, meaning an identity on the microblog platform
Image		
Whether explicitly disclose verified status	No	Yes
Whether explicitly endow credibility	No	Yes
Preferred verification methods	Phone numbers	Phone numbers
Cost for verification	Not differentially costly	

Identify Verification Policies

In this study, we leverage different verification policies in Weibo (viz. verification with/ without a verification badge), similar to the policies adopted by most popular platforms in the United States, such as Twitter or Facebook. This similarity supports the generalizability of our findings.

In 2010, Weibo introduced its first verification policy with no verification badges (the first verification policy). To pass this verification process, a user needs to verify her identity with a phone number.[7] After verification, a badge called *Rulaishenzhang* automatically

---

[7]To pass this verification process, users need to supply a valid phone number to the platform and promptly enter a 4-digit code sent to that phone number.

appeared on the user's profile page (Table 2). This badge is not strictly a verification badge, as its name refers to a "movement" in Chinese martial arts, and its image, which presents a hand palm, is not associated with identity verification. Therefore, we categorize this identity verification process as identity verification without a verification badge (see support in the MTurk survey in Section *Robustness Checks*).

In 2012, the platform introduced the second verification policy with a verification badge. Upon verification, a badge called *Micro Identity* automatically appears on a user's profile page (Table 2). This badge functions as an explicit disclosure of the user's verified status, as its Chinese name refers to "identity," and its image resembles a government-issued photo ID. In addition, this badge has the word "Credible" on the icon. While this policy allows users to choose either their phone numbers or their government-issued IDs to verify their accounts, users naturally prefer to pass this verification with the same method (phone numbers) they would use for the first verification policy (see support in Section *Robustness Checks*), given the lower costs and the lower risk of disclosing a phone number to the platform than disclosing an ID. Hence, the only major difference between the first and second identity verification policy is whether verified users receive an explicit verification badge.

We note that identity verification without a verification badge was introduced earlier (in 2010) than the one with a verification badge (in 2012). It is possible that the order in which these badges were introduced had different impacts of the identity verification policies. As a robustness check, we replicate our analysis by only including users who passed the 2nd policy first. The results are consistent with the main findings. A detailed discussion can be found in *Robustness Checks*.

An Exogenous Shock to Identity Verification

Our focal social media platform implemented a policy change in 2011 in which it mandated users to verify their accounts. We leverage this policy change as an exogenous shock to users' verification decisions to alleviate the concern of potential self-selection bias.

The timeframe for the exogenous shock is from October 2011 to March 2012. In October 2011, Weibo instituted a site-wide identity verification policy and demanded that all users verify their identities by March 2012. Both types of identity verification policies mentioned earlier (viz. verification with and without a verification badge) were mandated.[8] Due to technical challenges and the size of the user population, Weibo failed to fully verify all users before the self-imposed deadline (March 2012) [66]. We display the timeline of key events in our study in Figure 1.

Figure 2 shows the distribution of daily identity verification volume in our sample. We can see that while some users verified their accounts before October 2011 or after March 2012, the volume of identity verification spiked during the October 2011~March 2012 period. Our data show that 38% of the identity verifications were conducted during this 6-month period, with the remaining verifications conducted during the rest of the 7-year period of our data. We treat this spike, where a verification

---

[8]During October 2011 - January 2012, the platform required users to pass the first verification policy (verification without a verification badge) by restricting them from posting, sharing, and commenting at the platform (*Newhua* 2012). During February 2012 - March 2012, the platform changed its policy by requiring unverified users to pass the second verification policy (verification with a verification badge).

Figure 1. Timeline of the Key Events in the Exogenous Shock

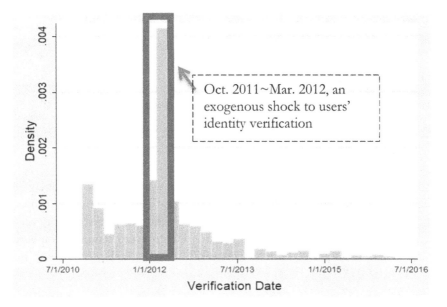

Figure 2. An Exogenous Shock to Identity Verification Note: The vertical axis indicates the percentage of identity verification in each day as a fraction of the total incidence of identity verification in our sample.

decision is less subject to unobserved individual characteristics, as an exogenous shock to identity verification. Users who verified their accounts during the period of the exogenous shock (October 2011 ~ March 2012) are considered as the treatment group, while the other users who did not verify their accounts during this period are as the control group.

The platform's decision to implement this policy change may be related to its desire to combat fake news. If this is the case, the shock might not necessarily be exogenous to the posting of fake news. To address this concern, we included time-fixed effects to tease out unobserved time-variant factors that may relate to the implementation of this policy change. Another concern is that this treatment may not be perfectly random. We reviewed Weibo users' online discussions; they indicate that the platform did not strategically select certain users for the treatment (i.e., identity verification) during this policy change. In addition, our t-tests reveal no pre-treatment difference between the treatment and the control group (Table 3). To further alleviate this concern, we replicated our main analysis with a propensity score matching (PSM) method to further ensure the similarity of the treatment and the control group. Details are available in *Robustness Checks*.

Table 3. Descriptive Statistics of Users Who Verified During the Exogenous Shock and Others Who Did Not

	Users Who Verified Identities during the Exogenous Shock		Users Who Did Not Verify Identities during the Exogenous Shock		
Variable	Mean	Std. Dev	Mean	Std. Dev	T-Test (p-value)
CumPreviousPostFake	0.12	0.41	0.10	0.30	0.9
CumPreviousSharedFake	0.19	0.64	0.13	0.38	0.9
WeeklyPosts	1.78	3.30	2.38	3.92	0.9
Ln(WeeklySharesOfPosts)	0.25	0.71	0.22	0.66	0.9
Ln(WeeklyLikesOfPosts)	0.01	0.12	0.02	0.13	0.9
Ln(WeeklySharesOfShared)	4.10	3.41	5.20	3.38	0.8
Ln(WeeklyLikesOfShared)	0.00	0.04	0.04	0.03	0.9
Ln(WeeksSinceRegist)	4.21	0.49	4.20	0.58	0.9

Note: Based on Data One Week before the Exogenous Shock

Table 4. Percentage of Users under Each Verification Policy

Users Passed Identity Verification (62%)			
Verification without a verification badge (40%)		Verification with a verification badge (59%)	
Verification out of the Exogenous Shock (29%)	Verification within the Exogenous Shock (11%)	Verification out of the Exogenous Shock (32%)	Verification within the Exogenous Shock (27%)

Note: 37% of the users passed both of the two identity verification policies.

To better understand identity verification behavior, we display the percentage of users under each verification policy in Table 4. It shows that 62% of the users in our sample verified their identities. In addition, 40% of users in our sample passed identity verification without a verification badge, 59% of them passed identity verification with a verification badge, and 37% of them passed both identity verification methods.

Data

Our dataset was collected in May 2016. To reduce bias, we focused on fake news posts determined and disclosed by Weibo.[9] We started collecting all records of fake news announced on Weibo. Next, we focused on users that posted fake news and went to their personal pages to collect their posting history. Our data include detailed information on each fake news post, such as content, time of posting and number of shares/likes/comments, and data on the users who posted the fake news, including demographic information and posting histories from their first posts to May 2016.

During data collection, we selected our sample as follows. *First*, as our interest lies in users' propensity to post fake news and posting fake news is a rare event throughout the platform,[10] we restricted our sample to 11,546 users who have ever been accused of posting at least one instance of fake news before the time of our data collection,[11] as suggested by the

---

[9]One might argue that fake posts could be posted by social bots that are controlled by computer algorithms and take no responsibility. After manually checking the profile of fake news creators in our sample, we are assured that the majority of the fake news creators in our sample are not bots as we clearly see they have real fans who organically interact with their posts. One potential reason is that our study focuses on fake news creators who have been reported to the platform by other users. In this case, those fake news authors should have real audiences and be less likely to be social bots.

[10]Weibo has 340 million active monthly users, but only 30,000 fake news have been reported in 7 years.

[11]A key assumption here is that the determination of fake news on Weibo is largely accurate. To validate this assumption, we randomly selected 200 fake news from our sample and manually validate them by investigating the legitimacy of the evidence provided by the accusers of each fake news. Despite a few ones about personal affairs that we cannot validate with external sources, the majority of the fake news are confirmed as fake.

literature on logistic regressions with rare events data. Commonly-used sampling strategies (e.g., randomly selecting a sample from the entire population) are grossly inefficient for rare events data [43, 72]. Our first attempt to collect data of a random sample (15,000 users) included only 13 users who were accused of posting fake news at the platform. Notably, sampling only the users with fake news should not bias our estimation. The data of users that did not post fake news would have been omitted in the estimation of our fixed-effects logit model, as there is no variation in the dependent variable (posting of fake news) for these users [48].

Second, as we leveraged an exogenous shock caused by the policy change in October 2011, we restricted our sample to those who had registered their accounts before October 2011. By doing so, we were able to gather each user' data before and after the policy change, ruling out the concern that the policy change might influence new users' decision to register on this platform. The second restriction shrinks the sample size to 6,649 users.

Third, as celebrities and opinion leaders might exhibit different behavior over social media, we removed users recognized by the platform as celebrities or opinion leaders. This restriction further reduces the sample size to about 5,000 users, which is the full sample relevant to our study.

After selecting this sample, we collected individual-level data of fake news posters. Due to technical issues, we successfully collected the posting data (from each user's registration to May 2016) of 1,335 users. Our attempt to collect additional data in 2017 was not successful, as users' badge information (e.g., time of verification) is no longer publicly available. Although 1,335 users are not a big sample in its absolute value, our sample comprised 25% of the user sample relevant to our study and 11% of all users who have ever been caught posting fake news on the platform. We believe that our data is sufficient to produce unbiased estimations.

Empirical Models and Results

Key Variables

The dependent variable in our study is $DummyPostFake_{it}$. This dummy variable equals to 1 if user i posted fake news in week t and 0 if otherwise, and accordingly, we use a logit model to estimate the coefficients. We decided to use a dummy variable rather than the actual number of weekly fake news of each user as our dependent variable, as only 111 out of 245,635 observations had the value of weekly fake news greater than 1. To ensure robustness, we replicated the analysis using $NumberPostFake_{it}$ (i.e. the actual number of fake news posted by user i in week t) as the dependent variable and a negative binomial model. These results are consistent.

We have two independent variables: $VerificationWithBadge_{it}$ and $VerificationWithNoBadge_{it}$, which equal to 1 if user i verified her identity with or without a verification badge, respectively, before or in week t.

The prior studies informed the set of controls we incorporated. First, we controlled for $DummySharedFake_{it}$ as users' behavior of posting fake news may relate to their sharing of fake news posted by other users.[12] Second, we controlled for $CumPreviousPostFake_{it}$, as users'

---

[12]As the platform does not report users' sharing of fake news, we identity whether a shared post is fake or not by matching the content of the post to that of all fake news disclosed on the platform.

Table 5. Summary for the Key Variables

Key Variables	Description
Dependent Variable:	
DummyPostFake$_{it}$	1 if individual i posted any fake news in week t; 0 otherwise
Explanatory Variables and Controls:	
VerificationWithBadge$_{it}$	1 if individual i verified her identity and got a verification badge before or in week t; 0 otherwise
VerificationWithNoBadge$_{it}$	1 if individual i verified her identity but did not get a verification badge before or in week t; 0 otherwise
DummySharedFake$_{it}$	1 if individual i shared any fake news in week t; 0 otherwise
CumPreviousPostFake$_{it}$	The total number of fake posts individual i has posted before week t
WeeklyPosts$_{it}$	The total number of posts individual i has posted in week t
Ln(WeeklyLikesOfPosts)$_{i(t-1)}$	Log of the number of likes individual i has received for all posts she posted in week $(t-1)$
Ln(WeeklySharesOfPosts)$_{i(t-1)}$	Log of the number of shares individual i has received for all posts she posted in week $(t-1)$
Ln(WeeksSinceRegist)$_{it}$	Log of how many weeks have passed since individual i registered on the platform up to week t

Table 6. Descriptive Statistics

Variable	Obs	Mean	Std. Dev.	Min	Max
DummyPostFake	246,985	0.100	0.099	0	1
VerificationWithBadge	246,985	0.448	0.497	0	1
VerificationWithNoBadge	246,985	0.333	0.471	0	1
DummySharedFake	246,985	0.004	0.035	0	1
CumPreviousPostFake	246,985	1.112	1.574	0	24
WeeklyPosts	246,985	1.444	3.824	0	191
Ln(WeeklyLikesOfPosts)	246,985	0.201	0.749	0	11.193
Ln(WeeklySharesOfPosts)	246,985	0.229	0.846	0	12.097
Ln(WeeksSinceRegist)	246,985	5.001	0.731	0	5.911

previous history of posting fake news is related to their likelihood of being verified and their future decision of posting fake news. Third, we included $WeeklyPosts_{it}$, the number of all posts (fake or not) posted by user i in week t, as identity verification may affect overall posting activity [18]. Fourth, we controlled for $Ln(WeeklyLikesOfPosts)_{i(t-1)}$ and $Ln(WeeklySharesOfPosts)_{i(t-1)}$ to account for the amount of attention user i received for her posts in the prior week [11]. Fifth, we controlled for users' posting trend over time with $Ln(WeeksSinceRegist)_{it}$. Sixth, we accounted for unobservable time-invariant individual heterogeneity (e.g., age or gender of users) with user-fixed effects and control for unobserved time-variant factors (e.g., the platform's willingness to combat fake news and seasonality) with week dummies. Table 5 summarizes the definitions of our key variables, Table 6 offers the summary statistics, and Table B1 in Online Appendix B shows the correlations among our key variables.

Models with the Exogenous Shock

In testing H1 and H2, we are mindful of the potential omitted variable bias because some users may have self-selected for identity verification. To address this concern, we leverage the policy change (October 2011-March 2012) as an exogenous shock to users' verification decisions.[13] Empirically, Weibo strongly mandated users to verify their identities during the exogenous shock period, and thus identity verification during this period is less subject to

---

[13]In the main analysis, we set the period of the exogenous shock to Oct. 2011-Mar. 2012. Considering that the platform pushed its verification policies more intensively during the last two months of the exogenous shock (Feb. 2012 - March 2012) (see Figure 2), we replicate our analysis with this shorter period as the timeframe of the exogenous shock (Section *Contributions*). Results are consistent.

self-selection bias than outside of the shock. As technical challenges prevented Weibo from mandating identity verification from all users, we identified a treatment group and a control group in this exogenous shock. In addition, whether verified users obtained a verification badge during the exogenous shock is less subject to users' self-selection, as the platform first mandated users to pass the first verification policy without a verification badge since Oct. 2011 – Jan. 2012 and then mandated users to undergo the second verification policy with a verification badge during Feb. – Mar. 2012.

To leverage this exogenous shock, we split *VerificationWithBadge* and *VerificationWithNoBadge* into four independent variables: *VerificationWithBadge (**ExoShock**)* and *VerificationWithNoBadge(**ExoShock**)* to indicate identity verification with and without a verification badge, respectively, conducted during the exogenous shock; and *VerificationWithBadge(**NoExoShock**)* and *VerificationWithNoBadge(**NoExoShock**)* to indicate identity verification with and without a verification badge, respectively, conducted out of the exogenous shock period. We rely on the coefficient of *VerificationWithNoBadge (**ExoShock**)* to test H1. We compare the coefficients of *VerificationWithNoBadge(**ExoShock**)* and *VerificationWithBadge(**ExoShock**)* to test H2, which predicts that the coefficient of *VerificationWithNoBadge(**ExoShock**)* is significantly more negative than that of *VerificationWithBadge(**ExoShock**)*. The empirical model is defined as the following:

$$P(DummyPostFake_{it} = 1|\mathrm{x}) =$$
$$\mathrm{f}(\beta_1 VerificationWithBadge(ExoShock)_{it} + \beta_2 VerificationWithNoBadge(ExoShock)_{it} +$$
$$\beta_1 VerificationWithBadge(NoExoShock)_{it} +$$
$$\beta_2 VerificationWithNoBadge(NoExoShock)_{it} + ControlVariables + H'_1 + R'\chi_1 + \varepsilon_{it})$$

$$(1)$$

where H is the vector of individual-fixed effects, R is the vector of week dummies, and ε indicates the error term. Because the dependent variable is dichotomous, we used a logit model. To reduce heteroscedasticity concerns, we used robust standard errors clustered at the user level.

Results

Estimation results are shown in Table 7. In Table 7, Column 1 presents the result without the exogenous shock. It shows that the coefficient of *VerificationWithNoBadge* is negative and significant, while the coefficient of *VerificationWithBadge* is positive and significant. This result suggests that users' propensity to post fake news decreases after identity verification without a verification badge, but increases after verification with a verification badge. Again, we acknowledge that the coefficients of verification in Column 1 could be affected by self-selection bias. Thus, we rely on Column 2, which uses the exogenous shock to infer the impact of identity verification. Here, the coefficient of *VerificationWithNoBadge(**ExoShock**)* is significantly negative. In addition, it is significantly more negative than that of *VerificationWithBadge (**ExoShock**)*. This result demonstrates that identity verification without a verification badge negatively impacts users' propensity to post fake news, thus supporting H1. However, this impact is significantly weakened when users receive a verification badge, thus supporting H2.

Interestingly, while the coefficient of *VerificationWithBadge(**ExoShock**)* is not significant in Column 2 of Table 7, the coefficient of *VerificationWithBadge(**NoExoShock**)* is positive and significant ($p < 0.01$). This result suggests that when users volunteer to verify their identities

Table 7. Impact of Identity Verification on Users' Propensity to Post Fake News

VARIABLES	(1) DummyPostFake	(2) DummyPostFake
VerificationWithNoBadge	-1.046**	
	(0.467)	
VerificationWithBadge	0.601***	
	(0.142)	
VerificationWithNoBadge(ExoShock)		-1.105**
		(0.531)
VerificationWithBadge(ExoShock)		0.407
		(0.259)
VerificationWithNoBadge(NoExoShock)		-0.359
		(1.072)
VerificationWithBadge(NoExoShock)		0.671***
		(0.163)
Control Variables:		
DummySharedFake	1.539***	1.023***
	(0.140)	(0.104)
CumPreviousPostFake	-0.620***	-0.451***
	(0.0253)	(0.0259)
WeeklyPosts	0.0380***	0.0379***
	(0.00157)	(0.00393)
Lag.Ln(WeeklyLikesOfPosts)	0.152***	0.142***
	(0.0377)	(0.0401)
Lag.Ln(WeeklySharesOfPosts)	0.172***	0.218***
	(0.0286)	(0.0284)
Ln(WeeksSinceRegist)	0.722***	0.303
	(0.234)	(0.214)
Observations	245,635	245,635
Number of Users	1,335	1,335
Individual Fixed-Effects	Yes	Yes
Week Fixed-Effects	Yes	Yes

Standard errors clustered in individuals in parentheses *** $p<0.01$, ** $p<0.05$, * $p<0.1$

and the verified status is explicitly disclosed with a badge, users are more likely to post fake news after verification. One potential explanation is that when users realize that their verified status will be disclosed by a badge after verification, the increased benefit of posting fake news (given by the badge as a signal of credibility) may incentivize some users to actively verify their identities and take more risks to post fake news. This indicates that a verification badge produces a perverse incentive to post fake news, as proposed in our theoretical discussion.

Robustness Checks

Our theory relies on several assumptions, the violation of which could challenge the robustness of our study. Therefore, we conducted additional robustness checks to rule out alternate possibilities. These include: 1) a survey on crowdsourcing platforms to support the mechanisms proposed in our theoretical discussion; 2) a replication of our main analysis using propensity score matching (PSM); 3) an analysis of users who passed two verification policies in a reversed order; 4) an analysis of the impact of identity verification on users' propensity to share fake news. Each of these robustness tests consistently supports the findings in our main analysis.

Mechanical Turk Survey

To support the mechanisms proposed in our theoretical discussion, we designed a survey about users' reactions to identity verification and their decisions relevant to posting fake news, and sent the survey to both American users of Twitter and Chinese users of Weibo. Detailed survey information can be found in Online Appendix A. The goal of the survey is to find support for the following assumptions we made that are critical to our theorization:

(1) When users have the option to verify their accounts with phone numbers or IDs, they prefer to verify their accounts with phone numbers. Therefore, the second verification policy (which requires either phone numbers or IDs) is not significantly more costly than the first policy (which requires only phone numbers).

(2) A *Micro Identity* badge in the second verification policy serves as an explicit disclosure of users' verified status (namely, a verification badge), while a *Rulaishenzhen* badge in the first verification policy does not. In other words, the second verification policy has a verification badge, and the first verification policy does not.

We also leverage the survey to validate the theoretical arguments we made in the hypotheses:

(1) Users generally validate the credibility of news before they post it from their accounts.

(2) After identity verification, users would be more willing to validate the credibility of news and be less willing to post suspicious news.

(3) Users expect that a verification badge endows extra credibility and attracts more engagement for their posts.

(4) After identity verification, if users know that suspicious news is likely to receive a lot of engagement due to the verification badge, they will be more willing to post the suspicious news.

We recruited Weibo users for our survey using a leading crowdsourcing platform in China (wenjuan.com[14]). We chose a more commonly-used website in China than Amazon Mechanical Turk (MTurk), as our trials on MTurk had difficulties to hire enough participants who use Weibo. We listed our task on the crowdsourcing platform in October 2020 and paid 2 Chinese Yuan (around 0.3 US dollars) for each participant. To ensure quality, each unique IP address is allowed to participate only once and careless participants are excluded from the sample. Next, we recruited Twitter users by listing this survey on MTurk in October 2020 and paid 0.3 US dollars for each response. We also excluded careless participants based on validity of their answers. In total, we collected about 200 valid responses from Weibo and Twitter users, respectively.

---

[14]Wenjuan.com boasts over 600,000 users and has helped over 100 million online participants to be reached by companies, media, governments and colleges. Its customers include Alibaba, Tsinghua University, and other well-known corporations and institutions.

Results in Table A1 (Online Appendix A1) support our assumptions in this study: 1) the participants predominately prefer to verify with phone numbers (84%) than IDs (16%); 2) they are substantially more likely to consider the *Micro Identity* badge (55%) as a verification badge than the *Rulaishenzhen* badge (8%). More importantly, results also support our arguments in the hypotheses: 1) most users (92%) validate the credibility of news before they post; 2) users become more willing (95% vs. 92%) to validate fake news and less willing (43% vs. 62%) to post suspicious news after identity verification than before; 3) half of the surveyed users (47%) expect that a verification badge can bring more credibility and engagement for their posts; and 4) users' willingness to post suspicious news after identity verification becomes stronger (66% vs. 43%) if they know the suspicious news is likely to receive a lot of engagement due to the verification badge than if not.

Propensity Score Matching

In Equation 1, we leverage a policy change as an exogenous shock to users' verification decisions, which was implemented in batches and not applied to all users. If the platform selected certain users for verification during this shock in a non-random manner, our estimation would be biased. Although users' online discussion and the descriptive statistics suggest no pre-treatment difference between the treated and the untreated users (Table 3), we employed a propensity score matching (PSM) to further ensure robustness.

We executed the PSM for identity verification with and without badges, respectively. First, we used logit models to predict each user's propensity to verify her identity without a verification badge in week t with user characteristics in week $(t-1)$ such as *gender, availability of age information, age, paid member, CumPreviousPostFake, CumPreviousSharedFake, Lag.WeeklyPosts, Lag.WeeklySharedPosts, Lag. Ln(WeeklyLikesOfPosts), Lag.Ln(WeeklySharesOfPosts), Lag.Ln(WeeklyLikesOfShared), Lag.Ln(WeeklySharesOfShared),* and *Ln(WeeksSinceRegist)*. Based on the predicted propensity, we then used one-to-one dynamic matching (with replacement) and a caliper width of 0.01. We used the PSM results to estimate the impact of identity without a verification badge. Second, we repeated this process to match each user's propensity to verify her identity with a verification badge in week t and use the PSM results to estimate the impact of identity with a verification badge. To ensure the success of our matching, we compared the differences in covariates across the matched sets (Online Appendix B: Table B2 and Table B3). Results suggest no difference across groups.

Results of the PSM are in Table 8. Column 1 shows the PSM estimation of the impact of verification without a verification badge. Here, the coefficient of *VerificationWithNoBadge* is negative and significant, indicating a negative impact of identity verification without a verification badge on users' posting of fake news. This result supports H1. Column 2 shows the PSM estimation for the impact of verification with a verification badge. The coefficient of *VerificationWithBadge* is insignificant and significantly less negative than that of *VerificationWithNoBadge*, supporting H2.

The results consistently suggest that while identity verification without a badge has a significantly negative impact on users' propensity to post fake news, a verification badge could weaken this impact of identity verification. Thus, H1 and H2 are supported.

Table 8. Propensity Score Matching (PSM)

VARIABLES	(1) PSM Match Users Who Verified without A Verification Badge to Others Who Did Not Verify DummyPostFake	(2) PSM Match Users Who Verified with A Verification Badge to Others Who Did Not Verify DummyPostFake
VerificationWithNoBadge	-4.256***	
	(1.253)	
VerificationWithBadge		0.337
		(0.236)
Observations	25,167	32,622
Number of Users	977	1,415

Standard errors clustered in individuals in parentheses *** p<0.01, ** p<0.05, * p<0.1
Note: we use logit models to predict each user's propensity to take the treatment in week *t* with user characteristics in week *t*-1 such as *gender, age, availability of age information, whether user is a paid member, CumPreviousPostFake, CumPreviousSharedFake, Lag.WeeklyPosts, Lag.WeeklyShared, Lag.Ln(WeeklyLikesOfPost), Lag.Ln(WeeklySharesOfPost), Lag. Ln(WeeklyLikesOfShared), Lag.Ln(WeeklySharesOfShared),* and *Ln(WeeksSinceRegist).*

Order of Passing the Two Verification Policies

We recognize two concerns about our main analysis on the verification badge. First of all, since not all users in our sample passed the two identity verification policies (with and without a verification badge), our method to test the moderating effect of a verification badge may reflect the heterogeneous impacts of individual characteristics rather than the role of a verification badge itself, if users' preference of a verification policy is determined by their unobserved characteristics. Second, since the identity verification without a verification badge was introduced earlier (in 2010) than the one with a verification badge (in 2012), the different impacts of these two verification methods may be a byproduct of this particular ordering. For example, before users underwent the second verification policy (with a verification badge), they may have already passed the first verification policy (without a verification badge). In this case, the first verification policy should reduce the posting of fake news due to the restrictions it put on users. But, the second verification policy might not have any effect because it did not cause any additional restrictions on those who had been verified.

To address the above two concerns, we replicated our main analysis by only including users 1) who passed both verification policies, and 2) who passed the 2nd policy first.[15] Table 9 shows that the results of this analysis are consistent with our main analysis in Table 7. Thus, H1 and H2 are consistently supported.

Impact of Identity Verification on Users' Propensity to Share Fake News

To further examine the effect of identity verification on the spread of fake news, we replicated our analyses with users' propensity to share fake news. Ideally, we should see a similar (possibly smaller) impact of identity verification on users' propensity to share fake news, given the same types of benefits, costs, and risks for posting and sharing fake news on social media.

---

[15] We note that the platform did not remove the first verification method after the second one was introduced. While data suggest that most users verified their accounts with only the second method after February 2011, some users still verified with the first method after they already verified with the second method, potentially due to a misunderstanding of the policies. We had 86 such users in our sample, who passed the second verification policy and later passed the first verification policy again.

Table 9. Analysis of the Users Who Passed Both Identity Verification in A Reversed Order

VARIABLES	(1) DummyPostFake	(2)
VerificationWithNoBadge	-0.150	
	(0.223)	
VerificationWithBadge	0.714***	
	(0.159)	
VerificationWithNoBadge (ExoShock)		-1.864***
		(0.580)
VerificationWithBadge (ExoShock)		0.673**
		(0.329)
VerificationWithNoBadge (NoExoShock)		0.00835
		(0.234)
VerificationWithBadge (NoExoShock)		0.742***
		(0.178)
Control Variables:		
DummySharedFake	1.375***	1.382***
	(0.439)	(0.439)
CumPreviousPostFake	-0.491***	-0.491***
	(0.0648)	(0.0648)
WeeklyPosts	0.0300***	0.0301***
	(0.00438)	(0.00439)
Lag.Ln(WeeklyLikesOfPosts)	0.143*	0.145*
	(0.0742)	(0.0743)
Lag.Ln(WeeklySharesOfPosts)	0.116	0.112
	(0.108)	(0.108)
Ln(WeeksSinceRegist)	1.122	1.237*
	(0.724)	(0.732)
Observations	15,731	15,731
Number of Users	86	86
Individual Fixed-Effects	Yes	Yes
Week Fixed-Effects	Yes	Yes

Standard errors clustered in individuals in parentheses *** $p<0.01$, ** $p<0.05$, * $p<0.1$

Empirically, we used a new dependent variable, $DummyShareFake_{it}$, which equals to 1 if user i shared someone else's fake news on her account in week t, and 0 otherwise. The results are in Table 10, which provides a consistent result with our main analysis. The significantly negative coefficient of *VerificationWithNoBadge(**ExoShock**)* in Column 2 indicates that identity verification without a verification badge reduces users' propensity to share fake news. The coefficient of *VerificationWithNoBadge(**ExoShock**)* is significantly more negative than that of *VerificationWithBadge(**ExoShock**)* in Column 2, suggesting that a verification badge significantly undermines the effect of verification on users' propensity to share fake news. These results consistently support our arguments for H1 and H2.

Discussion

Key Findings

In this study, we examined how identity verification affects users' posting of fake news on social media. We used a novel dataset from a large micro-blog website, a robust identification strategy based on an exogenous policy change, and propensity score matching. Our study found that, while identity verification without a verification badge reduces users' propensity to post fake news, identity verification with a verification badge does not. These mixed effects suggest that the presence of a verification badge for verified accounts significantly weakens

Table 10. Impact of Identity Verification on Users' Propensity to Share Fake News

VARIABLES	(1)	(2)
	DummyShareFake	
VerificationWithNoBadge	-0.667***	
	(0.204)	
VerificationWithBadge	0.314**	
	(0.144)	
VerificationWithNoBadge (ExoShock)		-1.631***
		(0.559)
VerificationWithBadge (ExoShock)		0.0431
		(0.341)
VerificationWithNoBadge (NoExoShock)		0.135
		(0.209)
VerificationWithBadge (NoExoShock)		0.0841
		(0.170)
Control Variables:		
DummyPostFake	0.685***	0.684***
	(0.116)	(0.116)
CumPreviousSharedFake	0.593***	0.599***
	(0.0300)	(0.0300)
WeeklySharedPosts	0.0408***	0.0412***
	(0.00167)	(0.00167)
Lag.Ln(WeeklyLikesOf SharedPosts)	0.253***	0.254***
	(0.0299)	(0.0299)
Lag.Ln(WeeklySharesOf SharedPosts)	-0.0236	-0.0257
	(0.0423)	(0.0424)
Ln(WeeksSinceRegist)	0.364	0.334
	(0.235)	(0.233)
Observations	245,635	245,635
Number of Users	1,335	1,335
Individual Fixed-Effects	Yes	Yes
Week Fixed-Effects	Yes	Yes

Standard errors clustered in individuals in parentheses
*** $p<0.01$, ** $p<0.05$, * $p<0.1$

the impact of identity verification. More interestingly, we found that when users volunteer to pass identity verification with a verification badge, they post more fake news after verification. Our results underscore the potential of leveraging identity verification to deter the spread of fake news on social media and highlight the negative consequences if the platforms publicly disclose users' verified status in their design of identity verification policies.

Generalizability

Given the idiosyncrasies of the empirical investigation, we take several precautions to ensure the generalizability of our findings. As suggested by the idea of structural causal models [3], we discuss the generalizability from three angles: 1) the Weibo setting, 2) the selection of fake news, and 3) the proposed mechanisms across platforms and countries.

We believe that the observed effects should not be limited to the Weibo setting. As discussed, we compared the interface and functions of platforms, definitions of fake news, and the designs of identity verification policies on Weibo and Twitter, the two leading microblogging platforms in the world. We found no observable differences across the settings of these platforms. Specifically, users can write a post with up to 140 characters (before the time of data collection), follow other users' posts, and share/comment/like others' posts. In addition, both Weibo and Twitter define fake news as news posts that are completely false or misleading due to the inclusion of exaggerated, outdated, or incomplete information. The identity verification policies are also similarly implemented on both platforms, using equivalent verification methods (viz. phone numbers or government-issued IDs) and comparable designs (viz. with versus without a verification badge) (see the discussions in §3.1).

It is also worth considering if the fake news we selected in the sample is representative. Our study excluded all fake news relevant to the government or politics from our sample, considering the sensitivity of fake political news, albeit only a few. In doing so, we aim to alleviate the concern that our findings are not generalizable across countries with different political environments.

To ensure that our theoretical mechanisms on identity verification and verification badges can be generalized outside of Weibo and China, we surveyed American and Chinese users of Twitter and Weibo (discussed in §5.1). Details of the survey are in Online Appendix A1. The results support the key assumptions critical to our theorization and the theoretical arguments we made in the hypotheses. This evidence assures us that the proposed effects are not unique to Chinese users.

Contributions

We contribute to the IS literature in three key ways. *First*, we contribute to the burgeoning literature on fake news diffusion over social media [7, 68, 74]. While scholars have examined the spread of fake news [12, 26, 40, 74], an issue that is damaging society by eroding public trust [4], most of the current literature has focused on how to detect fake news after it has been posted and spread. To our knowledge, few studies have investigated how to design an information system to address this issue before it happens, viz. the posting of fake news over social media. Our study fills this gap in the literature.

Second, although prior studies have investigated the general impact of identity verification policies on social media users [17, 18, 39], we contribute to the literature by specifically focusing on a design component in identity verification that has received scant attention to date from IS scholars: the verification badge. This study offers an important insight into how a verification badge moderates the effectiveness of identity verification. Given that many social media platforms disclose users' verified status by giving users a badge after identity verification, an initial assessment of the role of such badge can help the platforms better design their verification systems to deter fake news.

Third, while prior work on identity verification generally suggests that identity verification can effectively deter user misconduct on social media [18, 29], we show both the positive and negative consequences of identity verification. Specifically, our findings illustrate the possibility that a verification badge may incentivize malicious users to "game" the verification system and thereafter engage in misconduct more frequently. This finding highlights a need for future work in this area to further investigate the unintended consequences that may appear when the platforms allow voluntary verification and privilege users with erroneous endorsements at the same time. Our finding of the mixed effects of identity verification on fake news extends and deepens our knowledge of how to implement comprehensive and robust identity verification strategies.

Implications for Practice

Our findings yield important implications for social media managers. First, our study offers practical insights into the trade-off in leveraging identity verification to combat fake news. Social media platforms are increasingly using identity verification to combat the proliferation of fake news, despite user resistance [17]. Platforms aim to suppress the spread of fake news by holding users responsible for their actions while on the platform [39]. However, as this study shows, identity verification may not always work as platforms expect. With findings of a significant impact of identity verification without verification badges and an insignificant impact of identity verification with verification badges, our study highlights that social media platforms must re-evaluate the effectiveness of their current identity verification systems.

Second, the finding that a verification badge weakens the effectiveness of identity verification raises concerns about badges in identity verification systems. Our study suggests that the platforms should be more careful in using badges to encourage identity verification, as an explicit status disclosure may steer user behavior in other unintended ways. Given the moderating effect of a verification badge in weakening the impact of identity verification, as well as the possibility that malicious users may voluntarily verify their identities to obtain the verification badge and post more fake news, platforms should consider not disclosing verified status, especially when users volunteer to verify their accounts.

Third, the implications of this study can be extended to other platforms where user credibility is essential for the sustainability of these platforms, such as dating websites (i.e., Match.com), professional networking websites (i.e., LinkedIn), and crowdfunding platforms (i.e., Kickstarter). Many of these platforms rely on a verification policy to ensure the reliability of their users; moreover, they often employ badges to disclose users' verified status and allow voluntary verification as well. Our findings suggest that these digital platforms should reconsider awarding verified users. Platform managers should be aware that a verification badge or any other form of privilege for verified users may undermine the restrictions on user behavior placed by identity verification and even incentivize user misconduct.

Limitations and Suggestions for Future Research

We note several limitations with our study. First, our data on fake news may be incomplete, as not all fake news has been detected and announced by Weibo. However, as long as the incompleteness of fake news detection is not related to our independent variable (identity verification), our estimations are unlikely to be biased. Second, we recognize that the platform's ability to accurately determine fake news is unlikely to be perfect due to the nature of fake news. While we believe the determination of fake news in our sample is accurate mainly based on the platforms' process and our manual validation, we include time-fixed effects to further alleviate potential bias due to detection inaccuracy at the platform level. Third, we make several assumptions in our analysis. For example, we assumed that the impact of identity verification did not fundamentally change after our data collection (2016), and most users would naturally choose phone numbers over government ID to fulfill verification requirement. Although data limitations prevented us from testing our assumptions directly, we support our assumptions with manual reviews of the data and online surveys.

Our discussions of identity verification and the spread of fake news suggest many opportunities for future research. First, does the type (viz. political or non-political) of fake news matter? Specifically, will the impact of identity verification and verification badges we identified in this paper remain the same on users' posting of fake political news? For example, one key argument we made in the paper is that most users evaluate the credibility of the news they intent to post, and identity verification makes them more willing to validate and less willing to post suspicious news. However, one might argue that many people hold strong political bias that can be used heuristically when evaluating political news, making them less likely to suspect political news that is aligned with their bias. Thus, researchers can study if identity verification is effective in reducing users' posting of fake political news.

Second, we found that the impact of identity verification depends on whether users obtain a verification badge after identity verification. Future studies should explore how other factors, such as the characteristics of the verified users (e.g., reputation), influence the interplay between identity verification and the posting of fake news. For example, identity verification might discipline well-known users to a greater extent and offer fewer restrictions for relatively unknown accounts.

Third, researchers can investigate how a platform's verification policies influence users' other behaviors and interactions on the platform. For example, if a user verifies her identity, will she become more or less active in terms of posting, sharing, or engaging with other users?

Fourth, our study examines the impact of identity verification on the spread of fake news on social media, but it remains unclear how identity verification may influence user behavior on other platforms, such as online dating and online labor markets. Specifically, does identity verification influence the matching rate of online dating? Will it impact the efficiency of online recruiting?

Concluding Remarks

Although fake news is not a new problem, social media and the internet have certainly exacerbated it. Behind the curtain of anonymity the internet creates, social media users have largely participated in the process of posting and propagating fake news, intentionally and unintentionally. Identity verification is increasingly used as a *de facto* solution by many social media platforms to suppress the proliferation of fake news. Yet, the limited means by which empirical evidence can be gathered from social media has hitherto prevented the academic community from making data-driven concrete recommendations for designing effective identity verification systems. Presumably, due to the lack of knowledge of its effectiveness, social media platforms are still experimenting with different identity verification policies after many years of practice. For example, while Facebook and Instagram allow users to voluntarily request identity verification with a verification badge,[16] Twitter suspended this option.[17] In this context, our study offers important theoretical, practical, and policy implications. Our findings inform practitioners that an effective design of identity

---

[16]https://www.facebook.com/help/1288173394636262
[17]https://www.recode.net/2018/3/8/17098008/twitter-verification-jack-dorsey-all-users

verification systems can reduce users' posting of fake news, while a poorly-designed system may even exacerbate the fake news problem that social media platforms set out to solve.

Disclosure statement

No potential conflict of interest was reported by the author(s).

References

1. Akdeniz, Y. Anonymity, democracy, and cyberspace. *Social Research: An International Quarterly*, 69, 1 (2002), 223–237.
2. Albright, J. Welcome to the era of fake news. *Communication*, 5, 2 (2017), 87–89.
3. Ali, N., Chater, N., and Oaksford, M. The mental representation of causal conditional reasoning: Mental models or causal models. *Cognition*, 119, 3 (2011), 403–418.
4. Allcott, H., and Gentzkow, M. Social media and fake news in the 2016 election. *Journal of Economic Perspectives*, 31, 2 (2017), 211–236.
5. Aphiwongsophon, S., and Chongstitvatana, P. Detecting fake news with machine learning method. *2018 15th International Conference on Electrical Engineering/Electronics, Computer, Telecommunications and Information Technology (ECTI-CON): IEEE* (2018), pp. 528–531.
6. Armstrong, C., and McAdams, M. Blogs of information: How gender cues and individual motivations influence perceptions of credibility. *Journal of Computer-Mediated Communication* (2009)14(3), 435–456.
7. Bakir, V., and McStay, A. Fake news and the economy of emotions: Problems, causes, solutions. *Digital Journalism*, 6, 2 (2018), 154–175.
8. Baym, N., Zhang, Y., and Lin, M.-C. Social interactions across media: Interpersonal communication on the internet, telephone and face-to-face. *New Media & Society*, 6, 3 (2004), 299–318.

9. BBC. Twitter user numbers overtaken by China's Sina Weibo. (2017).

10. Bernard JG, Dennis A, Galletta D, Khan A, Webster J. The Tangled Web: Studying online fake news. A Working Paper (2019).

11. Bock, G, Zmud, R., Kim, Y., and Lee, J. Behavioral intention formation in knowledge sharing: Examining the roles of extrinsic motivators, social-psychological forces, and organizational climate. *MIS Quarterly* (2005), 87–111.

12. Borden, S., and Tew, C. The role of journalist and the performance of journalism: Ethical lessons from "fake" news (seriously). *Journal of Mass Media Ethics*, 22, 4 (2007), 300–314.

13. Cardoso, F., Vieira, R., and Garcia, A. Can machines learn to detect fake news? a survey focused on social media. *Proceedings of the 52nd Hawaii International Conference on System Sciences* (2019).

14. Chen, J., Xu, H., and Whinston, A.B. Moderated online communities and quality of user-generated content. *Journal of Management Information Systems*, 28, 2 (2011), 237–268.

15. Chen, S., and Pol'y, P. What's in a Name: Facebook's Real Name Policy and User Privacy. *Kan. JL & Pub. Pol'y* 28 (2018), 146.

16. Chiou, L., and Tucker, C. Fake news and advertising on social media: A study of the anti-vaccination movement. *National Bureau of Economic Research* (2018).

17. Cho, D. Real name verification law on the Internet: A poison or cure for privacy?. *Economics of Information Security and Privacy III: Springer* (2013), pp. 239–261.

18. Cho, D., Kim, S., and Acquisti, A. Empirical analysis of online anonymity and user behaviors: the impact of real name policy. *System Science (HICSS) (2012), 45th Hawaii International Conference on: IEEE* (2012) pp. 3041–3050.

19. Cho, D., and Kwon, K. The impacts of identity verification and disclosure of social cues on flaming in online user comments. *Computers in Human Behavior* (2015), 363–372.

20. Christopherson, K. The positive and negative implications of anonymity in Internet social interactions:"On the Internet, Nobody Knows You're a Dog". *Computers in Human Behavior*, 23, 6 (2007), 3038–3056.

21. Clarke, R., and Felson, M. Routine activity and rational choice. *Transaction Publishers* (1993).

22. Connelly, B., Certo, S., Ireland, R., and Reutzel, C. Signaling theory: A review and assessment. *Journal of Management*, 37, 1 (2011), 39–67.

23. Cornish, D., and Clarke, R. Understanding crime displacement: An application of rational choice theory. *Criminology*, 25, 4 (1987), 933–948.

24. Danielson, D. Web credibility. *Encyclopedia of human computer interaction: IGI Global* (2006), pp. 713–721.

25. Edwards, L., and McAuley, D. What's in a name? Real name policies and social networks. *Proceedings of 1st International Workshop on Internet Science and Web Science Synergies (INETWEBSCI)*, Paris, France (2013).

26. Farsetta, D. and Price, D. Fake TV News. *Center for Media and Democracy* (2006).

27. Flanagin, A., and Metzger, M. The role of site features, user attributes, and information verification behaviors on the perceived credibility of web-based information. *New Media & Society*, 9, 2 (2007), 319–342.

28. Friedman, B., Khan, P., and Howe, D. Trust online. *Communications of the ACM*, 43, 12 (2000), 34–40.

29. Fu, K., Chan, C., and Chau, M. Assessing censorship on microblogs in China: Discriminatory keyword analysis and the real-name registration policy. *IEEE Internet Computing*, 17, 3 (2013), 42–50.

30. Ge, R., Feng, J., Gu, B. and Zhang, P. Predicting and deterring default with social media information in peer-to-peer lending. *Journal of Management Information Systems*, 34 (2017), pp.401–424.

31. Gibson, D., Ostashewski, N., Flintoff, K., Grant, S., and Knight, E. Digital badges in education. *Education and Information Technologies*, 20, 2 (2015), 403–410.

32. Gilda, S. Evaluating machine learning algorithms for fake news detection. *2017 IEEE 15th Student Conference on Research and Development (SCOReD): IEEE* (2017), pp. 110–115.

33. Gimpel, H., Heger, S., Olenberger, C., and Utz, L. The effectiveness of social norms in fighting fake news on social media. *Journal of Management Information Systems*, 38, 1 (2021), 196–221.

34. Gintis, H., Smith, E., and Bowles, S. Costly signaling and cooperation. *Journal of Theoretical Biology*, 213, 1 (2001), 103–119.

35. Granik, M., and Mesyura, V. Fake news detection using naive Bayes classifier. *2017 IEEE First Ukraine Conference on Electrical and Computer Engineering (UKRCON): IEEE* (2017), pp. 900–903.

36. Grinberg, N., Joseph, K., Friedland, L., Swire-Thompson, B., and Lazer, D. Fake news on Twitter during the 2016 US presidential election. *Science*, 363, 6425 (2019), 374–378.

37. Gsell, L. Comments anonymous: newspaper Web sites wrestle with offensive blog comments. *American Journalism Review*, 31, 1 (2009), 16–18.

38. Johnson, D. Ethics online. *Communications of the ACM*, 40, 1 (1997), 60–65.

39. Kaminski, M. Real masks and real name policies: Applying anti-mask case law to anonymous online speech. Fordham Intell. Prop. *Media & Ent. LJ*, 23 (2012), 815.

40. Khaldarova, I., and Pantti, M. Fake news: The narrative battle over the Ukrainian conflict. *Journalism Practice*, 10, 7 (2016), 891–901.

41. Kim, A., and Dennis, A. Says who? The effects of presentation format and source rating on fake news in social media. *MIS Quarterly*, 43, 3 (2019).

42. Kim, A., Moravec, P., and Dennis, A. Combating fake news on social media with source ratings: the effects of user and expert reputation ratings. *Journal of Management Information Systems*, 36, 3 (2019), 931–968.

43. King, G., and Zeng, L. Explaining rare events in international relations. *International Organization*, 55, 3 (2001), 693–715.

44. Kraut, R., Fish, R., Root, R., and Chalfonte, B. Informal communication in organizations: Form, function, and technology. *Human Reactions to Technology: Claremont Symposium on Applied Social Psychology: Citeseer* (1990), pp. 145–199.

45. Lazer, D., Baum, M., Benkler, Y., Berinsky, A., Greenhill, K., Menczer, F., Metzger, M., Nyhan, B., Pennycook, G., and Rothschild, D. The science of fake news. *Science*, 359, 6380 (2018), 1094–1096.

46. Li, J., and Su, M. Real Talk About Fake News: Identity Language and Disconnected Networks of the US Public's "Fake News" Discourse on Twitter. *Social Media+ Society*, 6, 2 (2020).

47. Mele, N., Lazer, D., Baum, M., Grinberg, N., Friedland, L., Joseph, K., Hobbs, W., and Mattsson, C. Combating fake news: An agenda for research and action. *Retrieved on October* (2017).

48. Menard, S. Applied Logistic Regression Analysis. *Sage*, 2002.

49. Moravec, P., Kim, A., and Dennis, A. Appealing to Sense and Sensibility: System 1 and System 2 Interventions for Fake News on Social Media. *Information Systems Research* (2020).

50. Mustafaraj, E., and Metaxas, P. The fake news spreading plague: was it preventable?. *Proceedings of the 2017 ACM on Web Science Conference* (2017), pp. 235–239.

51. Nagin, D., and Paternoster, R. Enduring individual differences and rational choice theories of crime. *Law and Society Review* (1993), 467–496.

52. Omernick, E., and Sood, S. The impact of anonymity in online communities. Social Computing (SocialCom), *2013 International Conference on: IEEE* (2013), pp. 526–535.

53. Rainie, H., Anderson, J., and Albright, J. The future of free speech, trolls, anonymity and fake news online. *Pew Research Center Washington* (2017).

54. Rainie, L., Kiesler, S., Kang, R., Madden, M., Duggan, M., Brown, S., and Dabbish, L. Anonymity, privacy, and security online. *Pew Research Center Washington* (2013).

55. Reiter, M., and Rubin, A. Crowds: Anonymity for web transactions. *ACM Transactions on Information and System Security (TISSEC)*, 1, 1 (1998), 66–92.

56. Robinson, S., and Deshano, C. Citizen journalists and their third places: What makes people exchange information online (or not)?. *Journalism Studies*, 12, 5 (2011), 642–657.

57. Rosenberry, J. Users support online anonymity despite increasing negativity. *Newspaper Research Journal*, 32, 2 (2011), 6–19.

58. Rösner, L., and Krämer, N. Verbal venting in the social web: Effects of anonymity and group norms on aggressive language use in online comments. *Social Media+ Society*, 2, 3 (2016).

59. Rubin, V., Chen, Y., and Conroy, N. Deception detection for news: three types of fakes. Proceedings of the 78th ASIS&T Annual Meeting: Information Science with Impact: Research in and for the Community: *American Society for Information Science* (2015), pp. 83.

60. Ruesch, M., and Märker, O. Real name policy in E-participation. *Conference for E-democracy and Open Government* (2012), pp. 109.

61. Santana, A. Virtuous or vitriolic: The effect of anonymity on civility in online newspaper reader comment boards. *Journalism Practice*, 8, 1 (2014), 18–33.

62. Shao, C., Ciampaglia, G., Varol, O., Flammini, A., and Menczer, F. The spread of fake news by social bots. *arXiv preprint arXiv*, 96 (2017), 104.

63. Shu, K., Sliva, A., Wang, S., Tang, J., and Liu, H. Fake news detection on social media: A data mining perspective. *ACM SIGKDD Explorations Newsletter*, 19, 1 (2017), 22–36.

64. Shu, K., Wang, S., and Liu, H. Beyond news contents: The role of social context for fake news detection. *Proceedings of the Twelfth ACM International Conference on Web Search and Data Mining* (2019), pp. 312–320.

65. Shu, K., Mahudeswaran, D., Wang, S., & Liu, H. Hierarchical propagation networks for fake news detection: Investigation and exploitation. *In Proceedings of the International AAAI Conference on Web and Social Media (2020)*, Vol. 14, pp. 626–637.

66. SouthChinaMorningPost. China's Twitter-like Weibo orders users to register their real names. (2017).

67. Stieglitz, S. and Dang-Xuan, L. Emotions and information diffusion in social media—sentiment of microblogs and sharing behavior. *Journal of Management Information Systems*, 29 (2013), pp.217–248.

68. Susarla, A., Oh, J., and Tan, Y. Social networks and the diffusion of user-generated content: Evidence from YouTube. *Information Systems Research*, 23, 1 (2012), 23–41.

69. Sydell, L. We tracked down a fake-news creator in the suburbs. here's what we learned. *National Public Radio*, 23 (2016).

70. Tandoc, E., Lim, Z., and Ling, R. Defining "fake news" A typology of scholarly definitions. *National Public Radio*, 6, 2 (2018), 137–153.

71. Tandoc, E., and Vos, T. The journalist is marketing the news: Social media in the gatekeeping process. *Digital Journalism*, 10, 8 (2016), 950–966.

72. Van Den Eeckhaut, M., Vanwalleghem, T., Poesen, J., Govers, G., Verstraeten, G., and Vandekerckhove, L. Prediction of landslide susceptibility using rare events logistic regression: a case-study in the Flemish Ardennes (Belgium). *Geomorphology*, 76, 3–4 (2006), 392–410.

73. Vo, N., and Lee, K. The rise of guardians: Fact-checking url recommendation to combat fake news. *The 41st International ACM SIGIR Conference on Research & Development in Information Retrieval* (2018), pp. 275–284.

74. Vosoughi, S., Roy, D., and Aral, S. The spread of true and false news online. *Science*, 359, 6380 (2018), 1146–1151.

75. Wasko, M., and Faraj, S. "It is what one does": why people participate and help others in electronic communities of practice. *The Journal of Strategic Information Systems*, 9, 2–3 (2000), 155–173.

76. Waszak, P., Kasprzycka-Waszak, W., Kubanek, A. The spread of medical fake news in social media–the pilot quantitative study. *Health Policy and Technology*, 7, 2 (2018), 115–118.

77. Zhou, X., and Zafarani, R. Fake news detection: An interdisciplinary research. *Companion Proceedings of The 2019 World Wide Web Conference* (2019), pp. 1292–1292.

Emotions: The Unexplored Fuel of Fake News on Social Media

Christy Galletta Horner ⓘ, Dennis Galletta ⓘ, Jennifer Crawford ⓘ, and Abhijeet Shirsat ⓘ

ABSTRACT

Easy access to equipment, software, and platforms to create, distribute, and provide access to fake news stories has exacerbated the problem of fake news, making for a large number of highly biased sources that are reaching the mainstream through social networks. The economics of emotion theory proposes that fake news headlines are created to evoke emotional responses in readers that will cause them to interact with the article in a way that allows the creator to make a profit (through clicking on the link to the full article, by sharing the article, etc.). This mixed methods study investigates the process by which individuals experience discrete emotional reactions to fake news headlines, and how these emotions contribute to the perpetuation of fake news through sharing behaviors. U.S. participants (n=879 across two waves) viewed one of eight false news headlines and reported their emotional reactions, belief in the headline, and potential sharing behaviors. In general, participants were more likely to believe headlines that aligned with their existing beliefs (e.g., liberals were more likely to believe negative news about conservatives), reacted with more negative emotions to headlines that attacked their party, and were more likely to report intentions to suppress (e.g., post a link to a fact check) fake news that attacked their own party. Emotional reactivity of participants was associated with response behavior intentions such that participants who reported high levels of emotions were more likely to take actions that would spread or suppress the fake news, participants who reported low levels of emotions were more likely to ignore or disengage from the spread of false news, and participants who reported high levels of negative emotions and low levels of positive emotions were more likely to suppress the spread of fake news and less likely to contribute to the spread of fake news. Our findings are synthesized into a process model that explains how discrete emotions and beliefs influence sharing behaviors. Implications for mitigating the spread of fake news are discussed in terms of this model.

Introduction

The phrase "fake news," or news headlines and stories that are false but intended to mislead readers [1], has recently become part of the everyday global parlance. According to a recent Pew survey, about half (50%) of Americans believe that fake news is a serious problem today in the United States (US)–more so than climate change (46%), racism (40%), and terrorism (34%) [57]. The target is often political in nature, to influence voters in an upcoming

Access the Support Material: www.routledge.com/ 9781032561127

election by feeding, rather than challenging their biases. The 2020 election provided a unique and extremely rare opportunity to study fake news in the US, enabled by social networking, in a relatively constrained two-party system and a highly charged environment.

With our access to an unprecedented amount of information at our disposal, one might expect that people would make better decisions. However, people are repeatedly and constantly exposed to information that is slightly biased at best and blatantly false at worst. In their reactions, people move on to repost, retweet, and re-energize pernicious fake news items. We believe that two major forces have led to our current problem: media factors and psychological factors.

Media Factors: The widespread use of media has provided a foundation for fake news, and two centuries of development resulted in the powerhouse it is today. Newspapers before the 1840s were actually *expected* to have strong political biases [71]. However, the invention of the telegraph made possible syndication services such as the Associated Press, and national and international reports could be investigated, written, and edited to sell their stories to a large number of diverse local newspapers. The diversity of their customer base made it important for those syndicates to provide comprehensive, objective reporting so that the local news media could pick and choose stories or portions of stories they wanted to cover. Today, any expectation of objectivity has largely been extinguished by a swing of the pendulum back to biased reporting, as evidenced by several bias rating systems (for example, [50]).

How did the bias pendulum reverse direction so strongly? Two media developments contributed to that reversal. First, national and international cable TV channels and other news outlets gained popularity and developed a substantial enough base of resources to fly their own reporters virtually anywhere, to cover carefully chosen material with their specific preferred narrative. Most reporting that reaches mainstream households is biased at various levels of strength, and viewers can choose to be informed by their chosen platform in a large, diverse set, ranging from the far right to the far left and many gradations in between. This situation illustrates Anderson's [3] concept of a "long tail" of diverse choices with widely varying popularity.

The second media development, social media, has thrust the pendulum even more solidly towards extreme views, which we believe has created an Andersonian nightmare. Production tools such as desktop publishing, still and video cameras, and editing software are in the hands of a wide audience, resulting in an unprecedented amount of content globally available on publishing platforms such as YouTube. Social media platforms such as Facebook selectively provide headlines to members based on their preferences. The upshot is that any individuals who are unhappy with the current state of affairs, and wish to make themselves heard, can produce their own official-looking content [43][49][78], upload it quickly, and release it on social media [44].

The impact of creating and disseminating fake news is an IT-reliant process that has more subtle impacts than the superficial act of using technology. Without IT, it would be too expensive and time-consuming to create professional-looking false messages, and those messages would not reach a large population worldwide and convince them so thoroughly that they are true. Face-to-face communications would be too slow and their believability would be dependent on the person telling the story. Print resources are somewhat faster, but production and distribution costs are too high to support a large selection of highly-biased niche sources.

Thus, technology is a powerful *enabler* of fake news, through instant connections between like-minded friends on social networks, spreading these stories virally. The influence can be quite large and widespread, as Facebook alone reaches up to 190 million users in the USA [79]. Consumers appear hungry for these stories, and our technology is there to serve them at unprecedented speed and scale. A recent global study [90] found that fake news spreads more quickly than true news. Researchers have observed tangled and immersive stories in "rabbit holes" (e.g., [41]) filled with questionable but persuasive conspiracy theories. Social media technologies circulate them in minutes, and can have immediate impacts on voter intentions.

Psychological Factors: Underlying the hunger is the second of the two major forces driving fake news: psychological factors. Willing producers plant their seeds and eager social network users consume the bountiful harvest. According to one global study [88], those with extreme views appear to develop psychological distress, cognitive simplicity, overconfidence, feelings of moral superiority), and intolerance, which can even lead to "a willingness to use violence to reach ideological goals" (p. 162). Fortunately, most stop short of violence, but spread the word to others by creating "news" stories from their own imaginations, which in turn could stir up readers who are not so passive in their aggression. Studying what emotions drive an appetite for consuming and sharing fake news might help us learn how to prevent these stories. In Information Systems (IS) research, emotions have been found to predict beliefs [64][28] and to predict problematic use of social media far more strongly than typical factors such as usefulness and satisfaction [87].

In this article, we seek to better understand the fake news phenomenon, its emotional drivers, and its behavioral outcomes, as a step towards supporting potential future work in this area. We include quantitative and qualitative components to investigate how people react to, quash, and even play along with, fake news.

Research Questions

Fake news has been explored by researchers in several fields, including the information systems field. Alan Dennis and colleagues have conducted several fruitful studies in the area, ranging from nudging users to be more critical in reading social media posts [43][59][60] to using warning messages [44] to redesigning the warnings and training readers [60]. In those studies, there was evidence that emotion is a powerful antecedent to some of the actions taken by users. Facebook eventually abandoned their practice of flagging fake news postings (e.g., [54]) due to mixed results. This current study begins to open the black box of what fake news causes readers to think and feel, and in turn helps us understand in more detail how they intend to behave.

The occurrence of fake news is so widespread and rapidly changing that it has moved beyond elections to diverse reporting, including, for example, characterizations of racial inequality protests, COVID-19, and mask-wearing. A widely-watched cable news channel altered images in the June 2020 Seattle, Washington racial protests [12] to make them more alarming. Many falsified news reports about COVID-19 have been found [91], and they spread extremely quickly—"almost as fast as the virus itself" (para. 1). This exacerbates the danger as people begin to follow advice that is not medically sound. For example, politically-inspired false messages about dangerous reductions in oxygen intake from wearing a face mask led to social media postings persuading others to leave their protective masks behind

[13]. At the same time, hospital personnel, researchers, and epidemiologists were begging people to wear masks [36]. One of the two messages is incorrect, and believing the incorrect one can lead to a decision with a fatal outcome.

Mainstream scientists appeal to rationality through research results while the naysayers appeal to emotion. Unfortunately, the latter appears stronger than the former. Also, those sources are visited by people with common points of view, creating "echo chambers" [85]. More rational peers, who have recently been shown to be effective in discouraging sharing of fake news [27], are not generally present in those chambers. Nevertheless, peers might also play a role when noticing that others are sharing fake news. Left unchecked, the news can spread in a "viral" fashion, where people would send the message to others in their network, leading to further sharing in a geometric fashion [69]. During a pre-election period, undecided voters can be swayed by these headlines, which may unfairly and falsely endanger a candidate.

While it is important to study how to detect fake news and to remind individuals about being aware of the signs of fake news, understanding audiences' responses to false headlines will enable us to support the design of more strategies to stem their flow. To address this need, we explore how people with diverse political affiliations experience patterns of emotional responses to fake news headlines, how they make attributions about those emotional responses, and how these patterns of emotional responses are associated with response behavior intentions. We aim to contribute to existing research on emotional reactions to fake news by measuring evoked discrete emotions from headlines that might challenge or correspond to their beliefs. We also examine the role of a reader's belief in the validity of the news item. Our study is exploratory, and therefore we use a mixed methods approach and posit several non-directional hypotheses (due to the varied emotions measured) to address the following research questions:

> RQ1: What emotional responses do social media users report upon reading and upon envisioning the sharing of fabricated political headlines that are confirmed to be false (quantitative), and to what do they attribute these emotions (qualitative)?
>
> RQ2: What, if any, (quantitative) differences exist among social media users holding competing political stances in their ratings of believability in false political headlines, their emotional responses to the headlines, their emotional responses to envisioning the headlines being shared, and their (qualitative) attributions of these emotional responses?
>
> RQ3: How consistent are social media users' emotional response patterns with their intentions to respond with engagement behaviors (e.g., sharing or liking), or with inhibiting behaviors (like posting links for fact checking)?
>
> RQ4: How consistent are social media users' behavioral response intentions with their political stances related to the target of attack of fake news headlines?

We take an interdisciplinary approach to framing the current study. First, we are informed by a framework recently introduced by Bakir and McStay [6] to explain the forces behind the proliferation of fake news. The authors argue that the *economics of emotion* drives the spread of fake news, as "emotions are leveraged to generate attention and viewing time, which converts to advertising revenue" (p. 2). Thus, fake news creators deliberately write stories that evoke emotions to garner attention on social media [53] and produce revenue.

Taken together, concepts and theories we discuss below will provide insights into how emotion and cognition interact during information processing, such as that which occurs when reading fabricated content online.

Theoretical Background

The following discussion examines 1) the spread of fake news via social media, 2) fake news and emotions, 3) political stance and emotions, beliefs, and behavioral intentions.

The Spread of Fake News via Social media

Earlier, we established the role of social media to sow fake news and make it accessible to the public more rapidly and widely than ever before. Social media bots compound the problem, as they can overload fake news rapidly, dampening people's ability to engage in fact checking [49][85]. Merely seeing repeated stories from people representing diverse social ties serves as cognitive confirmation [58][86], as well as emotional support, taking advantage of the "mere exposure effect" that attitudes [10][92] and trust [48] tend to improve about an object merely through repeated exposure. Constant sharing of fake news, its acknowledgment by social media friends, and repeated information can make social media users accept fake news stories as true. Hordes of social media users experience and fall victim to this phenomenon daily [73], accounting for its rapid spread [91][49] and isolation into polarized echo-chambers that inhibit the ability of people to discern fake stories from real ones [85].

Fake News and Emotions

There is evidence that emotional components of fake news play a key role in deceiving readers [19][22][26] and that the emotional valence of a fake news article can differentially impact subsequent sharing behavior [9][21][81]. According to several studies, emotional states can be easily manipulated in individuals through online content [8][15][20][33][46]. For example, in a controversial experiment, Facebook modified the timelines of 689,003 users without their knowledge or consent to show either mostly positive or mostly negative content [46]. They found that users' subsequent interactions aligned with their assigned treatment; those in the "negative" group posted more negative messages and those in the "positive" group posted more positive messages [46]. These findings suggest that "emotional contagions" [34]— emotional states that are transferable from person to person—are also present in online media, allowing creators to manipulate readers into engaging with and perpetuating fake news.

Researchers suggest that understanding experienced emotions is key to predicting the subsequent beliefs and actions of online users. Studies have found that negative emotionally charged messages have powerful usage patterns; they tend to be shared more [9][21], are shared more often and more quickly [21][81], and are believed more readily [19][22][26]. However, little is understood about discrete emotional reactions to fake news headlines. Discrete emotions are specific, short-lived feelings that are elicited from some "stimulus event" and lead to distinct behavioral responses [4][66]. For example, anger has been described as an "other-directed" emotion, which motivates individuals to take action, while sadness has been described as a "situation-directed" emotion that elicits moderate withdrawal or avoidance [4][25][66].

Emotion cycles [31] can provide a deeper explanation of how people experience emotion and then behave by spreading the news further. One major cycle is feeling anger in response to sadness or fear. For example, people far apart on the political spectrum might feel fear initially, but after they find that they are powerless to make a direct change, their fear turns into anger at those perceived to be responsible. On the other hand, sadness, a powerless, deactivating emotion [68], would not as likely lead to actions such as sharing on social media. But if sadness is accompanied by someone to blame, anger could result. Anger, the activating emotion, is expected to be key in reacting to fake news, even when another emotion is initially responsible for the anger. As several emotions activate, interact, and even deactivate in a complex manner, the strength of the current political conflicts by large groups appears to indicate that there are likely widely-shared, distinct patterns of those emotions. H1, H2, and H4 are posited in a non-directional, exploratory manner given that we used a complete inventory of emotions that have not previously been reported. Addressing RQ1, we posit the first two exploratory hypotheses:

H1: Patterns of differences among emotions will emerge when social media users view a fake news item.

H2: Patterns of differences among emotions will emerge when social media users envision a fake news item being shared.

Political Stance and Emotions, Beliefs, and Behavioral Intentions

In the US, two major political parties combine diverse societal preferences into stances or platforms. People who are conservative are associated with the Republican party, and among many other things, tend to favor few regulations and a small role of government in the welfare of its citizens. Those who are liberal are associated with the Democratic party, and among many other things, tend to favor regulations and social benefits and services [74]. These two platforms are directly opposed to each other, paving a path towards strong emotions when the opposite side dogmatically describes its tenets as desirable or "correct."

Literature is scarce in the area of emotions and fake news. However, people with different political stances appear to experience emotions in different ways, dating back to work by Tomkins [84] in 1963. Since then, a promising collection of research has emerged on the relationship between political ideology and emotions; more recent work has found that conservatives experience negative emotions more strongly than liberals on a broad level [2] [18][51][77][76], particularly with respect to disgust, anger, and fear. Conservatives are said to have a "negativity bias" [67], where negative events receive more attention [14][17][63] and are experienced and remembered [56] more strongly than positive events. Exploring the prevalence of specific emotional states among conservatives and liberals can help us understand how individuals from different political parties make sense of and interact with the world.

This negativity bias extends to partisan differences in perception, motivation, and behavior. Studies have shown that, compared to liberals, conservatives tend to perceive the world as more dangerous [2][18], rate negative messages as being of higher quality than positive messages [51], recall more negative stimuli [77], are more susceptible to conditioning with negative stimuli [76], and tend to experience more feelings of anger [35] [42][89], fear [39][40][65], and disgust [37][38][82]. Little published research exists on other emotions, so we focus our inquiry on a wider range of possible patterns that emerge in a more diverse group of emotions occurring in differentiated patterns for people with different political stances.

Beliefs are a strong part of how people react to fake news. Stated succinctly, people sometimes so fervently want to believe a fake news item that they accept it as fact [72]. Beliefs have been found to correlate with emotions [52]. Conversely, readers who have one political stance might find it more difficult to believe a news item that attacks their political views than one that supports their political views. The next two hypotheses are informed by an understanding of a collection of theories and concepts that have been applied to both psychology and economics: confirmation bias, motivated reasoning, and cognitive dissonance regulation. *Confirmation bias* is the tendency to most readily seek and accept information that fits within existing belief systems, and to interpret information in a way that does not challenge those belief systems [62]. Recently, confirmation bias and *motivated reasoning*, the construction of justifications for arriving at desired conclusions [47], have together provided a useful framework for understanding political information processing before and after a presidential election [83]. Finally, when confronted with information that challenges ones' existing beliefs, *cognitive dissonance* causes discomfort and motivates action to reduce this discomfort [23]. Koole [45] provided the following examples of regulating actions individuals might take to reduce dissonance:

> selective criticism of threatening information ..., trivialize the information ..., selectively forget the information ..., make self-serving attributions ..., inflate their self-conceptions in a non-threatened domain ..., engage in downward social comparison ..., and derogate others (p. 20).

These theoretical bases could explain differences in how people with diverse political views consume fake news on social media. Guess et al. [29] observed that more fake news was targeted towards conservatives. They found that most of the fake news items supported Republican Donald Trump and that conservatives were disproportionately more likely to visit fake news websites and share more fake news stories [61][30]. Guess et al. [30] also reported that independent voters were almost equally likely to share fake news as conservatives.

Consequently, the next two hypotheses address RQ2:

H3: False headlines aligned with the reader's political stance will be more believable.

H4: Differences in strength and nature of emotions will exist among social media users with different political stances when reading false headlines and when envisioning them being shared.

Finally, emotions are expected to relate to users' behavioral responses. IS research has found high correlations among attitudes, intentions, and behavior [16]. Some are characterized as "engagement" behaviors such as clicking "like" or reposting/sharing the fake news items, while others are "inhibiting" behaviors, such as clicking a frowning or angry icon, clicking "thumbs down;" replying with fact checking advice; or even sending a private message to the original poster arguing or stating that it is fake. Therefore, addressing RQ3, we expect the following:

H5: Social media users with more intense emotional responses will have stronger behavioral response intentions.

These ideas can be drawn together to relate political stance and response patterns, in response to RQ4:

H6: Social media users' intentions to respond through either engagement or inhibiting behaviors will depend on their own political stance and the political target of the headlines.

Method

Design

To address our research questions, we chose a concurrent explanatory mixed methods design with a quantitative emphasis, in two sequential waves of data. In Wave 1, we collected qualitative and quantitative data concurrently, and conducted quantitative analyses first. Wave 2 provided additional quantitative data, resulting in a larger sample for more thorough quantitative analysis of some of the hypotheses. In our between-subjects design, we showed participants one false headline chosen at random and asked them to report on their emotional responses and response intentions quantitatively, and to explain their emotional attributions qualitatively. Subsequent systematic analysis of qualitative data allowed us to both corroborate and deepen our understanding of the quantitative findings. Hypothesis tests are not the complete story, as our open-ended qualitative probing informs our results in important ways.

Participants

We collected all data using Qualtrics and Amazon's Mechanical Turk (MTurk) during a two-month period, and corresponding to events in Washington, DC at the time of data collection. In both waves, all participants were told that the task normally took 10 minutes or less, and we paid those who successfully completed the HIT $1.20. To qualify, participants were required to be US residents and to have completed at least 50 successful HITs with an overall approval rating above 95%. Across both waves, we obtained usable results from a total of 879 participants.

Four pairs of headlines were used in Wave 1, completed on October 23, 2020, two weeks prior to the November 3 US presidential election. Because of the high number of participant disqualifications, two months later, Wave 2 re-used the fourth pair of headlines that were still relevant, open for two days, from January 4 to January 6. We concluded all data collection at 1:00 pm Eastern time on January 6, immediately before the Joint Session of U.S. Congress began, which was already expected to be a fiercely contested meeting to certify the voting results of the U.S. Electoral College. Wave 2 was thus closed well before the insurrection of the US Capitol.

Only participants who completed the questionnaire and passed all three objective attention checks were included. We subjected cases to a fourth attention check by evaluating the qualitative responses for signs that "bots" had completed them, such as repeating simple words across all fields or inserting random words or text copied from other sources. Multiple research team members reviewed the cases, and removed those they agreed were problematic. Finally, we used listwise deletion for missing values, so our sample size varied somewhat in testing each hypothesis. Appendix 1 provides a profile of the 879 participants across both waves.

In Wave 1, 1,108 participants began but only 884 completed the entire task. In addition, 337 failed the attention checks described above. Prior to analyzing othe pre-election data, we tested assumptions and removed 26 multivariate outliers, which included any case with a significant Mahalanobis distance (p-value <.001). Wave 1, therefore, provided a net sample of 521.

In Wave 2, we raised the MTurk qualification threshold to 100 successful HITs due to an extremely high number of disqualifications in Wave 1. This reduced the disqualification rate from 38% to 26%. 624 participants began the Wave 2 study, and 485 completed all questions. We removed an additional 127 who failed the screenings, leaving 358 participants, net.

Procedures

We created eight fake news headlines in text and added graphics to appear in the general fashion of a Facebook post. To focus attention on the headline and to remove any confounds, we created a generic "News" icon for the news service and blurred it, along with counts of "likes" or "views." The made-up headlines were created in four pairs. Each pair provided an identically-worded threat to each political candidate. For instance, Headlines 7 and 8 fictitiously reported that the candidate's campaign hired hackers to plant viruses in voting machines. See Figure 1 for these two headlines, and Appendix 2 for the images of all eight headlines shown to participants. The headline text was as follows (with candidate or party randomly assigned by Qualtrics):

- Headlines 1 & 2: *Campaign Insider: Newly Revealed Health Report Leads 32 Congressional (Republicans/Democrats) to Recommend (Trump/Biden) Quits Presidential Bid*
- Headlines 3 & 4: *Insider: Major Scandal Will be Revealed Two Days before Election that will Disqualify (Trump/Biden)*
- Headlines 5 & 6: *Big Pharma Firms Bribed Congressional (Republicans/Democrats) on COVID Medicine Plans*
- Headlines 7 & 8: *(Trump/Biden) Campaign Hired Hackers to Plant Viruses in Voting Machines in States Lacking Paper Ballot Backups*

Data collection (Waves 1 and 2)
We began by asking a series of demographic questions, including political stance (liberal to conservative), political party (Republican, Democrat, Independent, No Party, and Other), voting choices for 2016 and 2020, gender, ethnicity, education, social media site usage, and political news consumption. We also asked them to describe Republicans, Independents,

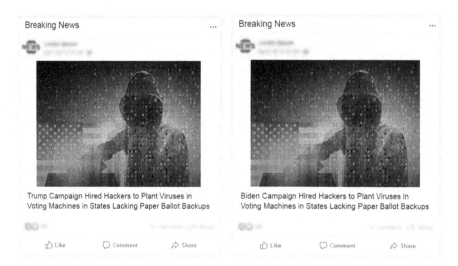

Figure 1. Sample Fake News Headlines – Headlines 7 and 8

and Democrats with three adjectives each. We operationalized political stance with the participants' stated political party membership, having found a very high correlation between political party, voting choices, and their reported liberal/conservative stance.

Emotional Responses to Headlines

Participants were prompted to assume the randomly-chosen headline was posted on social media, and then answered questions about: (1) their emotions upon reading the headline using an instrument described below, (2) their attributions of those emotions (open-ended, "why do you feel that way?"), and (3) their belief of whether the information relayed in the headline is true, using a Likert-type scale with the following response options: 7=virtually certain, 6=very likely, 5=likely, 4=about as likely as not, 3=unlikely, 2=very unlikely, and 1=exceptionally unlikely.

To prepare participants for the next step, we revealed that the headline was false, and then asked the participants to respond to the DEQ items again to reveal their emotional responses. We then showed the headline a third time and asked participants to respond to the DEQ with this question: "Knowing that this headline is FALSE, how would you feel if you saw it being shared on social media?" followed by an open-ended question asking why they felt that way.

We followed up by asking what they would do in response to seeing a) a close friend or family member and b) a casual acquaintance share this fake news on social media, and how they would respond using 9 possible behavioral responses we created as part of the qualitative analysis process. Those responses included replying, sharing, expressing approval, fact-checking, ignoring, unfriending (permanently or temporarily), debunking, or private messaging. Those reporting that they might comment were asked what they would write. Alternatively, those who reported that they would not comment were asked to explain why not.

We used a truncated form of the *Discrete Emotions Questionnaire* (DEQ) [32], a commonly used 32-item self-report instrument with 8 subscales (Anger, Disgust, Fear, Anxiety, Sadness, Desire, Relaxation, Happiness) and 4 items per subscale. We conducted a pilot study to demonstrate the reliability of a shorter form of the DEQ to prevent fatigue from asking participants to go through the entire instrument three times. Each of the 8 emotions had four descriptors, and we chose the two descriptors for our truncated instrument that maximized Cronbach's alpha. The pilot also confirmed that the DEQ revealed significant emotional responses after participants read fake headlines.

Although it relies on self-reporting, the DEQ has been shown to be reliable, and was designed to be administered in response to a stimulus, which is the case in this study. While it is rather parsimonious and compact, it covers a wide gamut of emotions. The shorter form helped us avoid fatigue or time delays, as emotions tend to begin to dissipate in under one minute [11]. Fortunately, the truncated scale was reliable, with all alpha scores above .7 (see Appendix 3).

The instructions provided with the DEQ direct participants to report to what extent they experienced these emotions. Likert-type response options included: 1=Not at all, 2=Slightly, 3=Somewhat, 4=Moderately, 5=Quite a Bit, 6=Very Much, 7=An Extreme Amount.

Data collection: Wave 2
During the second wave, conducted to increase statistical power for some of our hypothesis testing, we repeated the procedure described above, but only included the fourth pair of headlines (shown in Figure 1)—that the (Trump/Biden) political campaign hired hackers to interfere in the election. We chose this headline pair because voting machines received growing attention following the election, and the other headlines were moot following the election.

Data Analysis Procedures

Quantitative Data Analysis (Waves 1 and 2)
Quantitative analyses included descriptive statistics, multivariate analysis of variance (MANOVA) or covariance (MANCOVA), and K-means cluster analysis. Some analyses, such as emotions evoked, were conducted across headlines for initial understanding of emotional response and for examining patterns of consequences from patterns of emotion. Some analyses were also conducted separately for each headline because of their potential differences—uncontrollable issues of the candidate (health), controllable issues of the candidate (scandal), the party (bribes), and transgressions of the campaign (hiring hackers).

Qualitative Analysis (Wave 1 only)
We sought to fully understand participants' attributional reasoning of their emotional reactions to two situations: Set (1) addresses the headlines as originally presented, and Set (2) addresses their reactions assuming the headlines are shared on social media (after being told they are false). We asked participants to respond to the open-ended question, "Why do you feel this way?" immediately after completing the DEQ for each set.

Two members of the research team divided the open-ended responses to "why do you feel this way" and independently conducted the recommended [70] first-cycle inductive coding to categorize the responses into distinct attributions of those emotions. The second member, who acted as primary coder, reviewed the independent codebooks and proposed a consolidated list of codes through axial coding (per [70]). The entire research team (all four authors) met to discuss and modify this code list. After the team reached consensus, the primary coder tested the draft codebook and proposed refinements. After editing the codebooks, the team used Dedoose, a qualitative, mixed methods software package, to establish high inter-rater reliability through iterative testing and collaborative codebook refinement. The coders reached final pooled Cohen's kappa scores (across all codes) for Set 1 and Set 2 of .85 and .91 respectively, indicating excellent agreement [24][55]. After achieving this level of inter-rater reliability, the two secondary coders divided the responses for the first set of responses to "why do you feel this way" and independently conducted focused coding on the full corpus of data.

The codes and themes in the codebooks (one per Set) are shown in Appendix 4, where we briefly describe the codes and themes that emerged from these responses. Appendix 5 provides the detailed codebooks that resulted.

Results

This section is organized by research question and hypotheses, and indicate data wave.

RQ1: Emotional Responses to False Headlines (Wave 1)

Research Question 1 asked what emotional responses social media users report upon reading and upon envisioning the sharing of fabricated political headlines that are confirmed to be false. H1 addressed patterns of different emotions in response to initially viewing the headlines; H2 addressed the patterns that would emerge in response to envisioning them being shared.

Figure 2 shows a graph of descriptive statistics for each of the emotions across headlines and parties upon initial presentation to participants ("assume you saw this headline posted on social media"). To compare the intensity of each of 8 discrete emotions, we conducted a repeated measures ANOVA comparing each emotion to the others in post-hoc

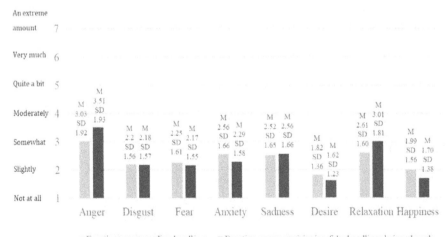

Figure 2. Emotional Responses to False Headlines; Overall Means for Wave 1

comparisons. The assumption of sphericity was violated (Mauchly's W=.016, p<.001), so we interpreted the Greenhouse-Geisser F statistic. The results indicated significant differences among the means of the 8 emotions, $F(2.427)=93.97$, p<.001. Pairwise comparisons using Bonferroni adjustment showed that 25 of 28 comparisons were significant: all except for Anxiety and Sadness (p=1.0), Anxiety and Relaxation (p=1.0), and Disgust and Fear (p=1.0). Thus, H1 was supported.

Figure 2 also shows similar emotion statistics upon asking participants to envision how they would feel, knowing that the headline is fake, if they saw it shared on social media. Again, the assumption of sphericity was violated (Mauchly's W=.024, p<.001). The Greenhouse-Geisser results indicated significant differences among the means of the 8 emotions, $F(3.53)=284.76$, p<.001. Pairwise comparisons using Bonferroni adjustment for multiple tests showed that 25 of 28 comparisons were significant: all except for Desire and Happiness (p=.117), Anxiety and Disgust (p=.079), and Disgust and Fear (p=1.0). Thus, H2 was supported.

Across headlines and parties, Anger and Relaxation were the highest-rated emotions, and Happiness and Desire were the lowest-rated emotions in response to reading the headline and in response to seeing the false headline shared on social media. However, variance within each emotion was relatively high; for example, anger and relaxation may have been both highly rated due to aggregation of emotional responses across political parties (i.e., a headline that angered one party may have relaxed another). We explored these nuances in detail in addressing the next research question.

RQ2: Belief in Headlines and Emotional Responses

We next examined the role of participants' believing the headline content upon first reading the headline. Research Question 2 asked: What, if any, quantitative differences exist among social media users holding competing political stances in their believing false political headlines, their emotional responses to the headlines, their emotional responses to envisioning the headlines being shared, and their qualitative attributions of these emotional responses?

Belief in False Headlines by Political Party (Wave 1)

We addressed the first part of RQ2 by comparing mean ratings of belief in the headlines among political parties; H3 posits differences among the parties. A one-way ANOVA indeed showed significant party differences on belief in these fake news headlines across headlines $F(2,970) = 7.065$; p = .001. Post hoc Bonferroni-adjusted comparisons indicated that Republicans (M= 3.00) rated the headlines higher than both Democrats (M=2.63; p=.009) and Independents (M=2.48, p=.001) on the likelihood that the information they contained was true (on a scale of 1-7, where 1=Exceptionally Unlikely and 7=Virtually Certain). However, for many individual headlines, either no difference was observed between parties, or Democrats believed the headlines more. When there were differences, participants were more likely to believe negative headlines about the opposite political party, and less likely to believe negative headlines about their own. We report specific belief by party results in Appendix 6b. These findings were corroborated with qualitative findings; participants more often expressed their disbelief in headlines attacking their opposing party in open-ended responses (see Appendix 6b). Thus, H3 was supported.

Emotions by Party and Headline (Wave 1)

We addressed the second and third parts of RQ3 by comparing the strength and nature of emotion responses to the false political headlines among parties (H4) with the expectation that patterns of differences will exist among people with different political stances. Because Anxiety and Fear, which are conceptually similar, presented a multicollinearity problem (r=.907), we created a composite variable (Anxiety/Fear) by calculating the mean of both scores (Cronbach's Alpha = .932). Box's M test suggested a violation of the assumption of equivalence of covariance matrices and group sizes were nonequivalent; therefore, we interpreted the Wilks' Lambda test statistic, which is relatively robust to these conditions [5].

To determine whether party and false headline content had an effect on the 7 emotions in response to reading the false headlines, we conducted a MANCOVA, controlling for belief in the headline and engagement with political news. There was a significant interaction between party and false headline content, indicating that emotional responses to different headlines depended on party affiliation: $F(14, 1924) = 3.563$, $p < .001$, Wilks' $\Lambda = 0.950$, partial $\eta^2 = .025$. Appendix 6a provides a set of tests after abstracting across the headlines. The significant interactions in both of these two-way multivariate analyses indicated that the mean differences on the emotion variables among parties depended on the nature of the headline content in terms of which party was being attacked, but also potentially based on other aspects of the headline (e.g., whether a candidacy was being threatened or members of a campaign or party were being accused of wrongdoing). Therefore, we probed further by conducting follow up quantitative analyses and supplemented them with qualitative analyses.

Because the main effects in each of these MANOVAs could not be directly interpreted in light of the significant interactions between independent variables, we performed individual MANOVAs to compare means on the emotion variables among parties for each individual headline pair. In other words, we compared emotional responses to each headline among political parties. We summarize these results in Table 1, and present detailed results in Appendix 6b.

Qualitative findings expand on these quantitative findings; responses to "Why do you feel this way [about the content of the headline]?" also differed by party and by headline, corroborating the quantitative findings. Though some findings were mostly stable across headlines (e.g., Republicans responded more often that they did not care about the content of the headlines regardless of the content), qualitative responses illustrated patterns of emotional response attributions related to the content of the headlines and the political stances of the participants. We summarize these below and in Table 2, and present detailed results in Appendix 6b.

Headlines 1 through 4 were similar in that they portrayed news that a presidential candidate's (Donald Trump's or Joe Biden's) bid for presidency may be in jeopardy. In explaining their emotional responses to these headlines, participants tended to align themselves with candidate over party when the party named in the headline matched their own political affiliation (i.e., Republicans aligned themselves with Trump more often than with Congressional Republicans, and Democrats aligned themselves with Biden more often than with Congressional Democrats). Democrats overwhelmingly stated that headlines about Biden losing presidential candidacy (Headlines 2 and 4) did not support their preferences, while Republicans overwhelmingly stated that these headlines

Table 1. Summary of Results by Wave and Headline (Repubs=Republicans; Dems=Democrats; Inds=Independents/No Party)

Data Collection Wave	Headline	Treatment	Party differences in ratings of headline believability	Significant party differences in emotional responses to reading headline	Significant party differences in emotional responses to envisioning headline being shared
Wave 1 (pre-election)	Campaign Insider: Newly Revealed Health Report Leads 32 Congressional ___ to Recommend ___ Quits Presidential Bid	Headline 1: Trump, Repubs	None	Repubs>Dems on Anger, Anxiety/Fear, Sadness. Repubs>Inds on Anger. Dems>Repubs on Happiness	Repubs>Dems on Anger. Inds>Dems on Sadness.
		Headline 2: Dems, Biden	None	Dems>Repubs & Inds on Anger, Anxiety/Fear, Sadness. Repubs>Dems & Inds on Relaxation, Desire, Happiness.	Repubs>Dems & Inds on Desire, Happiness
	Major Scandal Will be Revealed Two Days before Election that will Disqualify ___	Headline 3: Trump	None	Repubs>Dems & Inds on Anger, Anxiety/Fear, Disgust, Sadness. Dems>Inds on Happiness	None
		Headline 4: Biden	Repubs> Dems & Inds	None	Dems>Inds on Anger
	Big Pharma Firms Bribed Congressional ___ on COVID Medicine Plans	Headline 5: Repubs	None	None	None
		Headline 6: Dems	None	None	None
	___ Campaign Hired Hackers to Plant Viruses in Voting Machines in States Lacking Paper Ballot Backups	Headline 7: Trump	Dems>Repubs	None	None
		Headline 8: Biden	Repubs and Inds>Dems	None	None
Wave 2 (post-election, pre-certification)	___ Campaign Hired Hackers to Plant Viruses in Voting Machines in States Lacking Paper Ballot Backups	Headline 7: Trump	Dems>Repubs and Inds	Repubs & Dems>Inds on Anger, Desire, Sadness, Disgust, Anxiety/Fear. Repubs>Inds on happiness.	Repubs>Dems & Inds on Anger Repubs>Inds on Disgust Repubs & Dems>Inds on Desire, Relaxation, Happiness, and Anxiety/Fear. Dems & Repubs>Inds on Desire; Sadness; Happiness, Anxiety/Fear. Dems>Inds on Anger, Disgust
		Headline 8: Biden	Repubs & Inds>Dems	None	

Table 2. Summary of Research Questions, Hypotheses, and Findings

Research Questions	Hypotheses	Findings
RQ1: What emotional responses do social media users report upon reading and upon envisioning the sharing of fabricated political headlines that are confirmed to be false (quantitative), and to what do they attribute these emotions (qualitative)?	H1: Patterns of differences among emotions will emerge when social media users view a fake news item. H2: Patterns of differences among emotions will emerge when social media users envision a fake news item being shared.	These hypotheses were supported. Participants reported both negative and positive emotions (across 8 distinct emotions), and there were significant differences among the means of emotions. While many participants reported low levels of emotion in response to viewing these headlines, and envisioning them being shared cluster analyses revealed three distinct groups (those with high negative and positive emotions, low negative and positive emotions, and high negative and low positive emotions). Participants described a wide range of diverse reasons for experiencing the emotions they reported. Qualitative coding revealed 13 categories of statements explaining emotions in response to viewing headlines, and 9 categories of statements explaining emotions in response to envisioning the headlines being shared.
RQ2: What, if any, (quantitative) differences exist among social media users holding competing political stances in their ratings of believability in false political headlines, their emotional responses to the headlines, their emotional responses to envisioning the headlines being shared, and their (qualitative) attributions of these emotional responses?	H3: Differences in ratings of believability of false headlines will exist among social media users with different political stances. H4: Differences in strength and nature of emotions will exist among social media users with different political stances when reading false headlines and when envisioning them being shared.	This hypothesis was supported; Republicans rated headlines as more believable than Democrats and Independents across headlines. However, for many individual headlines, either no difference was observed among parties, or Democrats believed the headlines more. Where differences did exist, Democrats and Republicans rated the false headlines attacking the opposing political party as more believable than those attacking their own. Qualitative responses corroborated this; participants made more statements expressing disbelief in the headline when it was meant to attack their own political party. This hypothesis was partially supported; headline content and political party interacted and significant differences were observed within type of content (attacking Republicans versus attacking Democrats). However, there were no significant differences among parties on emotional response for many of the headlines. Qualitative response patterns also differed by party and headline; participants' attributions of these emotional responses provided a deeper understanding of these emotional response patterns (e.g., even when those with different political stances had similar emotional responses, their underlying reasoning differed).
RQ3: How consistent are social media users' emotional response patterns with their intentions to respond with engagement behaviors (e.g., sharing or liking), or with inhibiting behaviors (like posting links for fact checking)?	H5: Social media users with more intense emotional responses will have stronger behavioral response intentions.	This hypothesis was supported; MANOVAs comparing cluster groups (clustered by emotional response patterns) showed that the "upset" group and the "hot" group were more motivated to respond.
RQ4: How consistent are social media users' behavioral response intentions with their political stances related to the target of attack of fake news headlines?	H6: Social media users' intentions to respond through either engagement or inhibiting behaviors will depend on their own political stance and the political target of the headlines.	This hypothesis was mostly supported; we observed differences between parties across most of the response options that followed this pattern.

did support their preferences. The opposite was not true for headlines about Trump possibly losing presidential candidacy (Headlines 1 and 3). In fact, more Democrats stated that Headline 1 did not support their preferences than did Republicans. Additionally, both Democrats and Republicans stated that headlines about Trump would cause more unrest and uncertainty than headlines about Biden.

Headlines 5 and 6 portrayed news that Congressional Republicans (Headline 5) or Democrats (Headline 6) transgressed by accepting bribes. Most participants stated that the content of the headline was immoral or criminal, especially when the headline was about the opposing political party. Participants from both parties felt that the headline about Congressional Democrats would cause more unrest and uncertainty than the headline about Congressional Republicans.

Headlines 7 and 8 portrayed news that a presidential candidate's (Trump's or Biden's) campaign tampered with voting machines. Similar to all other headlines, both Republicans and Democrats were less likely to believe the headline about their own party, but stated that if the headline was true, it would cause great unrest in the country. Many Democrats also indicated that the headline about the Trump campaign (Headline 7) would be an immoral or criminal act if true.

We next determined whether Party and headline content had an effect on the same 7 discrete emotions after we told participants the content was false and to envision how they would feel if someone they knew shared the false information on social media. Again, we conducted a MANCOVA (interpreting Wilks' Lambda for the same reasons), controlling for engagement with political news. There was a significant interaction between party and headline content, indicating that emotional responses to different headlines depended on party affiliation: F (98, 2943) = 1.483, p < .002, Wilks' Λ = 0.737, partial η^2 = .043. We repeated the MANCOVA with Party versus Party Attacked and the interaction (results are shown in Appendix 6a, Table 1). Again, the interaction of Party and Party Attacked was significant (F=2.954 (14,962); p<.001; η^2 = .041), indicating that a social media users' emotional response patterns depended on their own party and the party attacked by the headline (Results are shown in Appendix 6a, Table 2). Again, we followed up by analyzing the headlines separately, comparing emotional responses to each headline among political parties. The results are summarized in Tables 1 and 2, and Figure 4 (the only headlines with significant ANOVA results), and detailed results covering all headlines appear in Appendix 6b.

Qualitative responses to "Why do you feel this way [about seeing the fake news article shared on social media]?" showed similar response patterns in coding categories across all headlines, but varied between political party. Overall, participants were most likely to say that they disliked that fake news was being shared. The next most common response was that they were concerned that the sharing of false headlines would result in more people believing the false content. The third most common response was that of apathy, reflecting disengagement or fake news fatigue. Headlines 5-8 also had a high incidence of stating that seeing fake news headlines shared on social media is indicative of a larger problem.

Emotions by Party and Headline (Wave 2: Post-Election Responses)

As described earlier, after the election, but prior to the certification of the outcome, we collected another wave of data that only included Headlines 7 and 8, which accused either the Trump or Biden campaign of hiring hackers to rig the election. Party differences in believability ratings were consistent with Wave 1 results (in short, participants were more

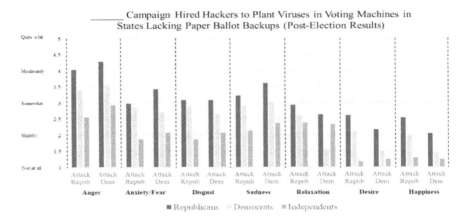

Figure 3. Graphical Summary Comparison for Headlines 7 and 8, Wave 2

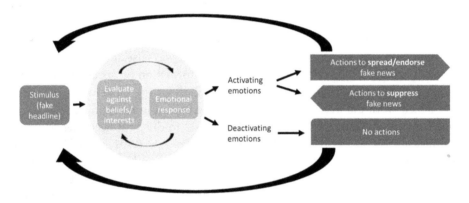

Figure 4. Process Model of Fake News and Emotions

likely to believe headlines meant to attack the opposing party). However, while in the previous analysis of these two headlines we did not find significant differences among the parties on emotional responses to the headline content or to envisioning the headlines being shared after they were confirmed to be false, results of this set of analyses (MANOVAS, follow up ANOVAS, and post hoc analyses) uncovered several differences. Independents tended to report significantly milder emotional responses than Republicans and Democrats, while the other results were mixed. The discrepant results could be due to the larger sample size and thus increased power in this analysis or to increased political polarization. These results are summarized in Table 1 and Figure 3, and presented in detail in Appendix 6c.

RQ 3: Emotional Responses and Response Intentions (Waves 1 and 2)

Next, we sought to determine if and how patterns of emotional responses to reading the headlines and envisioning the headlines being shared on social media relate to behavioral intentions to respond. Specifically, RQ3 asked: How do social media users' emotional response patterns impact their intentions to respond with engagement behaviors that can perpetuate the spread of fake news (like sharing or liking), or with inhibiting behaviors (like posting links for fact checking)? To identify patterns of emotional responses, we conducted a K-means cluster analysis using all of the emotional responses (to both the initial reading of headlines and to envisioning the headlines being shared on social media) as clustering variables. We included all of the emotion variables for both conditions (in response to initial reading and in response to envisioned sharing) because of the explora- tory nature of this work. This approach included as much information about emotional responses as possible, while being more parsimonious than alternative approaches such as conducting two different cluster analyses (one with initial responses and one with responses to imagined sharing), which would have necessitated two separate sets of follow up analyses and would have complicated the interpretation of results. We searched the literature for any indications that our use of these variables might be problematic, but found no indication of this, although discussion in the literature regarding selection of clustering variables is relatively sparse (for example, see the seminal review on K-means clustering in [80]).

After examining group means with two, three, and four cluster solutions, we selected the three cluster solution; four clusters returned two that were similar, and the two cluster solution eliminated a meaningful group. To test the validity of these groups, we compared them on clustering variables; significant differences existed among all groups on all cluster- ing variables (all p-values < .001). In addition, the elbow method (using R) [7][75] suggested 3 clusters as the best solution. Finally, we used the NbClust() function, which uses 30 fit indices to determine the best number of clusters based on majority rule; this method also suggested a 3 cluster solution.

Group 1 (n=128) was characterized by relatively high scores across emotions; we called this group the "hot" (emotionally reactive) group. The second group (n=542) was char- acterized by relatively low scores across emotions; we called this group the "cold" (emotionally unaffected) group. The third group (n=209) was characterized by relatively high negative emotion scores paired with low positive emotion scores; we called this the "upset" group.

Next, we tested H5, which stated that social media users with more intense emotional responses will have stronger behavioral response intentions, by conducting a MANCOVA comparing the hot, cold, and upset groups on all response behaviors controlling for belief in headline content and engagement with political news. Because Box's M test suggested a violation of the assumption of equivalence of covariance matrices and group sizes were nonequivalent, we use the Wilks' Lambda test statistic. The multivariate results showed that after controlling for belief in the headline (p<.001) and engagement with political news (p=.004), there was a significant difference among cluster groups on behavioral response intentions; $F(36, 2000)=22.386$, p<.001, Wilks' Λ =.508, partial η^2 = .287. Individual ANOVAs indicated significant differences among cluster groups on all 18 of the behavioral response intentions (all p-values<.001).

Pairwise comparisons using the Bonferroni adjustment (see Appendix 7 for means and post-hoc results) indicated that the "hot" (emotionally reactive) group tended to be con- sistently higher than the "cold" (emotionally unaffected) group on both spreading/endor- sing behaviors and suppressing behaviors. The "cold" group was lowest on all behaviors except Ignore, in which case they were higher than at least one of the other two groups (higher than both others when considering a casual acquaintance as the poster, and higher than the "upset" group when considering someone close to the poster). The "upset" (high negative and low positive emotions) group was higher than the "cold" group on suppressing behaviors, but not spreading/endorsing behaviors (which were low for both the "cold" and the "upset" groups). H5 was supported.

RQ 4: Behavioral Response Intentions by Party

Research Question 4 asked how social media users' behavioral response intentions differ along their political stances related to the target of attack of fake news headlines. We hypothesized (H6) that social media users' intentions to respond through either engagement or inhibiting behaviors would depend on their own political stance and the political target of the headlines. We conducted a two-way MANCOVA to compare response behaviors by political party (Republican, Democrat, Independent) and nature of headline content (Attack Republicans, Attack Democrats) while controlling for believing the headline and engagement with political news. Multivariate results indicated a significant interaction between political party and nature of the headline content, $F(36, 1630)=1.960$, $p=.001$, Wilks' $\Lambda =.919$, partial $\eta^2 = .041$. This supports H6.

Because of the interaction, we did not interpret main effects. We next conducted two separate MANCOVAs: one for headlines attacking Republicans (e.g., Trump hacking headline), and one for headlines attacking Democrats (e.g., Biden hacking headline). We opted to use the "attack" variables that collapsed across multiple headlines for the sake of parsimony as well as statistical power, and because our hypothesis directly addressed the direction of the attack in relation to participants' own political stance.

Headlines Attacking Republicans
Multivariate results indicated significant differences on behavioral response intentions among political parties $F(36, 780)=2.338$, $p<.001$, Wilks' $\Lambda =.815$, partial $\eta^2 = .097$. Individual ANOVAs indicated differences among most (13 of 18) response behaviors among parties; post hoc analyses (Bonferroni) are presented in Appendix 8, Table 1, along with means and standard deviations, as well as which contrasts are (non)significant.

Headlines Attacking Democrats
Multivariate results indicated significant differences on behavioral response intentions among political parties $F(36, 816)=2.706$, $p<.001$, Wilks' $\Lambda =.798$, partial $\eta^2 = .107$. Most of the individual ANOVAs supported H6, indicating differences among most (14 of 18) response behaviors among parties; post hoc analyses (Bonferroni) are presented in Appendix 8, Table 8-2, along with means and standard deviations. We also indicate contrasts that are (non)significant.

Discussion

Our results indicate that negative false stories about politicians/political parties can effectively trigger discrete experiences of emotions, and these do indeed relate to response behaviors such as liking, sharing, and commenting.

A summary of our hypotheses and findings is shown in Table 2. In short, we expected and found varied emotional responses from users who saw fake news headlines. In our quantitative and qualitative results, we found patterns of emotional responses from users who were told their viewed headline was fake (H1) and that someone was sharing it (H2). We also expected and found that political stance would have impacts on beliefs in (H3) and emotions (H4) from false headlines that differed by headline content and political party attacked by the headline. We expected and found that the more intense the emotional response, the stronger the behavioral response intentions (H5). Finally, we expected and found that different political belief patterns would be associated with different intentions to respond through either engagement or inhibiting behaviors (H6).

Other findings were partly as expected. We expected both parties to push back against the fake news (e.g., by posting a fact check) for headlines attacking their own party and expected them to play along with fake news (e.g., by reposting) for headlines attacking the opposite party. However, we found that participants had negative feelings about fake news headlines even when they harmed the other party.

A deeper look at the data in the qualitative data helped us understand these results more clearly. Across many headlines, both qualitative and quantitative findings demonstrated that participants were more likely to believe the false content that upheld their existing belief systems; this is in alignment with confirmation bias [62]. In general, Republicans tended to believe the content of these headlines more readily than Democrats; this could help to explain previous findings that fake news tend to be right-leaning and that conservatives engage more with fake news (e.g., visiting sites, sharing fake stories) [30][61]. Some insight can be gleaned by examining the regulation strategies individuals use when confronted with information that challenge their existing beliefs and considering the qualitative responses participants gave. Namely, participants seemed to avoid negative emotional responses to bad news about their own party by dismissing or disengaging with the content of the headline. Again, Republicans, in particular, disengaged with headlines that attacked their party (e.g., disbelieving them, 'caring' less about them, and/or declining to take actions to suppress them), consistent with the psychology literature (see [45]), presumably to escape cognitive dissonance.

Process Model

Based on our qualitative and quantitative results across research questions and informed by previous literature, we propose a process model to help drive future research (see Figure 6). In general, the stimulus of fake news appears to initiate an evaluation against beliefs/interests and emotional responses (which likely inform one another bi-directionally). Activating emotions (such as anger) tend to relate either to sharing/endorsing or to suppressing fake news. Deactivating emotions (such as relaxation) do not appear to prompt further actions. These actions (or inactions) in turn inform fake news outlets about what types of fake news stories are successful. Therefore, the actions of online social media users may create a feedback loop that continually shapes the stories propagated by fake news outlets.

Our finding that anger (a strong activating emotion) and relaxation (a deactivating emotion) were reported to be the strongest in response to envisioning the headlines being shared on social media—knowing they are false—illustrates the pathways in the model to guide future research. The model asserts that activating emotions stimulate action and deactivating emotions yield inaction. Our cluster analysis suggests that the largest group, the "cold" group, was emotionally unaffected by these headlines and by envisioning them being shared. Qualitatively, they washed their hands of responsibility for combating fake news and minimized the severity of the problem (e.g., "It is their business not mine," "It's not worth my time"). These participants were higher on Relaxation and likely to report that they would ignore fake news posts.

According to our process model, activating emotions like anger, fear, disgust, and happiness are expected to drive behaviors such as sharing on one extreme, and posting cautionary messages or even toxic messages on the other. To increase clicks, disseminators want to target the right groups of people. Even when members of major parties felt a similar amount of anger at reading a headline, the reasons underlying those emotions differed. For example, a Republican immediately disbelieving that Trump's campaign would hire hackers, feels anger at the existence of the slanderous headline, while a Democrat reading the same headline may feel anger towards the Trump campaign/Trump/Republicans because they find it plausible and infuriating.

Interestingly, many people did not "push back" against the fake news headlines, and simply ignored them as if there was no harm or it was up to someone else to handle the problem. Increasing society's understanding of the threat might help activate these individuals to fight against misinformation by posting links and/or stating in a reply post that the headlines are false.

In summary, our study demonstrated that patterns of emotions in political fake news headlines are evident and differ with the target of the false headline in terms of the political stance of the reader, the political party affected, and the subject of the headline. As logic would predict, when the party is depicted as being endangered in the headline, the reader supporting that party generally reacts negatively. Emotional reactions can follow a path of activation, where the headlines are spread or endorsed, or a deactivation, where no action is taken. If the headlines are spread or no action is taken, more headlines appear, and the cycle continues.

Beyond the logical differences, Republicans generally rated headlines as more believable than Democrats and Independents across headlines, but for some headlines, either no difference was observed among parties, or Democrats believed the headlines more. Where differences did exist, Democrats and Republicans found the false headlines attacking the opposing political party more believable than those attacking their own. Headline content and political party interacted, and significant differences were observed within type of content (attacking Republicans versus attacking Democrats); however, there were no significant differences among parties on emotional response for many of the headlines. We observed differences in behavioral intentions between parties across most of the response options that followed a similar reader party vs. party attacked pattern. MANOVAs comparing cluster groups (clustered by emotional response patterns) showed that the "upset" group and the "hot" group were more motivated to respond.

Limitations and Further Research

As with all studies, ours has important limitations. First and foremost, the headlines all addressed issues in the US, and we sampled only individuals residing in the US given the opportunity for collecting data just before a major election. Additional research is needed to extend the work on emotions and fake news to other countries and cultures. Those with only one party and those with more than two major parties alike could exhibit very different mechanisms. Country size and cultural differences might be important as well to uncover additional vivid differences.

Second, the headlines were all political in nature. Future research should be conducted in non-political arenas. In the US, however, during the past two years, science, healthcare, education, and religion have all been politicized. One might be hard-pressed to find an arena of fake news that is as large as politics. Society's choices are impacted by lawmakers who represent parties that have well-formed and well-communicated policies in many areas of life.

Third, the study was conducted using a platform that appeared to have little control over its participants. Mechanical Turk is widely used, however, the researcher is forced to examine responses closely. We found it necessary to have multiple and diverse attention checks, and found nearly 25% of the entries to fail our scrutiny. In some cases, respondents who appeared to answer properly within a quantitative questionnaire, appeared to use "bots" to respond to essay text entry fields. It will be crucial for future researchers to improve the screening of participants or the time-related cost will force them to use corporate panel providers at much higher cost.

Conclusions

Emotional reactions to political fake news headlines were striking and followed interesting patterns. People who were more emotional about the headlines expressed intentions to engage more actively with the content or the poster. This means that, from the perspective of the original creator, activating emotions to either spread or fight fake news might boost revenue through increased visits. Combatting fake news is a complex task, and those headlines that become visible can have significant emotional and behavioral consequences.

We found that most people in this sample followed a "deactivating emotions" path and acted as bystanders who did not seem to care and did not provide intentions to "fight back" against fake news posts by fact-checking or contradicting the stories. Such passivity will do little to stem the tide of fake news. Others who exhibit either positive or negative emotions from reading the headlines could spread the false stories because the stories feed their own emotions and fact-checking would work against their wishes. Confirmation bias appears to strongly lead them to this complacency, when their unfavored candidate is damaged by a headline.

This study has identified some of the emotional and behavioral issues of this serious social issue. We saw evidence that conservatives more often believed fake news even when their own party or candidate was threatened. We also saw that several emotions appear to be strongly influential in this epidemic of fake news, which could explain why platform designers are having persistent difficulties in their attempts to reduce the introduction and spread of fake news. The problem is complex; reactions depend on the interactions between the political stance of the readers, the party attacked, and the actual targets of the fake news headlines. Because the problem is complex, more research is needed. However, because emotions are at the root of much of the problem, future research needs to take them into account to provide more thorough understanding, a necessary step to finding future solutions.

Disclosure statement

No potential conflict of interest was reported by the author(s).

ORCID

Christy Galletta Horner ⓘ http://orcid.org/0000-0003-2368-6984
Dennis Galletta ⓘ http://orcid.org/0000-0003-0442-5500
Jennifer Crawford ⓘ http://orcid.org/0000-0002-1507-8818
Abhijeet Shirsat ⓘ http://orcid.org/0000-0001-8882-5661

References

1. Allcott, Hunt, and Matthew Gentzkow. Social media and fake news in the 2016 election. *Journal of Economic Perspectives*, 31, 2 (2017), 211–36.
2. Altemeyer, R.A. The other "authoritarian personality." *Advances in Experimental Social Psychology*, 30, (1998), 47–92.
3. Anderson, C. *The long tail: Why the future of business is selling less of more.* Lebanon, IN: Hachette Books, 2006.
4. Angie, A.D., Connelly, S., Waples, E.P., & Kligyte, V. The influence of discrete emotions on judgement and decision-making: A meta-analytic review. *Cognition and Emotion*, 25, 8 (2011), 1393–1422.

5. Ateş, C., Kaymaz, Ö., Kale, H. E., & Tekindal, M. A. Comparison of test statistics of nonnormal and unbalanced samples for multivariate analysis of variance in terms of Type-I error rates. *Computational and Mathematical Methods in Medicine*, Volume 2019, Article 2173638, 1–8.

6. Bakir, V., & McStay, A. Fake news and the economy of emotions: Problems, causes, solutions. *Digital Journalism*, 6, 2 (2018), 154–175.

7. Barlow, J. B., & Dennis, A. R. Not as smart as we think: A study of collective intelligence in virtual groups. *Journal of Management Information Systems*, 33, 3 (2016), 684–712.

8. Beasley, A., & Mason, W. Emotional states vs. emotional words in social media. *In Proceedings of the ACM Web Science Conference, Oxford, United Kingdom*, 2015 (1–10)

9. Bebbington, K., MacLeod, C., Ellison, M.T., & Fay, N. The sky is falling: Evidence of a negativity bias in the social transmission of information. *Evolution and Human Behavior*, 38, 1 (2017), 92–101.

10. Bornstein, R. F. Exposure and affect: overview and meta-analysis of research, 1968–1987. *Psychological Bulletin*, 106, 2 (1989), 265.

11. Brans, K., & Verduyn, P. Intensity and duration of negative emotions: Comparing the role of appraisals and regulation strategies. *PLoS One*, 9, 3 (2014), e92410.

12. Brunner, J. Fox News runs digitally altered images in coverage of Seattle's protests, Capitol Hill Autonomous Zone, *Seattle Times*, June 14, 2020, http://www.seattletimes.com/seattle-news/politics/fox-news-runs-digitally-altered-images-in-coverage-of-seattles-protests-capitol-hill-autonomous-zone/

13. Burling, S. Some people think face masks are dangerous. Can that be true? *The Philadephia Inquirer*, June 23, 2020, available at https://medicalxpress.com/news/2020-06-people-masks-dangerous-true.html

14. Carraro, L. Castelli, L., & Macchiella, C. The automatic conservative: Ideology-based attentional asymmetries in the processing of valenced information. *PLoS One* 6, 11 (2011), e26456, 1–6.

15. Choudhury, M.D., Counts, S., & Gamon, M. Not all moods are created equal! Exploring human emotional states in social media [Paper presentation]. In *Proceedings of the Sixth International AAAI Conference on Weblogs and Social Media*. AAAI Conference on Artificial Intelligence, AAAI Press, Dublin, Ireland, June 2012, 66–73.

16. Conner, M., & Armitage, C. J. Extending the theory of planned behavior: A review and avenues for further research. *Journal of Applied Social Psychology*, 28, 15 (1998), 1429–1464.

17. Dodd, M.D., Balzer, A., Jacobs, C.M., Gruszczynski, M.W., Smith, K.B., & Hibbing, J.R. (2012). The political left rolls with the good and the political right confronts the bad: Connecting physiology and cognition to preferences. *Philosophical Transactions of the Royal Society B: Biological Sciences*, 367, 1589, 640–649.

18. Duckitt, J. A cognitive-motivational theory of ideology and prejudice. In M. P. Zanna (Ed.), Academic Press: *Advances in Experimental Social Psychology*, 2001, 41-113.

19. Fernández-López, M., & Perea, M. Language does not modulate fake news credibility, but emotion does. *Psicológica*, 41, 2 (2020), 84–102.

20. Ferrara, E., & Yang, Z. Measuring emotional contagion in social media. *PloS One*, 10, 11 (2015a) 1–10.

21. Ferrara, E., & Yang, Z. Quantifying the effect of sentiment on information diffusion in social media. *PeerJ Computer Science*, 1, 26 (2015b), 1–15.

22. Fessler, D.M., Pisor, A.C., & Mavarrete, C.D. Negatively-biased credulity and the cultural evolution of beliefs. *PLoS One*, 9, 4 (2014), e95167, 1–8.

23. Festinger, L. *A theory of cognitive dissonance* (Vol. 2). Stanford University Press, 1957.

24. Fleiss, J. L. Measuring nominal scale agreement among many raters. *Psychological Bulletin*, 76, 5 (1971), 378–382.

25. George, J.M., & Dane, E. Affect, emotion, and decision making. *Organizational Behavior and Human Decision Processes*, 136 (2016), 47–55.

26. Ghanem, B., Rosso, P., & Rangel, F. An emotional analysis of false information in social media and news articles. *ACM Transactions on Internet Technology*, 20, 2 (2020), 1–18.

27. Gimpel, H., Heger, S., Olenberger, C., & Utz, L. The effectiveness of social norms in fighting fake news on social media. *Journal of Management Information Systems*, 38, 1 (2021), 196–221.

28. Gregor, S., Lin, A. C., Gedeon, T., Riaz, A., & Zhu, D. Neuroscience and a nomological network for the understanding and assessment of emotions in information systems research. *Journal of Management Information Systems*, 30, 4 (2014), 13–48.

29. Guess, A., Nyhan, B., & Reifler, J. Selective exposure to misinformation: Evidence from the consumption of fake news during the 2016 US presidential campaign. European Research Council, 9, 3 (2018), 4.

30. Guess, A., Nagler, J., & Tucker, J. Less than you think: Prevalence and predictors of fake news dissemination on Facebook. *Science Advances*, 5, 1 (2019), eaau4586.

31. Hareli, S., & Rafaeli, A. Emotion cycles: On the social influence of emotion in organizations. *Research in Organizational Behavior*, 28, (2008) 35–59.

32. Harmon-Jones, C., Bastian, B., & Harmon-Jones, E. The discrete emotions questionnaire: A new tool for measuring state self-reported emotions. PloS One, 11, 8 (2016), e0159915.

33. Harris, R., & Paradice, D. An investigation of the computer-mediated communication of emotions. *Journal of Applied Sciences Research*, 3, 12 (2007), 2081–2090.

34. Hatfield, E., Cacioppo, J.T., & Rapson, R.L. Emotional contagion. *Current Directions in Psychological Science*, 2, 3 (1993), 96–99.

35. Huber, M., Van Boven, L., Park, B., & Pizzi, W.T. Seeing red: Anger increases how much republican identification predicts partisan attitudes and perceived polarization. *PloS One*, 10, 9 (2015),e0139193.

36. Imlay, A. Utah hospital leaders beg residents to wear face masks amid COVID-19 surge, *Deseret News*, June 23,2020. Retrieved from https://www.deseret.com/utah/2020/6/23/21300523

37. Inbar, Y., Pizarro, D.A., & Bloom, P. Conservatives are more easily disgusted than liberals. *Cognition and Emotion*, 23, 4 (2009), 714–725.

38. Inbar, Y., Pizarro, D.A., Iyer, R., & Haidt, J. Disgust sensitivity, political conservatism, and voting. *Social Psychological and Personality Science*, 3, 5 (2012), 537–544.

39. Jost, J.T., Glaser, J., Kruglanski, A.W., & Sulloway, F.J. Political conservatism as motivated social cognition. *Psychological Bulletin*, 129, 3 (2003), 339–375.

40. Jost, J.T., Stern, C., Rule, N.O., & Sterling, J. The politics of fear: Is there an ideological asymmetry in existential motivation? Social Cognition, 35, 4 (2017), 324–353.

41. Kaiser, J., & Rauchfleisch, A. The implications of venturing down the rabbit hole. *Internet Policy Review*, 8, 2 (2019), 1406.

42. Kettle, K.L., & Salerno, A. Anger promotes economic conservatism. *Personality and Social Psychology Bulletin*, 43, 10 (2017), 1440–1454.

43. Kim, A., & Dennis, A.R. Says who? The effects of presentation format and source rating on fake news in social media. *MIS Quarterly*, 43, 3 (2019), 1025–1039.

44. Kim, A., Moravec, P.L., & Dennis, A.R. Combating fake news on social media with source ratings: the effects of user and expert reputation ratings. *Journal of Management Information Systems*, 36, 3 (2019), 931–968.

45. Koole, S. L. The psychology of emotion regulation: An integrative review. *Cognition and Emotion*, 23, 1 (2009), 4–41

46. Kramer, A.D.I., Guillory, J.E., & Hancock, J.T. Experimental evidence of massive-scale emotional contagion through social networks. *PNAS*, 111, 24 (2014), 8788–8790.

47. Kunda, Z. The case for motivated reasoning. *Psychological Bulletin*, 108, 3 (1990), 480.

48. Kwan, L. Y. Y., Yap, S., & Chiu, C. Y. Mere exposure affects perceived descriptive norms: Implications for personal preferences and trust. *Organizational Behavior and Human Decision Processes*, 129 (2015), 48–58.

49. Langin, K. Fake news spreads faster than true news on Twitter—thanks to people, not bots. *Science Magazine*, March 8, 2018. Retrieved from https://www.sciencemag.org/news/2018/03/fake-news-spreads-faster-true-news-twitter-thanks-people-not-bots

50. Langlois, S. "How biased is your news source? You probably won't agree with this chart," April 21, 2018, Retrieve from https://www.marketwatch.com/story/how-biased-is-your-news-source-you-probably-wont-agree-with-this-chart-2018-02-28

51. Lavine, H., Burgess, D., Snyder, M., Transue, J., Sullivan, J.L., Haney, B., & Wagner, S.H. Threat, authoritarianism, and voting: An investigation of personality and persuasion. *Personality and Social Psychology Bulletin*, 25, 3 (1999), 337–347.

52. Lazarus, R.S. Emotion and Adaptation. New York: Oxford University Press, 1991.

53. Long, Y. Fake news detection through multi-perspective speaker profiles. Association for Computational Linguistics, (Volume 2: Short Papers), (2017), 252–256.

54. Meixler, E. Facebook is dropping its fake news red flag warning after finding it had the opposite effect. Time (2017), available at https://time.com/5077002/facebook-fake-news-articles/#:~:text=The%20Facebook%20app%20is%20seen,1%2C%202017.

55. Miles, M. B., & Huberman, A. M. *Qualitative data analysis: An expanded sourcebook* (2nd ed.). Sage Publications, Inc., 1994.

56. Mills, M., Gonzalez, F.J., Giuseffi, K., Sievert, B., Smith, K.B., Hibbing, J.R., & Dodd, M.D. Political conservatism predicts asymmetries in emotional scene memory. *Behavioral Brain Research*, 306, (2016), 84–90.

57. Mitchell, A., Gottfried, J., Stocking, G., Walker, M., & Fedeli, S. Many Americans say made-up news is a critical problem that needs to be fixed. *Pew Research Center*, (June 2019), retrieved from https://www.journalism.org/wp-content/uploads/sites/8/2019/06/PJ_2019.06.05_Misinformation_FINAL-1.pdf

58. Mitnick, B. M. Credibility and the theory of testaments. In *annual meeting of the Academy of Management, SIM Division, Chicago, IL, August*, 1999 (pp. 8-11).

59. Moravec, P.L., Kim, A., and Dennis, A.R. "Flagging Fake News: System 1 vs. System 2," Proceedings of the Thirty Ninth International Conference on Information Systems, San Francisco 2018.

60. Moravec, P. L., Kim, A., & Dennis, A. R. Appealing to Sense and Sensibility: System 1 and System 2 Interventions for Fake News on Social Media. *Information Systems Research*, 31, 3 (2020), 987–1006.

61. Narayanan, V., Barash, V., Kelly, J., Kollanyi, B., Neudert, L. M., & Howard, P. N. Polarization, partisanship and junk news consumption over social media in the us. preprint arXiv:1803.01845, 2018.

62. Nickerson, R. S. (1998). Confirmation bias: A ubiquitous phenomenon in many guises. *Review of General Psychology*, 2, 2 175–220.

63. Oosterhoff, B., Shook, N.J., & Ford, C. Is that disgust I see? Political ideology and biased visual attention. *Behavioral Brain Research*, 336 (2018), 227–235.

64. Ortiz de Guinea, A., Titah, R., & Léger, P. M. Explicit and implicit antecedents of users' behavioral beliefs in information systems: A neuropsychological investigation. *Journal of Management Information Systems*, 30, 4 (2014), 179–210.

65. Oxley, D.R., Smith, K.B., Alford, J.R., Hibbing, M.V., Miller, J.L., Scalora, M., Hatemi, P.K., & Hibbing, J.R. Political attitudes vary with physiological traits. *Science*, 321, 5896, (2008), 1667–1670.

66. Roseman, I.J., Wiest, C., & Swartz, T. Phenomenology, behaviors, and goals differentiate discrete emotions. *Journal of Personality and Social Psychology*, 67, 2 (1994), 206–221.

67. Rozin, P. & Royzman, E.B. Negativity bias, negativity dominance, and contagion. *Personality and Social Psychology Review* 5, 4 (2001), 296–320.

68. Russell J. A. A circumplex model of affect. *Journal of Personality and Social Psychology*, 39(6), 1161, 1980.

69. Sadiku, M. N., Eze, T. P., & Musa, S. M. Fake news and misinformation. International Journal of Advances in Scientific Research and Engineering, 4, 5 (2018), 187–190.

70. Saldaña, J. The coding manual for qualitative researchers (3rd ed.). Newbury Park, CA: Sage, 2016.

71. Schudson, Michael. *Discovering the News: A Social History of American Newspapers*. New York: Basic Books, 1981.

72. Schwarz, N., Newman, E., & Leach, W. Making the truth stick & the myths fade: Lessons from cognitive psychology. *Behavioral Science & Policy*, 2, 1 (2016), 85–95.

73. Shao, C., Ciampaglia, G. L., Varol, O., Yang, K. C., Flammini, A., & Menczer, F. The spread of low-credibility content by social bots. *Nature Communications*, 9, 1, (2018), 1–9.

74. Sharp, C., & Lodge, M. (1985). Partisan and ideological belief systems: Do they differ?. *Political Behavior*, 7, 2, 147–166.

75. Shi, D., Guan, J., Zurada, J., & Manikas, A. A data-mining approach to identification of risk factors in safety management systems. *Journal of Management Information Systems*, 34, 4 (2017), 1054–1081.

76. Shook, N.J., & Clay., Valence asymmetry in attitude formation: A correlate of political ideology. *Social Psychological and Personality Science*, 2, 6 (2011), 650–655.

77. Shook, N.J., & Fazio, R.H. Political ideology, exploration of novel stimuli, and attitude formation. *Journal of Experimental Social Psychology*, 45, 4 (2009), 995–998.

78. Shu, K., Sliva, A., Wang, S., Tang, J., & Liu, H. Fake news detection on social media: A data mining perspective. ACM SIGKDD explorations newsletter, 19, 1 (2017), 22–36

79. Statista. "Leading countries based on Facebook audience size as of October 2020," Retrieved from https://www.statista.com/statistics/268136/top-15-countries-based-on-number-of-facebook-users/

80. Steinley, D. K-means clustering: a half-century synthesis. *British Journal of Mathematical and Statistical Psychology*, 59, 1 (2006), 1–34.

81. Stieglitz, S., & Dang-Xuan, L. Emotions and information diffusion in social media—Sentiment of microblogs and sharing behavior. *Journal of Management Information Systems*, 29, 4 (2013), 217–248.

82. Terrizzi, J.A., Shook, N.J., & McDaniel, M.A. The behavioral immune system and social conservatism: A meta-analysis. *Evolution and Human Behavior*, 34, 2 (2013), 99–108.

83. Thibodeau, P., Peebles, M. M., Grodner, D. J., & Durgin, F. H. The Wished-For Always Wins Until the Winner Was Inevitable All Along: Motivated Reasoning and Belief Bias Regulate Emotion During Elections. *Political Psychology*, 36, 4 (2015), 431–448.

84. Tomkins, S. Left and right: A basic dimension of ideology and personality. In R. W. White (Ed.), *The study of lives: Essays on personality in honor of Henry A. Murray* (pp. 388–411). Atherton Press, 1963.

85. Törnberg, P. Echo chambers and viral misinformation: Modeling fake news as complex contagion. PLoS One, 13, 9 (2018), e0203958.

86. Torres, R., Gerhart, N., & Negahban, A. Epistemology in the era of fake news: An exploration of information verification behaviors among social networking site users. *ACM SIGMIS Database: the DATABASE for Advances in Information Systems*, 49, 3 (2018), 78–97.

87. Turel, O., & Qahri-Saremi, H. Problematic use of social networking sites: Antecedents and consequence from a dual-system theory perspective. *Journal of Management Information Systems*, 33, 4 (2016), 1087–1116.

88. van Prooijen, J. W., & Krouwel, A. P. Psychological features of extreme political ideologies. *Current Directions in Psychological Science*, 28, 2 (2019), 159–163.

89. Vasilopoulos, P., Marcus, G.E., & Foucault, M. Emotional responses to the *Charlie Hebdo* attacks: Addressing the authoritarianism puzzle. *Political Psychology*, 39, 3 (2017), 557–575.

90. Vosoughi, S., Roy, D., and Aral, S. The Spread of True and False News Online, *Science*, 359, 6380 (2018), 1146–1151.

91. Wright, C.L. COVID-19 Fake News and Its Impact on Consumers, *Psychology Today*, April 30, 2020, retrieved from https://www.psychologytoday.com/us/blog/everyday-media/202004/covid-19-fake-news-and-its-impact-consumers

92. Zajonc, R. B. Attitudinal effects of mere exposure. *Journal of Personality and Social Psychology*, 9, 2p2 (1968), 1.

Uncovering the Truth about Fake News: A Research Model Grounded in Multi-Disciplinary Literature

Jordana George, Natalie Gerhart, and Russell Torres

ABSTRACT

Many diverse fields across academia are interested in the fake news (FN) phenomenon. A multidisciplinary literature review can provide researchers with new insights, alternative methods, and theories from other fields. The present review incorporates FN research across fields and organizes it into three categories: FN Stimuli, the triggers and impetus for people and organizations to engage with FN; FN Actions, which encompass the activities and processes undertaken in FN; and FN Outcomes, the effects and consequences of FN Actions. Within these categories, we systematize research topics into major themes. Stimuli: motivation; Actions: fabrication, propagation, mitigation; and Outcomes: persuasion, conviction, polarization, and aversion. We identify relationships that are important in understanding the impact on society: the cycle of amplification, the cycle of fragmentation, and the progression from social polarization and aversion into motivation for more fake news. Last, we distinguish FN roles, including creators, consumers, influencers, endorsers, propagators, and resistors.

Introduction

Thanks to the novel coronavirus, the earth is healing itself and animals are returning to overrun habitats; or are they? According to National Geographic [31], fake news (FN) surrounding the impacts of COVID-19 on climate change is rampant on social networks, and this is only one of a myriad of contemporary topics where FN abounds. Many scholars define FN as false information intentionally created and distributed to mislead [5, 71, 142]. FN is an important contemporary concern, primarily due to the technological affordances of social networks, which allow individuals to act not only as news consumers, but also as news creators (through first-hand accounts) and news propagators (by sharing or interacting with news) [69, 111, 141]. Because FN often masquerades as legitimate news, and with no effective means for the traditional media to play the role of gatekeeper and lend credibility to news stories, FN and legitimate news stories intermingle and can be easily mistaken for one another [44]. As a result, "news" no longer implies the impartiality of trained journalists, and its consumption may result in users incorporating falsehoods into their belief structures. Despite mitigation efforts and the emergence of a number of online

Access the Support Material: www.routledge.com/ 9781032561127

fact checking services, over half of 6127 respondents of a recent US survey admitted sharing FN online. Only 10% realized it at the time, but that also begs the question of why known FN would be shared at all [136].

History is riddled with examples of falsehoods used to achieve a goal. For instance, the term "disinformation," commonly used in discussions of FN today, is credited to Stalin ('Dezinformatsiya') who set up an official department for FN to influence the public and mislead opponents [105, 145]. Due in part to this history, the evolution of language, the development of new modes of communication, and the variety of social and academic perspectives on the topic, there is significant disagreement on exactly what constitutes FN. To some, all news is fake if it originates from a vilified source, such as liberals maligning Fox News or conservatives eschewing *The New York Times* [9, 29]. Others consider news to be fake if it opposes their personal worldviews or values [17, 71]. Alternative definitions have been voiced which broaden the notion to include news satire and parody, misinformation (inadvertent untruths), manipulated images such as deep fakes, advertisements masquerading as news, and propaganda [142]. We define fake news as information perceived as news which is *both factually incorrect and explicitly created to deceive* [5, 78, 141]. This definition requires the creator's deliberate intent to mislead and excludes inadvertent false information (e.g., misinformation) as well as alternative forms of false information with goals other than deception (e.g., satire and parody).

In this paper we answer the call to promote interdisciplinary research on FN [23, 78] with a multidisciplinary review of the FN literature. In doing so, we provide an organizing framework for existing FN research which can serve as a foundation for future FN scholars across fields. The goal of our review is not only to provide the current state of FN literature, but to curate a practical body of literature [55, 77, 147], identify where research in particular areas has and has not been conducted, and lay a foundation for scholars to distinguish new contributions from prior work [139]. This review was devised to answer the following research questions: (1) What is the current state of FN research? (2) What are the major streams? (3) What can we learn from viewing FN across multiple disciplines? (4) How can we guide future FN research?

Through our synthesis we contribute to the current understanding of FN in several ways. First, we provide a framework of categories and themes found in FN research across disciplines, which provides a consistent language for future investigations of FN. Second, we propose relationships within these themes that amplify FN and promote the fragmentation of society. Third, we describe a typology of FN roles related to these themes. We then provide a research agenda that highlights opportunities both in IS and across disciplines. Last, we contribute to literature review methodology with a detailed process for multidisciplinary research, identifying high quality research, and using grounded theory for a standalone literature review.

Methodology

Standalone literature reviews are a tradition in many academic fields and provide important support for research [129, 146]. To our knowledge, however, there are comparatively few FN standalone literature reviews and relatively few multidisciplinary literature reviews in general. Kapantai et al. (2020) examined the FN literature to establish a taxonomy of FN types, characterized by the underlying motive, facticity, and verifiability [66]. This useful and focused work draws on a smaller corpus of relevant papers. Zhou and Zafarani (2020) conducted a multidisciplinary review focused on FN detection techniques [166] and employed literature from psychology, philosophy, and economics. Our review extends these conversations by synthesizing research from numerous disciplines and discussing FN topics not previously covered. Furthermore, we utilize a combination of searches to ensure inclusion. First, we scoured top journals in each field. Next, we searched for specific articles across multiple journals and disciplines. Last, we searched the major IS journals and conferences. An overview of the process is described below and a detailed description of the method may be found in the Appendix.

Our search was multi-pronged looking for both plausible journals and conferences to include as well as article searches. We employed the SCImago Journal Rank (SJR), the Web of Science Journal Citation Rank (JCR), searches within top journals, searches within the Association of Information Systems (AIS) Basket of Eight, and Google Scholar. Backward/ forward searches were also conducted to identify additional literature which may have otherwise been missed.

While the topic of FN is of significant interest across a wide variety of fields, it was necessary to constrain the fields included in this review to both manage the size of the resultant corpus and to maintain a degree of consistency. We included Information Science, Information Systems & Technology (which includes computer science), Communications (journalism and communications), and Social Sciences (social science, sociology, political science, psychology, economics, and business). The included disciplines and related journals are summarized in the Appendix in Table A1. The keywords included "fake news," "falsified news," "false news," and "disinformation." The term "disinformation" was chosen over "misinformation" to capture the deceptive intent present in our definition of FN. Misinformation is a term used most often for poorly communicated or inadvertently incorrect information, rather than deceptive information [65, 158]. The Appendix presents additional details on the method used to select and analyze papers including the search process, number of papers identified and excluded during each step, and the final list of selected papers (Table A3).

We used grounded theory method (GTM) for this interpretive theoretical review [112]. The GTM approach to literature reviews is useful to ensure theoretical relevance and comprehensiveness and for building theory, although it is a relatively uncommon method for literature reviews [25, 139, 163]. GTM is helpful for research across disparate disciplines [163], which is our primary motivation for employing this method. Given the complexity of FN, we contend that the structure and process identified for GTM reviews is well-suited to meet established criteria for both rigor (in systematicity) and relevance (in interpretation) [146]. We felt that the key elements of Glaserian GTM (avoidance of preconceived notions, theoretical sampling, constant comparison, and theory building) provided a solid strategy, along with approaching FN with theoretical sensitivity [151]. In addition to GTM, we also drew upon standalone literature review papers to inform our selection and analysis methods [79, 146, 161]. The analysis process included open coding, memoing, selective coding, and theoretical coding with several iterations as theoretical saturation was in each area was reached, and further papers served for theoretical sampling. This resulted in fifty-three open codes, fourteen selective codes, and eight theoretical codes. The final codes include motivation, fabrication, propagation, mitigation, persuasion, conviction, aversion, and polarization. The iterations continued throughout paper development, resulting in one more abstraction: three main categories of FN Stimuli, FN Actions, and FN Outcomes. The Appendix contains a visual depiction of the coding process, presented in Figure A2, inspired by Seidel et al. 2013 [131] and the theoretical codes are presented in Table A3 in the form of a concept map [161].

Review of the Fake News Literature

Our analysis of fake news research indicates that interest in the topic has grown dramatically in recent years across a number of disciplines (see Figure A3 in the Appendix). In looking at the corpus of literature as a whole, we identified three primary topic categories: FN Stimuli, FN Actions, and FN Outcomes. FN Stimuli are the triggers and impetus for people and organizations to engage with FN. FN Actions are the activities and processes undertaken in dealing with FN. FN Outcomes describe the effects and consequences of FN. Within these three categories FN can be further broken down into eight major themes: Stimuli: motivation; Actions: fabrication, propagation, mitigation; and Outcomes: persuasion, conviction, polarization, and aversion. Each is discussed in detail below.

Fake News Stimuli

Motivation to Create

Motivation encapsulates the underlying reasons individuals and organizations engage in FN fabrication. Motivation as presented here does not address individual motivations to consume or share FN but, rather, why FN is created in the first place. Of the 228 papers examined, motivation is present in 57 (see Table A4 in the Appendix). The literature on motivation suggests that action is preceded by attitude toward a given behavior and perceptions about engaging in it [4]. Motivation research employs theories related to choice (e.g. rational choice theory [160], theories of program choice [116]), but this stream is somewhat inconsistent in its theoretical grounding. The motivation research focuses heavily on the economic and power-related incentives which make the creation of FN appealing. Such research highlights monetary inducements inherent in social media and digital advertising [6, 26] as well as political or ideological power-related incentives [9, 123]. Structural elements of both the online advertising industry [26] and the traditional broadcast and print media industry [85] lead to the creation of FN, as well. Revenue generation opportunities from advertising, combined with low barriers to entry and low operating costs make FN a lucrative opportunity [6, 105]. Politically, governments and partisans use FN for political framing [16, 30]. We also found that FN is most potent in the early days of an event when information asymmetry abounds [16, 19].

Some argue that the internet enables *fictitious information blends* (FIBs), which "gain plausibility from a nucleus of truth around which orbit speculations driven by partisan polarization, the resistance of citizens to information that contradicts them, and the reluctance of self-interested elites to reject them outright" [124:28]. While FIBs may have agenda setting power, others argue that FN is intertwined with partisan media but does not set the media agenda [154]. What is clear from these studies is that the co-mingling of truth and fiction at the heart of most FN is among the most problematic and least understood characteristics of the phenomenon.

Fake News Actions

Fabrication

Fabrication includes the various actors, methods, and tactics used to create FN. Just over half of the papers analyzed in the review addressed fabrication (see Table A4 in the Appendix). Fabrication is treated in a variety of ways in FN research; however, most address the design and manufacture of FN or focus on strategic messaging. Examples of the former include investigations of the operations of state-run FN factories [83] or the practices of FN websites [121]. The examination of strategic messaging is evident in research which finds that FN is created with truth-subversive language [2] designed to play on emotion [30] and connect with recipients by signaling authenticity and homophilic characteristics on the part of the originator [164]. The objective of such strategies is to seed FN content effectively, and to increase the propagation of FN messages through social networks. Strategies employed by Russia's Internet Research Agency demonstrate FN as a highly structured process designed to play on human tendencies. Using industrialized processes and specialized roles [83], the Internet Research Agency employs agents of influence [148] whose online messages contain cues to signal authenticity and cultural competence in order to develop credibility [164]. Additional creation research examines the use of cloaked websites that mimic opponent websites to incite aggressive reactions [41] and the potential of fake images [74]. Due to the practical focus of assessing why fabrication exists in specific situations, there is no dominant underlying theory that significantly guides the fabrication theme.

Propagation

Propagation is the distribution of FN. Despite popular fascination with the "spread" of FN, only 100 of the 228 papers reviewed placed significant focus on the propagation of FN. Propagation research often focuses on technological contributions to the propagation of FN, both in terms of platform capabilities that enable the spread of FN [24] and as a means for the direct distribution of FN such as bots [162, 165]. As a result, much of this theme relies on features of platforms and is therefore not explicitly driven by any theory. Social networks enable easy propagation of FN through sharing that requires little thought or effort [6]. FN is enabled by minimal barriers to market entry and the technological capabilities of publishing "news" are easily accessible [12, 99]. Dissemination occurs fluidly across multiple social network platforms [85] and is influenced by the presence of high virality metrics such as like and share counts [72], as well as factors related to group norms [47]. Other investigators focus on the role of media and social network platform regulation in sharing behaviors [21] and the use of strategies designed to attract additional views of FN [84]. Legitimate news may pounce on social network story leads and reduce time for intensive vetting and verification in the rush to be first with a headline [137]. Still others examine the characteristics of FN sharers and the underlying causes of sharing [43, 83], or reasons why an individual might choose to avoid sharing FN [8].

Mitigation

Mitigation includes attempts to reduce the amount, spread, or impact of FN. Mitigation is a highly studied topic, and the research is primarily focused on disrupting amplification of FN, either through human or machine intervention. Human inventions include increasing information literacy that enables FN recipients to evaluate authenticity more accurately [39, 88]. Personal detection of FN is important as research suggests that identification of FN alters subsequent behaviors [33]. Other FN deterrence research focuses on *ex post* methods, such as flagging [95, 97], rating news sources [70, 71], social norms [51] or fact checking [61, 89]. The research shows inconsistent results, indicating that further study in this area is needed. Some authors find that flagging has a positive impact on user behavior [50, 69, 94], while others find that flagging provides no FN protection [126]. Still others show that indicators may reduce the believability of flagged content, but do not change user engagement [43, 95]. Fact checking is shown to have a positive effect on curbing FN-related behaviors [159]. Citizen curation, a process in which individuals in a social network fact check each other, can be effective [35, 114], although efficacy depends on the social tie strength between the two [89]. Another mitigation research stream finds that information bias is unavoidable and simple disclosure would allow readers to better evaluate FN [36], although other research indicates that individuals are ill equipped to evaluate the quality of online information or its source(s) [40, 125]. At the same time, there is a paradox in which those most engaged with social network news, and presumably the most literate, may be more likely to encounter and share FN [152, 157]. Overall, findings suggest that the intent to verify news is often based on a combination of message features and perceptions of the news provider [11, 150]. Recipients of FN use both internal and external authentication strategies [142], and the skills and experience of social network users is influential in FN detection [134], though virality metrics may serve as a *de facto* indicator of the wisdom of the crowd [72]. Based on these approaches, the elaboration likelihood model (ELM) is heavily employed in this theme (e.g., [11, 63, 94–97, 138]). The ELM asserts that the persuasiveness of information is evaluated through two psychological paths; a central path focused on evaluations of argument quality and requires high cognition, and a peripheral path relying on heuristics or cues with low cognition [64]. Researchers are trying to better understand the effect of FN on individuals' central and peripheral processing.

Research on the algorithmic detection of FN is dominated by IS. Such research details the development of machine learning (ML) models using the design science paradigm [46, 75]. Classification and text mining are demonstrated as potentially useful for identifying and segregating FN from other news content [49]. Much of the research on automatic detection seeks to outperform prior attempts in terms of accuracy. However, given that model performance metrics are fundamentally tied to the unique data set from which they are derived, such claims of superior accuracy are dubious. Inputs to these algorithms include both the semantic content of the message, which can expose deceptive cues through text mining [49, 75], and external features collected through sources such as the Google API [107]. Some research suggests FN can be identified by associated meta-data, and other authors have considered the composition of the network and extracted information about both the news sender and receiver to inform predictive models [63]. Each approach adds to the body of knowledge on algorithmic detection of FN, and many authors have found encouraging results. However, detection remains a significant challenge and the variety of approaches in use suggests that no single paradigm governs this type of research, and it warrants continued exploration [162]. That notwithstanding, Twitter is the most popular data source used in IS FN detection research [162], and text mining is the most common method for detecting FN [46]. Other approaches have looked at how user characteristics such as culture [98] or education [155] influence detection or sharing behavior. Still others, building on the theory of planned behavior, explore intent to verify news encountered on social networks [150]. Less commonly, authors have explored the effect of national governance approaches as mitigating factors for FN [56, 128].

Fake News Outcomes

Persuasion

The persuasion theme captures the epistemological judgements made by an individual and is related to the influence of FN on the beliefs of a recipient. Persuasion is the most represented theme in the literature with 166 of the 228 papers included in this review, and it is the most uniformly studied across fields. FN is a tool used to influence public opinion, support preferred candidates, damage opponents, or promote or harm a particular cause or organization [1, 118]. FN is particularly effective when combined with government censorship to manipulate public sentiment and promote government legitimacy [52] and governments and partisans use FN for political framing in order to gain public support [16, 30]. This effect is reduced over time as new information becomes available to fill in the blanks and offer different narratives [16]. Those who use FN for persuasion have learned to strike early when public interest is high. This diverse research stream investigates how belief is established and takes a variety of forms, including recipients' political knowledge [92, 116] and affiliation [127] and how that influences susceptibility to FN. Tensions around news in general arise when people are exposed to news that is difficult to understand, when they are overwhelmed by too many choices, and when news conflicts with their worldviews [17, 81]. Confirmation bias, people's tendency to positively judge information that matches their personal worldviews [140], is a common thread.

Confirmation bias is also related to the psychological utility that consumers receive from news that validates their personal ideology, such as pleasure or satisfaction [6]. Add to this the enjoyment afforded by entertaining soft news treatments of traditionally hard news topics, and news stories fashioned as entertainment become a source of psychological utility. It is important to understand the concepts behind soft and hard news as many FN stories employ soft news tactics. Hard news is straight-forward, facts-only, verifiable news while soft news generally takes a humanistic view, often highlighting tales of individual heroics and injustice or impacts on local communities [20]. Soft news effectively influences behavior with appealing stories [15]. When soft news expands to hard news, we see the "Oprah Effect" where people are swayed by celebrities, especially those who peddle soft news along with lifestyle entertainment [18]. The transformation of hard news into entertainment via soft news strategies is a strong factor in enabling FN. Nearly all news is now presented in a considerably "softer" format than in previous decades as news agencies analyze which formats earn the most clicks [18, 45].

A common theory employed in FN articles focused on persuasion is the Elaboration Likelihood Model [95, 138], which asserts that information persuasiveness is evaluated through two paths; a central path evaluating argument quality that requires higher cognition, and a peripheral path relying on heuristics or cues with low cognitive effort The research suggests that motivating the central path should be beneficial for individual FN detection. Similarly, the theory of motivated reasoning is commonly employed in this theme [14, 92, 159], as FN consumers use confirmation bias to determine what news items with which to engage. Other persuasion research investigates the role of binary thinking in the establishment of belief [106], factors influencing the likelihood of validation [142, 149], or the role of technical skills in the ability to identify deceptive content [134]. Social identity differences can also play a role in as those with greater relational identities may lean more towards reinforcing FN, while those with higher social identifies may lean towards more variety [110].

Conviction

Conviction represents the incorporation of a given FN narrative into an individual's mental model as a deeply held belief and is thus the result of the persuasive effect of FN. Conviction is characterized by both longevity and strong commitment. As the information conveyed by FN is amplified within social networks, it transitions from the "news" realm to the realm of public knowledge [130] and becomes axiomatic for those that incorporate it into their belief system. The conviction theme is present in 107 of the papers included in this review and incorporates a broad range of theories. The 'convicted' individual "participates in their own victimization" through a "lack of acceptance for opposing viewpoints" [27:12]. Existing biases in the convicted individual cause resistance to disconfirming evidence [82] such as flags indicating a particular news item is false [95]. Such individuals may venture into the long tail of the web [100] in search of sources that provide information congruent with existing beliefs [14], as their faith in traditional news outlets drops. Media bias and media hostility are relatively new social phenomena. Historically, people in democracies tended to believe what they saw, read, or heard in the mainstream news [122]. Today, news from democracies is under just as much suspicion as state-run media [9, 52]. Hostility against the media is focused on the premise that the media is biased, sets agendas, and produces news that is either slanted or outright fake to support their view [17, 81]. Research also suggests that some individuals are more susceptible to incorporating false information into their beliefs. Differential educational backgrounds and personality traits [76], as well as political knowledge and trust [92] have been identified as influential factors. In addition, older individuals may be more likely to become convicted due to cognitive changes associated with aging [54]. Unlike persuasion which we characterize as the epistemic evaluation of a single FN item, conviction occurs over time as FN themes are amplified in the social network and the focal FN recipient is repeatedly exposed to the false narrative [115]. As conviction grows within the network, the broader societal impacts of polarization and aversion arise.

Polarization

We characterize polarization as a social phenomenon in which a sharp division in beliefs occurs, creating factions with countervailing conceptualizations of truth. The resultant us-versus-them mindset further entrenches beliefs, and individuals increasingly identify as a member of a distinct belief group. This division is best captured in social identity theory, which is heavily used in this them [62, 120, 153, 165]. Polarization is addressed in 103 of the 228 papers included in this review and is largely focused on political ideology, although some extend beyond the political sphere [62]. Market forces in the media and social networks exert considerable influence on FN, as much or more than personal characteristics [9, 101]. FN is highly related to partisan media, both responding to and setting their agendas [154], and purveyors of FN often represent themselves as openly ideological and in ways designed to appeal to partisan audiences [121]. Increased news market competition leads to specialty consumer focus in programming, resulting in both growth in the number of partisan media outlets and increasing extremity of views [9]. Changes in the recent political environment have resulted in new subversive campaign tactics that employ FN as a tool for polarization and division [123]. Political candidates today use more negative campaign strategies than in years past which increases polarization [62]. Against this backdrop, individuals seek membership in groups with congruent ideological beliefs, resulting in network partisan homophily and the self-selection of media silos which provide confirmatory news [80]. The resultant echo chambers reinforce polarization through further exposure to polarizing messages [81, 120]. Over time, polarized groups of individuals not only avoid opposing viewpoints, but actively attack them as described by the aversion theme.

Aversion

A step beyond polarization is aversion, the complete repudiation of opposing views and those that hold them. The aversion theme is evident in 73 of the 228 papers included in our analysis. Highly convicted individuals in polarized groups may transition from simple avoidance of information which runs counter to their beliefs to actively attacking those that supply such information. This phenomenon of distrust and suspicion of news agencies is known as "oppositional media hostility" [9:175]. Media brand bias is an example of this in action [17]. More striking is the evidence that partisans not only dislike those who share opposing information, but discriminate against them, and the level of that discrimination can exceed that of race or other common types of social discrimination [62]. Thus, while polarization is the formation of ideological groups and a largely passive undertaking, aversion is an active process in which opposing views are resisted or even antagonized. For this reason, similar to polarization, social identity theory is common in this theme [120, 153] when looking at who is "us" and who is "them" so it is clear who to be averse towards.

To summarize, this review breaks the extant FN literature down into causes of FN, how people and organizations interact with FN, and how FN impacts people, organizations, and society. We describe these as stimuli, actions, and outcomes. Within these categories we found eight major literature themes: motivation, fabrication, propagation, mitigation, persuasion, conviction, polarization, and aversion. This framework is illustrated in Figure 1 as a Descriptive Model of FN Research. Organizing the literature in this fashion provides researchers with both a macro view of the FN literature and a detailed examination of FN topics through research themes.

Discussion

The diverse fake news literature, when looked at as a whole, provides several insights for researchers. First, we develop a research framework and then propose an agenda to propel future IS research.

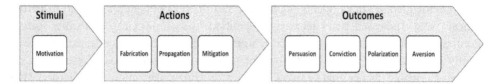

Figure 1. Descriptive Model of FN Research

A Framework for Fake News Research

Figure 2 illustrates our framework to help drive future fake news research. In it, we identify relationships between themes, and we discern specific roles that actors perform. We suggest several distinct relationships that promote FN acceleration, perpetuation, and increased societal impact. We refer to these as the cycle of amplification, the cycle of fragmentation, and the progression from aversion to motivation. These inter-theme relationships are important for researchers as they provide insights into the antecedents and consequences of their particular FN phenomenon of interest. Below we discuss these relationships and then elaborate on FN roles.

Along with FN categories and themes, we suggest that actors take on specific roles in FN processes. To our knowledge, there is no existing typology of FN roles in the extant literature, and FN research may not always explicitly identify the role(s) under investigation. Because FN is commonly transmitted via social networks and is, therefore, conveyance of (false) information in a computer-mediated environment, we began our interpretation of FN roles guided by existing IS theory which characterizes interlocutors as either senders or receivers [28, 34]. This view is consistent with the conceptualization of FN as a message transmitted from a creator to a consumer. However, we determined that more granularity would be helpful to fully depict human involvement in FN. Thus, based on the FN research and consistent with prior research demonstrating the centrality of roles in discussions of social media interactions [21], we derive FN roles based on their portrayal in the extant research: producers, who are the creators of FN, and consumers, who are the propagators,

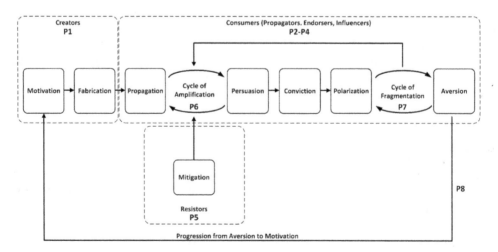

Figure 2. Framework for Fake News Research

endorsers, influencers, and resistors. These roles are summarized in Table 1 along with their associated themes. We also note that roles are not discrete, and people may take on more than one role.

FN creators are the actors responsible for FN formation and are portrayed in a variety of ways in FN investigations. While a creator is simply an individual involved in the manufacture of FN, the literature more commonly characterizes creators as members of ideological groups or state actors [66, 81, 83]. Research related to creators generally involves investigations about the impetus for, or manufacture of, FN. Thus, research featuring creators is heavily associated with the motivation and fabrication themes. For example, such research examines topics such as underlying financial or political motives [9, 26] and strategies and tactics employed in the creation of FN [40, 162]. Fundamentally, a creator is necessary for FN to exist and, therefore, may be viewed as the initiator of all subsequent actions. Hence, we suggest the following:

P1: Creators initiate and perpetuate FN

FN consumers include those who read, watch, or otherwise encounter FN, intentionally or inadvertently, whether or not they take action in regard to the FN. The literature suggests that the FN consumer is a meta-role composed of several more specific roles, primarily distinguished by epistemic judgments or assessments about the utility of the FN message made by the recipient. Our review suggests that research on consumers is more prevalent than that related to creators, likely due to the breadth of theoretical issues of interest related to the consumption and distribution of FN. Such research often presents FN consumers as critical to the overall FN process and as a key target of interest, because if no one consumed FN, it would quickly cease to exist. The persuasion theme plays an important part in research on FN consumers. Belief is often driven by deeply held ideological views and epistemic judgments are largely subject to confirmation bias [80, 138]. Thus, FN consumers decide if a given message conforms to their epistemological beliefs, and then ultimately adopt a supporting or refuting role. We identify four types of FN consumers: propagators, endorsers, influencers, and resistors.

FN propagators share FN items and contribute to its viral spread [56, 154], exacerbating the problem. Propagators also contribute to persuasion because they implicitly endorse the FN item when they share, ultimately aiding the cycle of amplification. While propagators may engage in the most passive FN activities, such as liking and sharing on social media also called clicktivism or slacktivism [48], and lack the prestige of endorsers and influencers, they are nevertheless a major force in the spread of FN. Thus, we suggest the following:

P2: FN propagators spread fake news through implicit positive engagement

FN endorsers take the next step by choosing to comment or otherwise positively engage with FN [69, 89]. As opposed to propagators who implicitly affirm FN through sharing and liking, endorsers are explicit. While FN propagators help to propagate FN, endorsers actively promote FN propagation. Many social media algorithms give preference to posts that have more engagement, thus endorsers help spread FN through their affirmation. Like propagators, endorsers are considered in the propagation theme and lead to amplification. FN endorsers demonstrate conviction with their actions, leading to the outcomes of polarization, aversion, and therefore the cycle of fragmentation. The outcomes of this role also lead to polarization, aversion, and the cycle of fragmentation. Therefore, we suggest the following:

P3: FN endorsers spread fake news through explicit positive engagement

FN influencers include famous, powerful, or otherwise authoritative FN supporters with a large social media following. While such individuals may participate in FN as propagators or endorsers, their status affords them extended social reach and the ability to greatly influence the outcome of FN campaigns [21]. Donald Trump is an example of a highly discussed influencer, mentioned by name in approximately one-quarter of the articles examined in this review. Influencers are often studied because of their ability to accelerate FN propagation and persuasion. FN influencers, endorsers, and propagators all contribute to the cycle of amplification, and their support of FN campaigns ultimately contributes to outcomes such as conviction, polarization, and aversion.

P4: FN influencers amplify fake news through explicit positive engagement

Propagation and persuasion form a cycle, which we term the cycle of amplification. The basis for this reciprocal relationship is the indication that message consistency and message volume (how many times a message is received) influences beliefs [115]. An individual who repeatedly encounters similar FN topics circulated within their network is more likely to be persuaded by its content and, ultimately, retransmit the message, thus extending its social reach and exposing new recipients. The amplifying effect is intensified by the fact that virality metrics, such as numbers of shares, themselves are taken as evidence of the normative expectations of the network and thereby increase behavioral intentions to share [94]. Thus, as it travels throughout social networks, the FN message persuades new consumers who then also like and share it. In this way, FN messages become magnified in both quantity and power. While not all FN will be amplified, these themes often build on each other and are a key element of the success of FN campaigns. To summarize, the amplification cycle is about FN propagation and FN persuasion. Based on this, we suggest the following:

P5: Fake news propagation and persuasion share a symbiotic cyclical relationship that results in the amplification of fake news.

Aversion, although magnified by polarization, can itself exacerbate polarization through its oppositional messaging [120], thus creating a symbiotic relationship between polarization and aversion that we identify as the cycle of fragmentation. We define fragmentation as extreme polarization that not only splits society further apart but creates more opportunities for extremist views [9, 54]. In this cycle, messages are often labeled "fake news" based on ideological reactions to content rather than strict facticity, deepening divisions and increasing the desire to respond [119]. Further, in highly charged and ideologically polarized environments, common FN propagation agents such as bots have increased influence [102, 126]. Thus, individuals in such environments are more likely to encounter FN [57] and to use it as an ideological weapon against those they perceive as having differing truths [53, 56]. Notably, as the cycle of fragmentation develops, a market for ideologically supportive news develops, increasing demand for FN messaging and serving as a motivation for additional FN creation. Thus, we posit the following:

Table 1. Fake News Themes and Roles

FN Themes	FN Roles Definition	Producers Make fake news	Consumers Interact with fake news				Exemplar Theme Articles
		Creator Those who create & develop FN	Propagator Those who disseminate FN	Endorser Those who support FN	Influencer Eminents who engage in FN	Resistor Those who fight against FN	
Motivation	Reasons and incentives for people to engage in FN creation	X					Allcott & Gentzkow (2017) [6]; Braun & Eklund (2019) [26]; Roemmele & Gibson (2020) [123]
Fabrication	Actors, methods, & tactics used in FN creation	X					Crabtree et al. (2019) [30]; Linvill & Warren (2020) [83]; Xia et al. (2019) [164]
Persuasion	Individuals judge the veracity of the news		X	X	X		Otto et al. (2017) [109]; Shen et al. (2019) [134]; Tandoc et al. (2018) [143]; Torres et al. (2018) [150]
Propagation	Distribution across channels by individuals, bots, or algorithms.		X	X	X		Bechmann (2020) [21]; Duffy et al. (2019) [38]; Hopp et al. (2020) [58]
Mitigation	Attempts to reduce the amount, spread, or impact of FN.					X	Kim et al. (2019) [71]; Kim & Dennis (2018) [69]; Margolin et al. (2018) [89]; Moravec et al. (2019) [95]
Conviction	Incorporation of a FN narrative as a deeply held belief.		X	X	X		Carlson (2018) [27]; Guess et al. (2019) [54]; Miller et al. (2016) [92]; Pennycook et al. (2018) [115]
Polarization	A sharp divide in beliefs based on FN consumption.		X	X	X		Iyengar & Westwood (2015) [62]; Lelkes et al. (2017) [80]; Robertson & Mourão (2020) [121]
Aversion	Rejection of opposing view due to FN consumption.		X	X	X		Arceneaux et al. (2012) [10]; Baum & Gussin (2008) [17]; Iyengar & Westwood (2015) [62]
Exemplar Role Articles		Arceneaux (2012) [9]; Keller et al. (2020) [68]; Xia et al. (2019) [164]	Hopp et al. (2020) [58]; Vosoughi et al. (2018) [156]	Kim et al. (2019) [71]; Masullo & Kim (2020) [90]	Bechmann (2020) [21]	Duffy et al. (2019) [38]; Torres et al. (2018) [150]	

P6: Fake news polarization and aversion share a symbiotic cyclical relationship that results in the fragmentation of society.

FN resistors identify deceit and disinformation in FN. The focus of much of the literature on FN mitigation is the facilitation of this identification and the subsequent transition of FN consumers to the resistor role [42, 157]. While the term "resistor" implies action in opposition to the FN, which could involve active campaigning against the FN narrative [58, 87] or rebuking those that share false information [8, 37], some resistors mitigate the FN influence by refusing to incorporate it into their belief system, thus derailing its propagation through the network [149].

P7: Fake news resistors are found along a spectrum, exhibiting a range of passive to proactive resistance behaviors to mitigate fake news.

We note a third relationship, the progression from aversion to motivation. At some point in time, a motivated individual begins their initial journey to produce FN. However, we suggest that it doesn't stop there, but becomes a self-actualizing long-term activity that repeats itself many times or even in perpetuity. As hate grows and tolerance wanes between those of differing viewpoints, affecting society at large, FN producers are incentivized at the individual level to create more news stories to garner clicks, ad revenue, and influence. Societal splits increase agenda setting, increase both confirmation bias and cognitive bias, and provide fertile ground for new FN products and greater spread [9, 12, 124]. Thus, we suggest the following:

P8: Aversion to differing others promotes new motivations for fake news

Future Research Agenda

The complex interactions that enable FN propagation, consequences, and societal impacts clearly position FN as a wicked problem. Fortunately, the IS research community is well-positioned to expand our understanding of FN phenomena and develop appropriate mitigation strategies. Also, while we believe our approach was unique and valuable, we identify some limitations in our study. Limitations may be present due to inclusion and exclusion choices and which keywords to use. We identified and attempted to include disciplines outside of IS that might have an important voice in FN research, but we recognize that not all relevant papers from all disciplines could be included due to sheer volume. We also acknowledge that, despite a rigorous search, some papers of note may have been overlooked. Many, if not all, of these research limitations may be addressed as authors continue to explore FN phenomena in future research as outlined below.

Based on the framework of FN developed herein, we highlight several future research directions. While this multidisciplinary review of the literature is an opportunity for bringing ideas from other disciplines to IS, we also acknowledge that the nature of FN offers an opportunity for home disciplinary research, cross, and interdisciplinary research [144]. Generally, half of the research identified in this literature review does not employ a specified underlying theory. As a result, we propose FN research could benefit from increased and cohesive theoretical guidance. Table 2 highlights potential theoretical perspectives and research questions, and we discuss some of these opportunities next.

Motivation Research on motivation is important, because to reduce FN, we must remove the impetus for its creation. The most common incentives are financial [6] or influential [148]. While this insight is useful, it is likely incomplete, and additional motivations for FN creation at both the individual and group levels of analysis remain unexplored. IS has a rich tradition of motivation research which examines factors that facilitate the use of various IS platforms, for both good and bad. What, for instance, might the IS social media research on motivations for information sharing behaviors bring to the discussion of FN research?

Fabrication While FN content is well researched, how the content is developed is relatively understudied across all fields. FN is largely studied in the context of social media and each FN item may be viewed as an instantiation of a digital artifact. To date, IS examinations of FN artifacts have largely considered their composition of that artifact only in terms of their contribution to algorithmic detection. However, IS researchers skilled in text analysis research might profitably apply these skills to FN fabrication investigations. Such research could explore, for instance, strategic design choices in FN messages and their impact on believability, the likelihood of verification, and intention to share.

Propagation The modest volume of FN propagation research represents an opportunity for IS scholars with expertise in social media research to examine information sharing and apply network analysis. The extant IS FN research primarily relies on Twitter for understanding FN phenomena [162], and research on other platforms may be fruitful. Mapping patterns of FN diffusion both within and among social networking sites may yield insights which enable the development of more robust FN control technologies.

Persuasion The persuasiveness of FN messaging is vital to the success of FN campaigns and FN employs tactics related to message content to increase believability [142]. Without such persuasiveness, the ability of FN to propagate may be impaired [85, 132]. We suggest that much remains to be learned about the persuasiveness of FN, as well as how individuals incorporate such knowledge into their belief system. IS has a rich tradition of research in relevant topics, such as deception in online product reviews and phishing emails. The insights, models, and underlying theoretical perspectives from such research is likely applicable to FN. Similarly, trust is intimately linked to epistemic judgements [149] and is a core concept in IS research [135]. Trust research related to e-commerce and online auctions might add useful insights to our understanding of veracity judgements made by FN recipients.

Amplification is a cycle that develops between persuasion and propagation. While much of the mitigation research focuses on disruption of this cycle, there may be additional amplification phenomena relevant to IS research. For instance, while research that uses ML often models engagement as distinct like and share features (corresponding to the endorser and propagator roles in our typology), propagation research often fails to distinguish between the two. While this may stem from the characteristics of the datasets available for such studies (see the discussion of the BuzzSumo dataset [7], diving deeply into the behavioral differences, attitudes and motivations of FN consumers would likely yield insights toward the development of appropriate social media interventions.

Mitigation research is common in IS, much of which focuses on automatic detection [59, 133] or FN notifications [70, 95]. Such research is generally focused on helping FN consumers adopt the resistor role, thereby disrupting the cycle of amplification. While this IS research shows promise, we propose that mitigation tactics could target any theme in our framework. For instance, consider the motivation theme. In addition to reactive strategies designed to interact with persuasion and propagation such as identification, flagging, and technological countermeasures, IS might explore strategies that could discourage FN from being created in the first place (i.e., motivations). How could the click maximization revenue paradigm of modern social media be changed? Alternatively, IS might look at who pays for the clicks on FN sites - advertisers - and how technology might improve accountability for their role in the monetary success of FN sites. Political motivations for creating FN are harder to address, yet scholars could research and build theories on how to make FN a less attractive political tool. Recent work on measuring internet influence such as that explored by Nimmo [102–104] may yield new strategies for mitigating politically motivated FN.

Conviction represents the tipping point at which point a given FN narrative is incorporated as a deeply held belief. In this conceptualization, conviction can be viewed as the aggregate effect of the persuasiveness of multiple individual FN messages. Literature in other fields have linked the notion of conviction and trust [24, 65]. As noted previously, there is a large body of extant work regarding trust in IS scholarship that may offer useful theoretical perspectives on the formation of conviction.

Polarization occurs when groups divide into opposing (and often acrimonious) camps [62]. In such circumstances, group members become insular and the lines between opinion and fact become blurred as group members reinforce each other [67]. We note that over time, consistent FN messages move consumers towards extremism and polarization, especially as similar FN themes are replayed through different FN channels [81, 101]. While IS research rarely evaluates political ideology [91], perhaps its inclusion could shed additional light on the role of technology in FN-related polarization. Another natural application of IS research to the investigation of polarization is echo chamber research, much of which involves the mining of social media text. Text mining approaches such as sentiment analysis are likely to shed light on polarization due to their ability to quantify the extremity of written language.

Aversion, which describes a state in which people not only disagree with those with alternative views, but actively avoid, ostracize, or attack them, is an often-overlooked consequence of FN. In IS, aversion might be enacted by FN consumers using privacy controls, altering the composition of their network, or abandoning digital services or platforms. While each of these behaviors would be of interest to IS scholars, relevant theoretical perspectives in IS on adoption, use, and discontinuance might shed light on aversion behaviors. Another issue well suited to examination in IS is related to technology use and affect. While some have considered the efficacy of corrections issued by other social media users [89] and the strategies employed in such communications [60], there is much to be learned about interactions between individuals who disagree about the veracity of social media posts.

Fragmentation Increased animosity and partisanship provide new impetus for FN as consumers provide ad revenues and are influenced through widespread propagation [80, 99]. As such, the interaction between polarization and aversion creates new opportunities for FN agendas, serving as motivation to start the cycle all over again. Fragmentation research in IS might examine the role of FN as an antecedent to violent social conflict. FN has become a weaponized form of social media [86, 93, 113]: it incites and magnifies connective action, the online connectedness that has expanded social activism mobilization beyond traditional political organizing and resources [22]. FN, which manifests itself in false virtual artifacts, appears to be particularly effective at provoking violent physical actions in the real world, as illustrated by the "stop the steal" Washington DC insurrection of January 2021 [13]. An additional area of possible interest is the long-term impact of FN on galleries, libraries, archives, and museums (GLAM) [117]. When FN is institutionalized, it can remain in history for generations. We posit that IS researchers can build on knowledge management as well as crowdsourcing to better comprehend the factors that impact, or are impacted by, FN.

Table 2. Future Research Summary

Themes/ Roles	Potential Theoretical Perspectives	Potential Research Questions
Motivation	• Self-Determination Theory and other theoretical perspectives on motivation • Economic theories on incentivization	• How can information sharing behavior research inform FN? • How do online trolls contribute to the FN problem? • How might the financial motivations of black hat hackers inform our understanding of FN fabricators? • Are there relevant intrinsic motivations for the creation of FN on social media?
Fabrication	• Semiotics • Impression Management • Media Synchronicity	• What is the impact of design on believability, the likelihood of verification, and intention to share? • What content makes FN believable and how can consumers use this to detect FN? • Does political FN content employ different strategic messaging than apolitical FN? • How do creators use deep fakes in FN? • How do digital FN creators impact the spread of FN?
Propagation	• Social contagion theory • Diffusion theory • Game theory	• What propagation patterns exist in FN? • To what extent do FN propagators knowingly propagate? • What do propagators gain from propagating FN? • Might the implementation of a simple retraction feature in social media interfaces help mitigate the aggregate flow of false information? • What is the efficacy of news rating and flagging solutions, given user experience differences across platforms? • How does the ideological composition of the network alter FN spread?
Persuasion	• Elaboration likelihood • Epistemological theories • Theories of trust	• How can trust research inform FN research? • Which deceptive FN practices are most commonly employed in online FN? • Which of these practices engender the most trust in FN consumers? • How does this influence further intentions to share FN items? • How do social media platform differences influence the persuasive effect of FN? • How do differences in computer self-efficacy and technological innovativeness influence FN susceptibility?
Amplification	• Social contagion theory • Diffusion theory • Game theory • Elaboration likelihood • Epistemological theories • Theories of trust	• How do behavioral differences, attitudes, and motivations of FN consumers impact FN consumption? • How does affective state influence FN engagement? • Are there common temporal delays between engagement actions which may be exploited for interventions? • What are the relationships between engagement levels, engagement types, technology efficacy, FN virality, and/or peer relationships?
Mitigation	• Deterrence theory • Protection motivation theory • Self-efficacy	• How can FN be a less attractive political tool. • What preemptive methods for mitigating FN exist? • Which of these methods is most efficacious? • How do non-mitigating (those other than flagging, rating, etc.) design elements on social media websites interact with user engagement? • How might the concepts of threat appraisal and coping appraisal from protection motivation theory be applied to FN phenomena? • What is the impact of technology mitigation beyond the focal FN consumer?

(Continued)

Table 2. (Continued).

Conviction	• Theories of trust • Cognitive dissonance theory • Social influence theory	• How can trust research inform FN research? • How does disposition to trust influence the conviction potential of FN consumers? • What role do flags and ratings have on FN consumers over long periods of time? • How do individuals reconcile differing levels of trust among the entities involved in FN-related discourse? • How do IT artifacts or platforms differentially influence conviction?
Polarization	• Homophily • Theories on party affiliation	• What do text mining approaches tell us about FN polarization? • How might FN engagement reflect identity management on the part of ideological groups? • How does engagement with FN vary among polarized social media members for apolitical content? • What role does polarization play in the composition and structure of social networks? • What impact does polarization have on the long-term trust of creator or endorser?
Aversion	• Cognitive dissonance • Theories of IS continuance • Generalized aggression model	• How might FN initiated and ideologically fueled interactions be influenced by the affective states of the individuals involved? • How is digitally mediated aversion enacted and what moderates it? • How does FN lead to IS continuance or discontinuance?
Fragmentation	• Homophily • Theories on party affiliation • Cognitive dissonance • Theories of IS continuance • Generalized aggression model	• How can knowledge management and crowdsourcing research inform FN research? • What makes virtual FN as inflammatory, or more so, than real world events? • How does fabricated information with no physical proof lead people to violent social action? • How might digital activism be used to reconcile differences among divided social media groups? • FN What is the impact of FN on knowledge management?
Roles	• Theory of Planned Behavior • Impression Management • Theory of Reasoned Action	• How do different personality types respond to and participate in FN? • How does FN participation impact a participant's social status? • What motivates individuals to continue to propagate FN? • What repercussions do individuals face for participating in FN? • How can the effect of endorsers and influencers be dampened?

Roles FN roles provide a clear opportunity for IS researchers. Do endorsers of one FN item resist others? If so, why? When do people take on multiple roles? When studied, engagement is often modeled as the dependent variable and is all-encompassing of the constituent behaviors and associated roles: sharing (propagators), liking (endorsers), or commenting (endorsers and resistors). Behavioral insights about how users adopt roles during FN discourse may improve our ability to design systems that encourage adoption of the resistor role. Additionally, extant research on FN ignores the agency of technology artifacts despite the regular reference to bots and AI algorithms which often operate autonomously once deployed. Example research questions to advance IS study in this area might include: What factors guide the behavior of FN recipients and dictate roles? What is the differential impact of roles on the propagation of FN?

What individual differences in FN consumers help resist FN spread? How do digital agents interact with humans in social media driven FN discourse? For example, IS research historically applies many different research methods. From our review, we find that quantitative and design science methods were used more frequently in the IS literature than the other fields examined in this study (See Appendix Table A5). We propose that IS can benefit from applying more qualitative or mixed method approaches to help answer how and why questions.

While the identification of these roles and their relationships to major themes within the FN literature provides insights into FN phenomena, there are two theoretically important observations to be made about such roles. First, multiple roles may be adopted by the same actor. For example, a single actor may be a propagator by sharing a post, and an endorser by "liking" the post. Alternatively, an individual might propagate one FN item, while resisting another. Thus, roles may be studied at a micro-level (FN event-specific) or a macro level (specific FN topics or particular groups/networks). Our analysis, while demonstrating the potential of the co-mingling of roles, reveals that it is important to be able to distinguish between actors and the roles they adopt in interactions with FN. As previously noted, studies in the extant FN literature may fail to clearly identify the role or roles addressed in each inquiry. We argue that this lack of clarity hinders the identification and application of relevant theory and ignores practical distinctions such as the fact that many detection algorithms treat likes and shares differently [132]. The exception to this would be design science research investigating the propagation of FN [32, 164, 165], which often distinguishes between engagements with FN as described in this typology, demonstrating the utility of distinguishing between these roles.

Another observation, which may be of particular interest to IS, is how technology is conceptualized in relation to roles. Our review suggests that, to date, technology has primarily been presented in conceptualizations consistent with the computational or tool views of technology [108]. Such research often highlights either the technological affordances of social media and their contributions to the spread of FN [24, 147] or considers the algorithmic potential of technology to identify FN and potentially disrupt its diffusion through social networks [73, 164]. However, such views often fail to fully recognize the possibility that technology may actively assume one or more of the roles described above. For instance, viewing the Facebook platform as an actor in the FN process may expose its role as both a propagator, whose algorithms reward virality and as a resistor, that actively employs automated fact-checking. Similarly, bots might be viewed as having agency and the ability to assume one or more of these roles, essentially independent of human actors once deployed. We argue that acknowledging the digital agency [3] of technological artifacts involved in FN will continue to gain importance as advances in AI expand the capacity of machines to act independently.

This investigation of FN has afforded a synthesized view of how these all relate to each other. We propose three levels with which to approach FN. First, there is the individual FN story, which is subsumed by the larger network level. The network is similarly a subset of the greater societal level. At the individual news story level, the roles include creators, consumers, and resistors. We observe individual news stories in the themes of motivation, fabrication, propagation, and mitigation. We also observe individual news stories in the progression from aversion to motivation. At the network level, the roles include influencers, endorsers, and propagators with themes around persuasion and conviction. The cycle of amplification comes into play here. Last, at the societal level, we find both creators and resistors, working within polarization and aversion, and trying either to promote or mitigate the cycle of fragmentation.

Conclusion

Unfortunately, fake news is unlikely to be eradicated anytime soon and we anticipate that FN research will continue to grow. This review contributes to the field in several ways. The descriptive model of FN provides a framework of FN research. We outline a typology of FN roles, and our review and tables provide resources for future researchers. We offer a research agenda that provides guidance and our details on developing a Grounded Theory literature review adds to literature review methodologies. Through these contributions, we provide a unifying FN framework and common language for researchers working across disciplinary silos. Although the future of fake news appears grim, we believe that with further understanding fake news can be better understood and the outlook for reducing its impact will improve.

Acknowledgments

The authors wish to thank Dorothy Leidner and Guy Paré for their guidance.

Disclosure statement

No potential conflict of interest was reported by the author(s).

References

1. 116TH Congress Senate. Report of The Select Committee on Intelligence United States Senate on Russian Active Measures Campaigns and Interference in the 2016 U.S. Election. 116TH Congress Senate, Washington, DC, 2020.

2. Adler, E. and Drieschova, A. The Epistemological Challenge of Truth-Subversion to the Liberal International Order. International Organization, Published Online (2020), 1–27.

3. Ågerfalk, P.J. Artificial intelligence as digital agency. European Journal of Information Systems, 29, 1 (January 2020), 1–8.

4. Ajzen, I. and Fishbein, M. Attitudinal and normative variables as predictors of specific behavior. Journal of Personality and Social Psychology, 27, 1 (July 1973), 41–57.

5. Albright, J. Welcome to the Era of Fake News. Media and Communication, 5, 2 (June 2017), 87.

6. Allcott, H. and Gentzkow, M. Social Media and Fake News in the 2016 Election. Journal of Economic Perspectives, 31, 2 (May 2017), 211–236.

7. Allcott, H., Gentzkow, M., and Yu, C. Trends in the diffusion of misinformation on social media. Research & Politics, Published Online (April 2019), 1–8.

8. Altay, S., Hacquin, A.-S., and Mercier, H. Why do so few people share fake news? It hurts their reputation. New Media & Society, Published Online (November 2020), 1–22.

9. Arceneaux, K. Cognitive Biases and the Strength of Political Arguments. American Journal of Political Science, 56, 2 (2012), 271–285.

10. Arceneaux, K., Johnson, M., and Murphy, C. Polarized Political Communication, Oppositional Media Hostility, and Selective Exposure. The Journal of Politics, 74, 1 (January 2012), 174–186.

11. Asadullah, A., Kankanhalli, A., and Faik, I. Understanding Users' Intention to Verify Content on Social Media Platforms. In Proceedings of the Pacific Asia Conference on Information Systems. Association for Information Systems, Yokohama, 2018, pp. 1–8.

12. Bakir, V. and McStay, A. Fake News and The Economy of Emotions. Digital Journalism, 6, 2 (February 2018), 154–175.

13. Barry, D. and Frenkel, S. "Be There. Will Be Wild!": Trump All but Circled the Date. The New York Times, 2021. https://www.nytimes.com/2021/01/06/us/politics/capitol-mob-trump-supporters.html.

14. Bauer, P.C. and Clemm von Hohenberg, B. Believing and Sharing Information by Fake Sources: An Experiment. Political Communication, 38:6, 647–671.

15. Baum, M.A. Sex, Lies, and War: How Soft News Brings Foreign Policy to the Inattentive Public. American Political Science Review, 96, 1 (March 2002), 91–109.

16. Baum, M.A. and Groeling, T. Reality Asserts Itself: Public Opinion on Iraq and the Elasticity of Reality. International Organization, 64, 3 (July 2010), 443–479.

17. Baum, M.A. and Gussin, P. In the Eye of the Beholder: How Information Shortcuts Shape Individual Perceptions of Bias in the Media. Quarterly Journal of Political Science, 3, 1 (March 2008), 1–31.

18. Baum, M.A. and Jamison, A.S. The Oprah Effect: How Soft News Helps Inattentive Citizens Vote Consistently. The Journal of Politics, 68, 4 (November 2006), 946–959.

19. Baum, M.A. and Potter, P.B.K. Media, Public Opinion, and Foreign Policy in the Age of Social Media. The Journal of Politics, 81, 2 (April 2019), 747–756.

20. Baumgartner, J. and Morris, J.S. The Daily Show Effect: Candidate Evaluations, Efficacy, and American Youth. American Politics Research, 34, 3 (May 2006), 341–367.

21. Bechmann, A. Tackling Disinformation and Infodemics Demands Media Policy Changes. Digital Journalism, 8, 6 (July 2020), 855–863.

22. Bennett, W.L. and Segerberg, A. The Logic of Connective Action - Digital media and the personalization of contentious politics. Information, Communication & Society, 15, 5 (2012), 739–768.

23. Bernard, J.-G., Dennis, A., Galletta, D., Khan, A., and Webster, J. The Tangled Web: Studying Online Fake News. In Proceedings of the International Conference on Information Systems. Association for Information Systems, Munich, 2019, pp. 1–7.

24. Bøggild, T., Aarøe, L., and Petersen, M.B. Citizens as Complicits: Distrust in Politicians and Biased Social Dissemination of Political Information. American Political Science Review, Published Online (2020), 1–16.

25. Bowers, A.W. and Creamer, E.G. Core principles of grounded theory in a systematic review of environmental education for secondary students. International Journal of Social Research Methodology, Published Online (September 2020), 1–14.

26. Braun, J.A. and Eklund, J.L. Fake News, Real Money: Ad Tech Platforms, Profit-Driven Hoaxes, and the Business of Journalism. Digital Journalism, 7, 1 (January 2019), 1–21.

27. Carlson, M. Fake news as an informational moral panic: the symbolic deviancy of social media during the 2016 US presidential election. Information, Communication & Society, Published Online (August 2018), 1–15.

28. Clemons, E.K., Dewan, R.M., Kauffman, R.J., and Weber, T.A. Understanding the Information-Based Transformation of Strategy and Society. Journal of Management Information Systems, 34, 2 (April 2017), 425–456.

29. Coe, K., Tewksbury, D., Bond, B.J., et al. Hostile News: Partisan Use and Perceptions of Cable News Programming. Journal of Communication, 58, 2 (June 2008), 201–219.

30. Crabtree, C., Golder, M., Gschwend, T., and Indriđason, I.H. It Is Not Only What You Say, It Is Also How You Say It: The Strategic Use of Campaign Sentiment. The Journal of Politics, 82, 3 (2020), 1044–1060.

31. Daly, N. Fake animal news abounds on social media as coronavirus upends life. National Geographic, 2020. https://www.nationalgeographic.com/animals/2020/03/coronavirus-pandemic-fake-animal-viral-social-media-posts/.

32. Dang, A., Moh'd, A., Islam, A., and Milios, E. Early Detection of Rumor Veracity in Social Media. In Proceedings of the Hawaii International Conference on System Sciences. IEEE Computer Society, Wailea, 2019, pp. 2355–2364.

33. Das, A. and Schroeder, R. Online disinformation in the run-up to the Indian 2019 election. Information, Communication & Society, Published Online (March 2020), 1–17.

34. Dennis, A.R., Fuller, R.M., and Valacich, J.S. Media, Tasks, and Communication Processes: A Theory of Media Synchronicity. MIS Quarterly, 32, 3 (September 2008), 575–600.

35. Downing, J. and Dron, R. Tweeting Grenfell: Discourse and networks in critical constructions of British Muslim social boundaries on social media. New Media & Society, Published Online (July 2019), 1–21.

36. Doyle, A. Analyzing the Laws of MIL: a Five-step Scientific Conversation on Critical Information Literacy. Communications in Information Literacy, 13, 1 (2019), 114–126.

37. Duffy, A. and Si, J.T.R. Naming the Dog on the Internet. Digital Journalism, 6, 7 (August 2018), 910–927.

38. Duffy, A., Tandoc, E., and Ling, R. Too good to be true, too good not to share: the social utility of fake news. Information, Communication & Society, Published Online (June 2019), 1–15.

39. Elmwood, V. The Journalistic Approach: Evaluating Web Sources in an Age of Mass Disinformation. Communications in Information Literacy, 14, 2 (December 2020), 269–286.

40. Evanson, C. and Sponsel, J. From Syndication to Misinformation: How Undergraduate Students Engage with and Evaluate Digital News. Communications in Information Literacy, 13, 2 (December 2019), 228–250.

41. Farkas, J., Schou, J., and Neumayer, C. Cloaked Facebook pages: Exploring fake Islamist propaganda in social media. New Media & Society, 20, 5 (May 2018), 1850–1867.

42. FEMA. Coronavirus Rumor Control. FEMA, 2020. https://www.fema.gov/coronavirus/rumor-control.

43. Figl, K., Kießling, S., Rank, C., and Vakulenko, S. Fake News Flags, Cognitive Dissonance, and the Believability of Social Media Posts. In Proceedings of the International Conference on Information Systems. Association for Information Systems, Munich, 2019, pp. 1–9.

44. Forestal, J. Beyond Gatekeeping: Propaganda, Democracy, and the Organization of Digital Publics. The Journal of Politics, Published Online (April 2020), 1–14.

45. Fox, R.L., Van Sickel, R.W., and Steiger, T.L. Tabloid justice: criminal justice in an age of media frenzy. Lynne Rienner Publishers, Boulder, 2007.

46. García Lozano, M., Brynielsson, J., Franke, U., et al. Veracity assessment of online data. Decision Support Systems, Published Online (February 2020), 1–14.

47. Garrett, R.K., Sude, D., and Riva, P. Toeing the Party Lie: Ostracism Promotes Endorsement of Partisan Election Falsehoods. Political Communication, 37, 2 (March 2020), 157–172.

48. George, J.J. and Leidner, D.E. From clicktivism to hacktivism: Understanding digital activism. Information and Organization, Published Online (May 2019), 1–45.
49. Ghosh, S. and Shah, C. Toward Automatic Fake News Classification. In Proceedings of the Hawaii International Conference on System Sciences. IEEE Computer Society, Wailea, 2019, pp. 2254–2263.
50. Gimpel, H., Heger, S., Kasper, J., and Schafer, R. The Power of Related Articles – Improving Fake News Detection on Social Media Platforms. In Proceedings of the Hawaii International Conference on System Sciences. IEEE Computer Society, Wailea, 2020, pp. 6063–6072.
51. Gimpel, H., Heger, S., Olenberger, C., and Utz, L. The Effectiveness of Social Norms in Fighting Fake News on Social Media. Journal of Management Information Systems, 38, 1 (January 2021), 196–221.
52. Gläßel, C. and Paula, K. Sometimes Less Is More: Censorship, News Falsification, and Disapproval in 1989 East Germany. American Journal of Political Science, Published Online (2019), 1–17.
53. Godler, Y. Post-Post-Truth: An Adaptationist Theory of Journalistic Verism. Communication Theory, Published Online (2019), 1–19.
54. Guess, A., Nagler, J., and Tucker, J. Less than you think: Prevalence and predictors of fake news dissemination on Facebook. Science Advances, 5, 1 (January 2019), 1–8.
55. Guinea, A.O. de and Paré, G. What literature review type should I conduct? Routledge Handbooks Online, 2017.
56. Helberger, N. The Political Power of Platforms: How Current Attempts to Regulate Misinformation Amplify Opinion Power. Digital Journalism, 8, 6 (July 2020), 842–854.
57. Hjorth, F. and Adler-Nissen, R. Ideological Asymmetry in the Reach of Pro-Russian Digital Disinformation to United States Audiences. Journal of Communication, 69, 2 (April 2019), 168–192.
58. Hopp, T., Ferrucci, P., and Vargo, C.J. Why Do People Share Ideologically Extreme, False, and Misleading Content on Social Media? A Self-Report and Trace Data–Based Analysis of Countermedia Content Dissemination on Facebook and Twitter. Human Communication Research, 46, 4 (October 2020), 357–384.
59. Hosni, A.I.E. and Li, K. Minimizing the influence of rumors during breaking news events in online social networks. Knowledge-Based Systems, Published Online (December 2019), 1–12.
60. Huang, Y. and Wang, W. When a story contradicts: correcting health misinformation on social media through different message formats and mechanisms. Information, Communication & Society, Published Online (November 2020), 1–18.
61. Humprecht, E. Where "fake news" flourishes: a comparison across four Western democracies. Information, Communication & Society, 22, 13 (November 2019), 1973–1988.
62. Iyengar, S. and Westwood, S.J. Fear and Loathing across Party Lines: New Evidence on Group Polarization. American Journal of Political Science, 59, 3 (2015), 690–707.
63. Janze, C. and Risius, M. Automatic Detection of Fake News on Social Media Platforms. In Proceedings of the Pacific Asia Conference on Information Systems. Association for Information Systems, Langkawi, 2017, pp. 1–15.
64. Jiang, J., Goonawardene, N., and Tan, S.S.-L. Do You Find Health Advice on Microblogging Platforms Credible? Role of Self-Efficacy and Health Threat in Credibility Assessment. In Proceedings of the Pacific Asia Conference on Information Systems. Association for Information Systems, Chengdu, 2014, pp. 1–10.
65. Jones-Jang, S.M., Kim, D.H., and Kenski, K. Perceptions of mis- or disinformation exposure predict political cynicism: Evidence from a two-wave survey during the 2018 US midterm elections. New Media & Society, Published Online (July 2020), 1–21.
66. Kapantai, E., Christopoulou, A., Berberidis, C., and Peristeras, V. A systematic literature review on disinformation: Toward a unified taxonomical framework. New Media & Society, Published Online (September 2020), 1–26.
67. Kavanagh, J. and Rich, M.D. Truth decay: an initial exploration of the diminishing role of facts and analysis in American public life. RAND, Santa Monica, California, 2018.

68. Keller, F.B., Schoch, D., Stier, S., and Yang, J. Political Astroturfing on Twitter: How to Coordinate a Disinformation Campaign. Political Communication, 37, 2 (March 2020), 256–280.

69. Kim, A. and Dennis, A.R. Says Who?: How News Presentation Format Influences Perceived Believability and the Engagement Level of Social Media Users. In Proceedings of the Hawaii International Conference on System Sciences. IEEE Computer Society, Waikoloa Village, 2018, pp. 3955–3965.

70. Kim, A. and Dennis, A.R. Says Who? The Effects of Presentation Format and Source Rating on Fake News in Social Media. MIS Quarterly, 43, 3 (September 2019), 1025–1039.

71. Kim, A., Moravec, P.L., and Dennis, A.R. Combating Fake News on Social Media with Source Ratings: The Effects of User and Expert Reputation Ratings. Journal of Management Information Systems, 36, 3 (July 2019), 931–968.

72. Kim, J.W. Rumor has it: The effects of virality metrics on rumor believability and transmission on Twitter. New Media & Society, 20, 12 (December 2018), 4807–4825.

73. Kormelink, T.G. and Meijer, I.C. Truthful or Engaging? Digital Journalism, 3, 2 (March 2015), 158–174.

74. Krafft, P.M. and Donovan, J. Disinformation by Design: The Use of Evidence Collages and Platform Filtering in a Media Manipulation Campaign. Political Communication, 37, 2 (March 2020), 194–214.

75. Kumar, N., Venugopal, D., Qiu, L., and Kumar, S. Detecting Anomalous Online Reviewers: An Unsupervised Approach Using Mixture Models. Journal of Management Information Systems, 36, 4 (October 2019), 1313–1346.

76. Landrum, A.R., Olshansky, A., and Richards, O. Differential susceptibility to misleading flat earth arguments on youtube. Media Psychology, Published Online (September 2019), 1–30.

77. Larsen, K.R., Hovorka, D.S., Dennis, A.R., and West, J.D. Understanding the Elephant: The Discourse Approach to Boundary Identification and Corpus Construction for Theory Review Articles. Journal of the Association for Information Systems, 20, 7 (2019), 887–927.

78. Lazer, D.M.J., Baum, M.A., Benkler, Y., et al. The science of fake news. Science, 359, 6380 (March 2018), 1094–1096.

79. Leidner, D. Review and Theory Symbiosis: An Introspective Retrospective. Journal of the Association for Information Systems, 19, 06 (June 2018), 552–567.

80. Lelkes, Y., Sood, G., and Iyengar, S. The Hostile Audience: The Effect of Access to Broadband Internet on Partisan Affect. American Journal of Political Science, 61, 1 (2017), 5–20.

81. Levendusky, M.S. Why Do Partisan Media Polarize Viewers? American Journal of Political Science, 57, 3 (2013), 611–623.

82. Ling, R. Confirmation Bias in the Era of Mobile News Consumption: The Social and Psychological Dimensions. Digital Journalism, 8, 5 (May 2020), 596–604.

83. Linvill, D.L. and Warren, P.L. Troll Factories: Manufacturing Specialized Disinformation on Twitter. Political Communication, Published Online (February 2020), 1–21.

84. Lu, Y. and Pan, J. Capturing Clicks: How the Chinese Government Uses Clickbait to Compete for Visibility. Political Communication, Published Online (July 2020), 1–32.

85. Lukito, J. Coordinating a Multi-Platform Disinformation Campaign: Internet Research Agency Activity on Three U.S. Social Media Platforms, 2015 to 2017. Political Communication, 37, 2 (March 2020), 238–255.

86. Maasberg, M., Ayaburi, E., Liu, C.Z., and Au, Y.A. Exploring the Propagation of Fake Cyber News: An Experimental Approach. In Proceedings of the Hawaii International Conference on System Sciences. IEEE Computer Society, Waikoloa Village, 2018, pp. 3717–3726.

87. MacFarquhar, N., Feuer, A., and Goldman, A. Federal Arrests Show No Sign That Antifa Plotted Protests. The New York Times, 2020. https://www.nytimes.com/2020/06/11/us/antifa-protests-george-floyd.html.

88. Mackey, T. Embedding Metaliteracy in the Design of a Post-Truth MOOC: Building Communities of Trust. Communications in Information Literacy, 14, 2 (December 2020), 346–361.

89. Margolin, D.B., Hannak, A., and Weber, I. Political Fact-Checking on Twitter: When Do Corrections Have an Effect? Political Communication, 35, 2 (April 2018), 196–219.

90. Masullo, G.M. and Kim, J. Exploring "Angry" and "Like" Reactions on Uncivil Facebook Comments That Correct Misinformation in the News. Digital Journalism, Published Online (October 2020), 1–20.

91. Mentzer, K., Fallon, K., Prichard, J., and Yates, D.J. Measuring and Unpacking Affective Polarization on Twitter: The Role of Party and Gender in the 2018 Senate Races. In Proceedings of the Hawaii International Conference on System Sciences. IEEE Computer Society, Wailea, 2020, pp. 2459–2468.

92. Miller, J.M., Saunders, K.L., and Farhart, C.E. Conspiracy Endorsement as Motivated Reasoning: The Moderating Roles of Political Knowledge and Trust. American Journal of Political Science, 60, 4 (2016), 824–844.

93. Molina, M.D., Sundar, S.S., Le, T., and Lee, D. "Fake News" Is Not Simply False Information: A Concept Explication and Taxonomy of Online Content. American Behavioral Scientist, Published Online (October 2019), 1–33.

94. Moravec, P., Kim, A., and Dennis, A. Flagging Fake News: System 1 vs. System 2. In Proceedings of the International Conference on Information Systems. Association for Information Systems, San Francisco, 2018, pp. 1–17.

95. Moravec, P., Minas, R., and Dennis, A.R. Fake News on Social Media: People Believe What They Want to Believe When it Makes No Sense at All. MIS Quarterly, 43, 4 (2019), 1343–1360.

96. Moravec, P.L., Kim, A., and Dennis, A.R. Appealing to Sense and Sensibility: System 1 and System 2 Interventions for Fake News on Social Media. Information Systems Research, 31, 3 (August 2020), 987–1006.

97. Moravec, P.L., Kim, A., Dennis, A.R., and Minas, R.K. Do You Really Know If It's True? How Asking Users to Rate Stories Affects Belief in Fake News on Social Media. In Proceedings of the Hawaii International Conference on System Sciences. IEEE Computer Society, Wailea, 2019, pp. 6602–6611.

98. Mousavizadeh, M., Hazarika, B., and Rea, A. A Study of News Credibility and Trust on Social Media – A Multi-Cultural Evaluation. In Proceedings of the Americas Conference on Information Systems. Association for Information Systems, New Orleans, 2018, pp. 1–5.

99. Munger, K. All the News That's Fit to Click: The Economics of Clickbait Media. Political Communication, Published Online (December 2019), 1–22.

100. Nelson, J.L. and Taneja, H. The small, disloyal fake news audience: The role of audience availability in fake news consumption. New Media & Society, 20, 10 (October 2018), 3720–3737.

101. Nie, N.H., Miller, D.W., Golde, S., Butler, D.M., and Winneg, K. The World Wide Web and the U.S. Political News Market. American Journal of Political Science, 54, 2 (2010), 428–439.

102. Nimmo, B. Robot Wars: How Bots Joined Battle in the Gulf. Journal of International Affairs, 71, 1.5 (2018), 87–96.

103. Nimmo, B. Measuring Traffic Manipulation on Twitter. University of Oxford Internet Institute, 2019.

104. Nimmo, B. The breakout scale: Measuring the impact of influence operations. Brookings Institute, 2020.

105. Nunberg, G. "Disinformation" Is The Word Of The Year — And A Sign Of What's To Come. Fresh Air, 2019. https://www.npr.org/2019/12/30/790144099/disinformation-is-the-word-of-the-year-and-a-sign-of-what-s-to-come.

106. Oliver, J.E. and Wood, T.J. Conspiracy Theories and the Paranoid Style(s) of Mass Opinion. American Journal of Political Science, 58, 4 (2014), 952–966.

107. Olivieri, A.C., Valais-Wallis, H.-S., and Cudre-Mauroux, P. Creating Task-Generic Features for Fake News Detection. In Proceedings of the Hawaii International Conference on System Sciences. IEEE Computer Society, Wailea, 2019, pp. 5196–5205.

108. Orlikowski, W.J. and Iacono, C.S. Research Commentary: Desperately Seeking the "IT" in IT Research–A Call to Theorizing the IT Artifact. Information Systems Research, 12, 2 (June 2001), 121–134.

109. Otto, L., Glogger, I., and Boukes, M. The Softening of Journalistic Political Communication: A Comprehensive Framework Model of Sensationalism, Soft News, Infotainment, and Tabloidization. Communication Theory, 27, 2 (May 2017), 136–155.

110. Pan, Z., Lu, Y., Wang, B., and Chau, P.Y.K. Who Do You Think You Are? Common and Differential Effects of Social Self-Identity on Social Media Usage. Journal of Management Information Systems, 34, 1 (January 2017), 71–101.

111. Papanastasiou, Y. Fake News Propagation and Detection: A Sequential Model. Management Science, 66, 5 (January 2020), 1826–1846.

112. Paré, G., Trudel, M.-C., Jaana, M., and Kitsiou, S. Synthesizing information systems knowledge: A typology of literature reviews. Information & Management, 52, 2 (March 2015), 183–199.

113. Patel, S. and Constantiou, I. Human Agency in the Propagation of False Information - A Conceptual Framework. In Proceedings of the European Conference on Information Systems. Association for Information Systems, Virtual, 2020, pp. 1–11.

114. Pedersen, S. and Burnett, S. "Citizen Curation" in Online Discussions of Donald Trump's Presidency. Digital Journalism, 6, 5 (May 2018), 545–562.

115. Pennycook, G., Cannon, T.D., and Rand, D.G. Prior exposure increases perceived accuracy of fake news. Journal of Experimental Psychology, 147, 12 (December 2018), 1865–1880.

116. Prior, M. News vs. Entertainment: How Increasing Media Choice Widens Gaps in Political Knowledge and Turnout. American Journal of Political Science, 49, 3 (2005), 577–592.

117. Qutab, S., Myers, M.D., and Gardner, L.A. Information Disorder in The Glam Sector: The Challenges of Crowd Sourced Contributions. In Proceedings of the European Conference on Information Systems. Association for Information Systems, Stockholm-Uppsala, 2019, pp. 1–12.

118. Rampal, K.R. and Adams, W.C. Credibility of the Asian News Broadcasts of the Voice of America and the British Broadcasting Corporation: Gazette (Leiden, Netherlands), 46, 2 (1990), 93–111.

119. Ribeiro, M.H., Calais, P.H., Almeida, V.A.F., and Meira Jr, W. "Everything I Disagree With is #FakeNews": Correlating Political Polarization and Spread of Misinformation. In Proceedings Data Science + Journalism. Halifax, Canada, 2017, pp. 1–8.

120. Risius, M., Aydinguel, O., and Haug, M. Towards an Understanding Of Conspiracy Echo Chambers On Facebook. In Proceedings of the European Conference on Information Systems. Association for Information Systems, Stockholm-Uppsala, 2019, pp. 1–11.

121. Robertson, C.T. and Mourão, R.R. Faking Alternative Journalism? An Analysis of Self-Presentations of "Fake News" Sites. Digital Journalism, 8, 8 (September 2020), 1011–1029.

122. Robinson, M.J. Public Affairs Television and the Growth of Political Malaise: The Case of "The Selling of the Pentagon." American Political Science Review, 70, 2 (June 1976), 409–432.

123. Roemmele, A. and Gibson, R. Scientific and subversive: The two faces of the fourth era of political campaigning. New Media & Society, 22, 4 (April 2020), 595–610.

124. Rojecki, A. and Meraz, S. Rumors and factitious informational blends: The role of the web in speculative politics. New Media & Society, 18, 1 (January 2016), 25–43.

125. Rosenzweig, J.W., Thill, M., and Lambert, F. Student Constructions of Authority in the Framework Era: A Bibliometric Pilot Study Using a Faceted Taxonomy. College and Research Libraries, 80, 3 (2019), 401–420.

126. Ross, B., Pilz, L., Cabrera, B., Brachten, F., Neubaum, G., and Stieglitz, S. Are social bots a real threat? An agent-based model of the spiral of silence to analyse the impact of manipulative actors in social networks. European Journal of Information Systems, 28, 4 (July 2019), 394–412.

127. Ryan, T. and Aziz, A. Is the Political Right More Credulous?: Experimental Evidence Against Asymmetric Motivations to Believe False Political Information. The Journal of Politics, Published Online (August 2020), 1–4.

128. Saurwein, F. and Spencer-Smith, C. Combating Disinformation on Social Media: Multilevel Governance and Distributed Accountability in Europe. Digital Journalism, 8, 6 (July 2020), 820–841.

129. Schryen, G., Wagner, G., Benlian, A., and Paré, G. A Knowledge Development Perspective on Literature Reviews: Validation of a New Typology in the IS Field. Communications of the AIS, 46, (2020), 134–186.

130. Schudson, M. The Power of News. Harvard University Press, 1995.

131. Seidel, S., Recker, J., and vom Brocke, J. Sensemaking and Sustainable Practicing: Functional Affordances of Information Systems in Green Transformations. MIS Quarterly, 37, 4 (December 2013), 1275–1299.

132. Seref, M. and Seref, O. Rhetoric Mining for Fake News: Identifying Moves of Persuasion and Disinformation. In Proceedings of the Americas Conference on Information Systems. Association for Information Systems, Cancún, 2019, pp. 1–5.

133. Shang, L., Zhang, D. (Yue), Wang, M., Lai, S., and Wang, D. Towards reliable online clickbait video detection: A content-agnostic approach. Knowledge-Based Systems, Published Online (October 2019), 1–11.

134. Shen, C., Kasra, M., Pan, W., Bassett, G.A., Malloch, Y., and O'Brien, J.F. Fake images: The effects of source, intermediary, and digital media literacy on contextual assessment of image credibility online. New Media & Society, 21, 2 (February 2019), 438–463.

135. Sidorova, A., Evangelopoulos, N., Torres, R., and Johnson, V. A Survey of Core Research in Information Systems. Springer US, New York, NY, US, 2013.

136. Statista. Online sharing of fake news U.S. 2019. 2019.

137. Steensen, S. Journalism's epistemic crisis and its solution: Disinformation, datafication and source criticism. Journalism, 20, 1 (January 2019), 185–189.

138. Suntwal, S., Brown, S.A., and Patton, M.W. How does Information Spread? A Study of True and Fake News. In Proceedings of the Hawaii International Conference on System Sciences. IEEE Computer Society, Wailea, 2020, pp. 5893–5902.

139. Sylvester, A., Tate, M., and Johnstone, D. Beyond synthesis: re-presenting heterogeneous research literature. Behaviour & Information Technology, 32, 12 (December 2013), 1199–1215.

140. Taber, C.S. and Lodge, M. Motivated Skepticism in the Evaluation of Political Beliefs. American Journal of Political Science, 50, 3 (2006), 755–769.

141. Tandoc, E.C. The facts of fake news: A research review. Sociology Compass, 13, 9 (September 2019), 1–9.

142. Tandoc, E.C., Lim, Z.W., and Ling, R. Defining "Fake News." Digital Journalism, 6, 2 (February 2018), 137–153.

143. Tandoc, E.C., Ling, R., Westlund, O., Duffy, A., Goh, D., and Zheng Wei, L. Audiences' acts of authentication in the age of fake news: A conceptual framework. New Media & Society, 20, 8 (August 2018), 2745–2763.

144. Tarafdar, M. and Davison, R.M. Research in Information Systems: Intra-Disciplinary and Inter-Disciplinary Approaches. Journal of the Association for Information Systems, 19, 6 (2018), 523–551.

145. Taylor, A. Before "fake news, " there was Soviet "disinformation." Washington Post, 2016. https://www.washingtonpost.com/news/worldviews/wp/2016/11/26/before-fake-news-there-was-soviet-disinformation/.

146. Templier, M. and Paré, G. A Framework for Guiding and Evaluating Literature Reviews. Communications of the Association for Information Systems, 37, 1 (August 2015), 112–137.

147. Templier, M. and Paré, G. Transparency in literature reviews: an assessment of reporting practices across review types and genres in top IS journals. European Journal of Information Systems, 27, 5 (September 2018), 503–550.

148. Till, C. Propaganda through "reflexive control" and the mediated construction of reality. New Media & Society, Published Online (January 2020), 1–17.

149. Torres, R., Gerhart, N., and Negahban, A. Combating Fake News: An Investigation of Information Verification Behaviors on Social Networking Sites. In Proceedings of the Hawaii International Conference on System Sciences. IEEE Computer Society, Waikoloa Village, 2018, pp. 3976–3985.

150. Torres, R., Gerhart, N., and Negahban, A. Epistemology in the Era of Fake News: An Exploration of Information Verification Behaviors among Social Networking Site Users. ACM SIGMIS Database: the DATABASE for Advances in Information Systems, 49, 3 (July 2018), 78–97.

151. Urquhart, C. Grounded theory for qualitative research: a practical guide. SAGE, Los Angeles, Calif.; London, 2013.

152. Valenzuela, S., Halpern, D., Katz, J.E., and Miranda, J.P. The Paradox of Participation Versus Misinformation: Social Media, Political Engagement, and the Spread of Misinformation. Digital Journalism, 7, 6 (July 2019), 802–823.

153. Van Bavel, J.J. and Pereira, A. The Partisan Brain: An Identity-Based Model of Political Belief. Trends in Cognitive Sciences, 22, 3 (March 2018), 213–224.

154. Vargo, C.J., Guo, L., and Amazeen, M.A. The agenda-setting power of fake news: A big data analysis of the online media landscape from 2014 to 2016. New Media & Society, 20, 5 (May 2018), 2028–2049.

155. Villafranca, E.S. and Peters, U. Smart and Blissful? Exploring the Characteristics of Individuals That Share Fake News on Social Networking Sites. In Proceedings of the Americas Conference on Information Systems. Association for Information Systems, Cancún, 2019, pp. 1–5.

156. Vosoughi, S., Roy, D., and Aral, S. The spread of true and false news online. Science, 359, 6380 (March 2018), 1146–1151.

157. Vraga, E.K. and Tully, M. Who Is Exposed to News? It Depends on How You Measure: Examining Self-Reported Versus Behavioral News Exposure Measures. Social Science Computer Review, Published Online (November 2018), 1–17.

158. Walker, S., Mercea, D., and Bastos, M. The disinformation landscape and the lockdown of social platforms. Information, Communication & Society, 22, 11 (September 2019), 1531–1543.

159. Walter, N., Cohen, J., Holbert, R.L., and Morag, Y. Fact-Checking: A Meta-Analysis of What Works and for Whom. Political Communication, Published Online (October 2019), 1–26.

160. Wang, S.A., Pang, M.-S., and Pavlou, P.A. Cure or Poison? Impact of Identity Verification on the Creation of Fake Posts on Social Media. In Proceedings of the International Conference on Information Systems. Association for Information Systems, Seoul, 2017, pp. 1–18.

161. Webster, J. and Watson, R.T. Analyzing the Past to Prepare for the Future: Writing a Literature Review. MIS Quarterly, 26, 2 (June 2002), XIII–XXIII.

162. Williamson, W. and Scrofani, J. Trends in Detection and Characterization of Propaganda Bots. In Proceedings of the Hawaii International Conference on System Sciences. IEEE Computer Society, Wailea, 2019, pp. 7118–7123.

163. Wolfswinkel, J.F., Furtmueller, E., and Wilderom, C.P. Using grounded theory as a method for rigorously reviewing literature. European Journal of Information Systems, 22, 1 (2013), 45–55.

164. Xia, Y., Lukito, J., Zhang, Y., Wells, C., Kim, S.J., and Tong, C. Disinformation, performed: self-presentation of a Russian IRA account on Twitter. Information, Communication & Society, 22, 11 (September 2019), 1646–1664.

165. Yan, H.Y., Yang, K.-C., Menczer, F., and Shanahan, J. Asymmetrical perceptions of partisan political bots. New Media & Society, Published Online (2020), 1–22.

166. Zhou, X. and Zafarani, R. A Survey of Fake News: Fundamental Theories, Detection Methods, and Opportunities. ACM Computing Surveys, 53, 5 (October 2020), 109:0–109: 40.

Index

Note: Figures are indicated by *italics*. Tables are indicated by **bold**. Endnotes are indicated by the page number followed by 'n' and the endnote number e.g., 20n1 refers to endnote 1 on page 20.

For Product Safety Concerns and Information please contact our EU
representative GPSR@taylorandfrancis.com
Taylor & Francis Verlag GmbH, Kaufingerstraße 24, 80331 München, Germany

www.ingramcontent.com/pod-product-compliance
Lightning Source LLC
Chambersburg PA
CBHW080407060326
40689CB00019B/4158

9 781032 561134